YALE STUDIES IN POLITICAL SCIENCE, 10

David Horne, Editor

Published under the direction
of the Department of Political Science

The Social Democratic Party
of Germany FROM WORKING-CLASS
MOVEMENT TO MODERN POLITICAL PARTY

BY DOUGLAS A. CHALMERS

New Haven and London, Yale University Press, 1964

Copyright © 1964 by Douglas A. Chalmers.
Designed by Crimilda Pontes.
Set in Times Roman type
and printed in the United States of America by
The Carl Purington Rollins Printing-Office
of the Yale University Press.

Library of Congress catalog card number: 64–12647

To Ruth Vinton Chalmers

Contents

Preface   ix
1. The Party's Past   3
2. Choices Facing the SPD—The Role of
   Parties in Political Systems   21
3. The Style of SPD Goals—Policy and Ideology   53
4. Party Objectives—Power and the Means to Achieve It   96
5. Policy Making   113
6. The Leadership   139
7. Organization and Membership   162
8. The Party and the Public   200
9. Conclusion   226
Appendix: Party Finances   235
Bibliography   241
Index   251

Preface

The post-World War II development of the Social Democratic Party, Germany's major opposition party, has attracted less attention than it deserves. The more dramatic Cold War struggle of East and West, the emergence of all-European institutions, and the rapid changes taking place in the non-Western world have shifted the focus of interest of political analysts away from the study of Western European domestic institutions. When German politics have taken the spotlight, it has been Chancellor Konrad Adenauer's success in holding together a loose coalition in and through the Christian Democratic Union for fourteen years which has drawn attention, and the Social Democrats have remained in the shadows.

This neglect is unfortunate, because the SPD has undergone changes recently which are of considerable significance. It has pruned its ideological foliage with the adoption of a new "fundamental program" in 1959, reoriented its post-World War II "nationalist" foreign policy, and chose the young, personable Berlin mayor, Willy Brandt, as its candidate in the elections of 1961 over the party stalwart and "organization man" Erich Ollenhauer. One reason these developments have not attracted more attention is that they appear on the surface to be largely negative. They could be (and have been) interpreted as signs of the decline of the almost century-old party, famous as leader of one of the first mass-based Socialist movements. It seems now to be throwing overboard everything that made it distinctive. However, the new, emergent structure deserves attention not only because the party is presently the second largest in Germany and will probably play an important role in German politics for years to come, but also because it presents us with an example of a situation not uncommon in contemporary politics: an ideological, class-based party adjusting to a political system increasingly different from the one in which it grew up.

In the case of the SPD the outstanding features of its new environment can be easily summarized. The collapse of Germany in 1945, its prosperity since the early '50s, and its division after the war have brought about a change both in the attitudes and ideas prevalent in German politics (its "political culture") and in the pattern of its political and social institutions. These changes in the political culture of Germany, especially the breakdown in the sharp cleavages of opinion that separated Germans on the question of the organization of the political system and the economy of the country, have resulted in a lowering of the intensity of political clashes and the emergence of what might be called a bargaining spirit or secularization of the values associated with politics. The most radical changes in political institutions have been the slow elimination since 1949 of the minor parties from the national scene and the emergence of a powerful chancellorship under Adenauer.

Less obvious, but equally important, has been the pluralization of organizations that articulate group interests, especially among those groups that deal with the interests of large masses of people —the trade unions, the refugees, the veterans, persons receiving various kinds of welfare, those who suffered in one way or another from the events of 1933 through 1945, and so forth. At the risk of oversimplification and consequent misunderstanding, one may say in general that Germany has moved toward what Gabriel Almond has referred to as the Anglo-American type of political system, although features of the old regime remain, producing a pattern that defies precise classification.

Within this new political system, the SPD is seeking a new formula for political success measured in votes and a majority mandate. For an organization of over half a million dues-paying members, and about the most elaborate tradition of any party in the West ingrained in the attitudes and behavior of many of those members, the change has not been easy, nor is the outcome obvious.

In order to meet the competition presented by Adenauer's CDU, the party has sought to loosen the ties that have traditionally bound it to working-class interests and a socialist ideology, while heightening the professional competence of its active members in such modern political specialities as brokerage between various political interests and manipulation of the means of modern mass communication and influence.

This transformation of the party, which is still going on (and is still in question, since the process might be reversed if the present leaders fail to deliver some substantial success) may be characterized as the change from the "party-as-movement" to the "party-as-cadre." The purpose of this study is to analyze the present structure of the SPD to discover what this cadre is and how the party's ideas and massive organization have adapted to the challenges of contemporary Germany.

From a broader point of view, a study of this kind provides an opportunity (subject to the limitations of a case study) to explore the increasingly complex problem of the role of parties in modern political systems and, in particular, the interrelation between this role and the party's internal structure of institutions and ideas. Much of the analysis of political parties, especially analysis that focuses on organization and ideology, has assumed that the party's primary function is the representation of some group within the population, and/or the promotion of some particular conception of the structure and goals of government. This representational model of political parties fails to take into account the highly variable roles political parties may play in a modern political system. The outstanding fact about the SPD is that its present "reformist" leadership (to be distinguished from the "revisionist" tendencies at the turn of the century) have begun to revise their own representational image and are seeking to redefine their role in German political society. In the process, they have found it necessary to modify and adapt the party's structure of ideas and organizations. The new orientation cannot be understood simply as a change in socialist ideology or as a simple broadening of the social base. Rather they are seeking a new relation between social groups, public opinion, and the party, more flexible, less demanding, less conditioned by fixed goals. The contemporary SPD therefore offers an excellent opportunity to explore the relatively unexplored territory of the complexities in the political means–ends relationship—when both are changing.

The pages that follow are roughly divisible into three sections. The first (Chapters 1 and 2) lays the groundwork for the study of the party by discussing first the historical development of the SPD, and secondly some tentative generalizations about the changes in the German political system which have forced the party leaders to abandon their traditional political outlooks and have conditioned the alternative paths the party may take from now on.

The second section (Chapters 3 and 4) discusses two aspects of the party's "political culture"—the significance of the recent abandonment of a full-scale socialist ideological program and the objectives the party sets out for itself. The latter is discussed with reference to the political power the party hopes to achieve and the methods of achieving it.

Finally, the third section (Chapters 5–8) deals with various aspects of the party's organization. The first two chapters take up the two important processes of policy making and leadership recruitment. An effort is made here to relate these processes, which are internal to the party, to the larger political system. The next chapter considers various aspects of the party's regional and local organizations, and the final one considers the organization and objectives of the party's appeal to the public.

I was able to carry out my studies in the academic year 1959–60 in Germany thanks to the generosity of the Social Science Research Council. I gathered material from interviews, SPD publications, and direct observation of party meetings and conventions. The principal material on which I have relied has been the opinions, attitudes, and goals of party members themselves, chiefly members who hold responsible positions in the party. The following pages could therefore be most accurately described as an outline and interpretation of the self-image of the party, i.e. the party structure and objectives as seen through the eyes of the party leadership. For the attitudes of top party leaders and the members of the central organization I have relied on material such as the yearbooks, protocols, pamphlets, and periodicals put out under their direction. For amplification and occasional contrast a series of interviews was conducted, ranging from one to three hours in length, with what might be called middle-range leaders of the party. These included 45 persons involved in *Land* (state) or *Bezirk* (district) politics. An effort was made to talk to approximately equal numbers who were primarily active (a) in parliamentary delegations or local administration, (b) in the party executives, or (c) in other organizations associated with the party, such as unions and youth groups. The actual figures are as follows:

- 8 members of the *Bundestag* (federal legislature)
- 25 members of *Landtage* (state legislatures)
- 15 members of local party executives
- 12 leaders of subordinate organizations
- 8 union leaders
- 3 *Burgermeistern* (mayors)
- 5 party secretaries

The numbers add up to more than 45 since, especially in the Landtage, individuals held two, and sometimes three, positions. This was not thought of as a sample of the leadership of the party, but rather as a counterweight to the material associated with the national party leadership.

I followed a similar program of using both national and Bezirk-level materials in going through yearbooks, party newspapers (for members), periodicals, protocols of party congresses, and pamphlets issued by the party. The documents found most useful are cited in the bibliography.

In the course of my research I asked for and received the assistance of many persons. I particularly wish to thank all those members of the party who generously gave of their time to respond to my questions. Without their sympathetic cooperation, this study would not have been possible.

D.A.C.

New York, New York
August 1963

The Social Democratic Party of Germany

1. The Party's Past

The history of Social Democracy and the labor movement in Germany is a long story, told often and for many different reasons. For the purposes of this study it is necessary only to pick out some of the highlights of this story, but these are important for an understanding of the attitudes of many members and the rationale behind many contemporary organizations and practices. The traditions of this century-old party have been handed down and carefully nurtured from generation to generation, and even today are written up and used as educational material in the courses the party conducts for its members.

From the standpoint of the study of the evolution of the structure of the party, which is our main concern here, it is useful to consider the party's history in four periods:

> The formative period—from the 1860s to 1891
> The period of successful political expansion—from 1891 to about 1905
> The consolidation of the mass organization—about 1905 to 1933
> The post-World War II reorganization period

Before 1891

In this early period the multiple, shifting organizations of the labor movement were growing, if somewhat hesitantly, in the paternalistic atmosphere of German authoritarianism. It was the era in which the formation of a united Germany was accomplished under Bismarck's imperious leadership. The precursors of the party at this time were spontaneous, and more or less local, *Arbeiterbildungsvereine* (workers' educational societies)—a fact often recalled to me in the interviews I conducted. They met to hear speeches and debates, to sing and to study—a form of entertainment and education which, judging from the lists of *Veranstaltungen* (locally organized meetings) in current German newspapers, is still widespread and popular in many social strata.

The workers' organizations grew with the increasing industrialization of Germany. Periodic economic crises made the situation of the German worker as close to that of the proletariat described by Marx as it ever would be. Slowly they acquired national organization.

The party received its first definitive shape as a result of the amalgamation of two organizations—the Lassalleaner (*Allgemeiner Deutscher Arbeiterverein*), founded in 1863 under the dominating leadership of Ferdinand Lassalle, and the Eisenacher (*Sozialdemokratische Arbeiterpartei*) led by August Bebel and Wilhelm Liebknecht. The new unified party, the *Sozialistische Arbeiterpartei Deutschlands,* was founded in Gotha in 1875, as Bismarck's countermeasures were growing in intensity. The hostility of the authorities to workers' organizations reached its peak in the so-called *Sozialistengesetze* ("socialist laws") of the years 1878 to 1890. A history of the party published recently by the SPD sums up the statistics of repression under these laws as follows:

Prohibition of 1,300 periodic and nonperiodic publications, 900 deportations of comrades, among them 500 fathers, 1,000 years of prison terms given to 1,500 persons, in addition to the 600 years of prison terms for supposed lèse majesté (*Majestätsbeleidigung*) after the 1878 attentat.[1]

To the jaded sensibilities of the twentieth-century observer, such figures seem mild indeed, but they were sufficient to rank those

1. Franz Osterroth, ed., *Chronik der Sozialistischen Bewegung Deutschlands* (Bonn, n.d., probably 1957), p. 41.

4

twelve years of the "laws" as the heroic years of exile and illegal activity in the annals of the party.

Organizationally, the most important consequence of the repression was to stunt temporarily the growth of the central party organization, forcing the party to build itself up through the establishment of more or less legal, informal, local groups, which depended on the viability and activity of the individuals who were there on the spot.[2] National organization was limited to mere symbols—the one or two dozen deputies who were still allowed to retain their seats in the Reichstag and the party journal, *Der Sozialdemokrat*, published principally in Zurich under the direction of Eduard Bernstein and smuggled into Germany in quantities of up to 12,000 copies.[3]

Despite this absence of formal national organization, the party was very successful throughout these years in winning the votes of the German working class. A most remarkable record is read in the electoral figures. After a brief setback, the party's vote almost tripled.[4]

Year	Votes	% of the total	Mandates
1877	493,447	9.0	12
1881	311,961	6.9	13
1884	549,400	9.7	24
1887	763,128	10.0	11
1890	1,427,298	20.0	35

The party's programs, from Lassalle's first declarations through the Gotha Program, were dominated by demands for the extension of democratic rights in the working class, such as free and

2. Fritz Bielgick et al., *Die Organisation im Klassenkampf* (Berlin, n.d., probably 1931), p. 32.

3. Osterroth, p. 35. See also Peter Gay, *The Dilemma of Democratic Socialism* (New York, 1952), Ch. 2.

4. Figures are taken from Osterroth. The figures for the mandates won do not vary proportionally with the percentage of popular vote due to the long-standing practice of manipulating the electoral system to minimize the seats won per vote by parties out of favor with those controlling the electoral laws.

equal suffrage. The party's activity was predominantly cultural and electoral. Trade unions were founded but were originally local organizations created as adjuncts to the parties.[5] Before Gotha, there were two sets of these trade unions, just as there were two sets of parties.

The ideology of the party, its picture of the society in which it acted, was unclear. Lassalle's ideas included at one point a plan for achieving the rights of the working classes through the cooperation of government and the aristocratic groups in society. Marxian ideas, which were at this time communicated to the active party members from the distant point of Marx's exile in Paris and London, influenced thinking in the Eisenacher wing of the party but were never fully accepted. General humanitarian ideas played a role, and there was even a strong dash of pro- and anti-Prussian sentiment mixed into the diffuse argumentation that went on among the organizers. Although the followers of Lassalle and Marx represented two shades of opinion, the hardening of the party into factions, which led ultimately to the splitting of the labor movement in Germany, did not occur until much later. In this period, the party was still dominated by personal ties to a variety of leaders.

This formative period, up to the lifting of the socialist laws, was a period which in many ways represents a romantic ideal, highlighting as it does the radical intellectual politicians and charismatic leaders. The structure of the party was a kaleidoscope—a moving one—unencumbered with a bureaucracy (thanks to Bismarck). Party activity was mildly dangerous and therefore very effective in drawing the attention of the public. The party was in a ferment of organizing activity and intellectual discussion which allowed just about as much free expression as is possible in a large organization, and much potential for development. To cap it all, the party's attempt to increase its popular vote and gain seats in the Reichstag—the immediate ambition of almost every wing of the party (no matter how much

5. Cf. Carl Schorske, *German Social Democracy, 1905–1917* (Cambridge, Mass., 1955), Ch. 1 and the references cited there.

some party theoreticians would argue against the usefulness of parliamentary activity)—was supremely successful; not enough, of course, for final victory, but enough to raise the hope that the day was not far off.

A good many of the ideals of the present-day party, especially the self-styled "leftists," seem to recall this period. Chancellor Adenauer, from his own point of view, has agreed on the importance of this period. He said in an interview:

> The trouble began with Bismarck, whose fault it was that there had been no healthy inner political development in Germany. Bismarck cruelly persecuted the Socialists . . . had he not done so . . . the Social Democratic Party would never have become what it is today. Every state gets the Socialist party it deserves.[6]

1891 to 1905

In 1890 the repressive socialist laws were allowed to lapse, and Bismarck was relieved of his office by the new emperor, Wilhelm II. The period that followed was marked by accelerated industrialization (although social insurance laws took the edge off its consequences for the working class), and by maneuvers to expand Germany's influence abroad, including attempts to create an empire. In the unhealthy air left by Bismarck, unreal Realpolitik flourished.

The first congresses of the party after the lifting of the laws, in Halle in 1890 and Erfurt in 1891, brought about the adoption of a new fundamental program,[7] the famous *Erfurterprogramm* which marked the high tide of Marxist thinking in the party

6. Paraphrased by George Bailey in "A Talk with der Alte," *The Reporter*, January 5, 1961.

7. At the convention of the party held in secret in Switzerland during the period of the socialist laws, the party delegates had considered revision of the program but had changed only one sentence, in which they had bound themselves to use only legal means to accomplish their objectives.

(without, however, mentioning his name). Even then, it was an amalgam. The preamble rang with Marxian phrases:

> The economic development of bourgeois society leads with natural necessity to the suppression of small business . . . separates the worker from his means of production and changes him into a propertyless proletarian . . . the gulf between the propertied and the propertyless will become still wider by the crisis founded on the essential nature of the capitalist mode of production.

History, according to this preamble, did not lead inevitably to a violent revolution, but only to a *Verwandlung* (transformation) of private property in the means of production into social property. On the other hand, the action program that laid out the immediate goals of the party emphasized the same demands as earlier programs for the extension of democratic political rights to the working classes, along with the expansion of the social welfare laws "to protect the working class."

The debate over the general tactics of the party was beginning to take on definite shape in this period. At the Erfurt Congress there was a debate on the value of parliamentary activity, and later, especially with the publication of articles and the book by Eduard Bernstein in the last half of the '90s, the lines hardened for the Revisionist versus Radical debates which were to become the characteristic ideological fare for the readers of party journals for many years to come.[8] These debates centered around such questions as the accuracy of Marxian predictions of the development of capitalist society, the extent to which the party could indulge in revolutionary-like activity (e.g., the general strike), and whether or not it was ultimately a "revolutionary" party. The practical party activity does not seem to have been much influenced by this discussion, however. It was a period marked by the optimism of a party that felt increasingly strong, despite the fact that an impotent Reichstag meant that its elec-

8. For an analysis of the ideological conflicts throughout this period see Gay and Schorske.

toral victories were more or less hollow, that is, useful only for increasing the size of the platform on which it could propagandize against the authoritarian government. As for winning votes, the party was still very successful:

Year	Votes	% of total	Mandates
1893	1,970,000	23.3	44
1898	2,110,000	27.2	56
1903	3,000,000 (approx.)	31.7	81

The party organization, too, was expanding. It had around 400,000 enrolled members by 1904, and 533,766 by 1907.

The party organization was constructed along lines that have been retained ever since—at least formally. Its basic units followed the boundaries of the election districts, and the "sovereign" (*oberster Instanz*) was the *Parteitag* (party congress), which was indirectly elected by the local organizations. To control the party's affairs between meetings of the convention, a party executive (*Parteivorstand*) was elected annually at the Parteitag by the delegates. A proposal had been made at the Halle Congress to make the *Fraktion* (parliamentary delegation) of the party the highest authority for policy, but this was defeated and the Fraktion remained formally subordinate to the party executive. The bureaucratic organization of the party—the officials who organized meetings, ran local elections, conducted the party's campaigns in local areas, and enrolled members—was growing substantially in this period, but the party does not seem to have been troubled with the evils of bureaucracy. The democratic nature of the party, based on a high level of enthusiasm and success, was apparently furthered in this period of expansion. The scope of its activity was centered around political agitation and the informal educational and cultural societies. The trade union organization was showing signs of the tremendous importance it was to have later on. In the last decade of the nineteenth century, it acquired a central organ, the General Commission, headed by Carl Legien, which proved to be a lever from which trade union leaders were later to make claims for leadership of the labor movement, or at least a controlling voice in its policy making.

1905 to 1933

It is perhaps unusual to group this long stretch of years together into one period, encompassing as it does the First World War, the Revolution of 1919, the temporary assumption of formal governmental power by the Socialists, and the splintering of the labor movement, which led to the creation of the *Kommunistische Partei Deutschlands* (KPD) in 1921. But concerned as we are with the structure of the SPD, these years form one continuum, which might be somewhat cumbersomely described as the period in which the party worked out the implications of its desires to organize the working class and experienced the unintended consequences of large-scale organization.

Ideologically, the party became almost brittle. Off and on after 1899 the Revisionist–Radical disputes had engaged party congresses. Presided over and mediated by the Center bloc of the leaders, headed by August Bebel and assisted by Karl Kautsky, editor of the *Neue Zeit* (the party's theoretical journal), they became something like a ritual. The prolonged debate, with first one side then the other claiming victory, led, for good or evil, to a great reduction in the influence of the party intellectuals and ideologues and helped to bring about the ascendancy of the lower-level politician and the party bureaucrat. The splits that finally did occur within the party revolved not so much about ideological positions, but about certain very concrete issues, such as loyalty to the German war effort and German political institutions. Later the break was made permanent when the KPD subordinated itself to the revolutionary regime in Russia.

In terms of party policy, the most important disputes centered on the tactics and strategy of day-to-day maneuvers, rather than contests over grand ideas on the development of society. Roughly three patterns appeared, generated by the various ways in which the organizations of the party fitted into the existing political structure. In south Germany, the party was represented by men who occasionally had an opportunity to influence the legislative policy of the government and, in addition, were dependent for their electoral chances on many nonworking-class groups in society, especially small farmers. They were oriented toward a more flexible and normal participation in the political system. In the north, especially Prussia, where the three-class electoral law prevented the party from gaining the number of deputies and amount of influence in government that its popular vote indicated, the party developed into a "state within a state," a world for proletarians neither Marx nor Bismarck had imagined, which provided for the worker a wide variety of services. The corresponding political attitudes, especially among the men who worked for the party in this establishment, were generally conservative (in the framework of radical rhetoric) and defensive. Out of these two groups flowed the influence that rendered the *Erfurterprogramm* meaningless for all practical purposes, except for the demands it made for extensions of the franchise in order to provide an even firmer basis for the party and its organization. The last remnant of classic radical socialism lingered on in the largest cities of the north, especially Hamburg and Berlin, but was partially decimated when the rhetorically even more radical Communists (with their own brand of conservatism) split off from the party.

This was, then, a period of rapid growth of the party organization. Some figures will make clear the extent of this growth:

In 1907, the party had 533,766 members, in 1911 it had 836,562, and in 1914 it had 1,085,905.

Its income in 1914 was 1.47 million marks.

In 1914, at all levels of government, the party had 12,332 elected representatives.

In the same year, it had 91 daily papers, with 1.5 million subscribers, employing 267 editors and over 8,000 other personnel.[9]

9. The figures are from Osterroth, pp. 62 ff. and Ch. 5.

11

This expansion was not limited to the party itself or to its purely political activities, however, and the period showed a tremendous increase in the size and activity of affiliated organizations:

A sample of 215 local organizations showed that 2,732 lectures had been given, and there were 80 trips to museums.

In 267 local organizations, almost 1,500 artistic, popular, or children's shows were staged.

1904 saw the foundation of the first factory owned by the cooperative movement.

In the same year Socialist youth movements were founded which by 1908 had over 10,000 members, with at least two journals of their own.

"Child Protective Commissions" were founded to oversee the application of child labor legislation and to organize vacations for children.

In 1912 the *Volksfürsorge* was founded as an insurance company owned and operated by the labor movement, which by 1922 had one million insured and by 1930, 2.2 million.

Women's subsidiaries of the party also became an honored part of the movement.

In the chaotic events of the Weimar Republic, the party also became involved in a paramilitary organization—the *Reichsbannar*—in 1924.

This immense organization became the core that made the SPD the best-organized party in the Western world, able to provide the most extensive protection, care, and education of the workers outside what was possible in state institutions. It built a core of faithful members whose numbers fluctuated under the pressure of war, the revolution, the party splits, and the inflation, but which rose to the million mark and beyond in 1914, 1919, and again in 1932.[10]

These loyalties and this organization, which crystallized in the period before the First World War and perpetuated themselves throughout the following decades (even on into the post-World War II period) were the background against which the games of left-wing politics and the tragedy of radical antidemocratic politics went on. The ideal of organizing the working class into an ever larger and ever more self-sufficient unit, accepted readily as the essential immediate goal of working-class parties in the earliest period of organization, was now reinforced, with little fundamental criticism even from the radicals.[11] After all, this huge organization provided a great deal of money for the party war chests and bound the party members more and more tightly to the organization. Besides, radicals who might have criticized it needed an alternative. Such an alternative would have required a reinterpretation of the party's role amidst the realities of the dramatic international disturbances stimulated by World War I, and of the more and more complex impact of industrialization on the way of life of the working class and the rapidly impoverished middle class. The party intellectuals had only the language of the nineteenth century with which to discuss these, and the result was, and is, uninspiring.[12]

Radical groups within the party continued to play a part, and a new splinter party at the end of the Weimar period—the SAP—showed that the old tensions had not been resolved, but also that they represented a diminishing segment of the SPD itself.

10. As Duverger points out, the stability of the membership was considerably higher than that of the party's popular vote. Cf. Maurice Duverger, *Political Parties* (London, 1954).

11. Even at this time, though, there were voices raised in opposition to this organizational pattern. See, for instance, the interesting series of essays by left-wing Social Democrats published in 1931 in Bielgick.

12. The reading provided by party journals such as *Gesellschaft* will bear this out—even, or perhaps particularly, the articles written by one of the leading thinkers of the party, Kautsky or Hilferding, for example. Cf., however, the essays in Bielgick.

The party has been criticized many times for its failures in the Weimar period—especially the failure to mobilize its forces against the Nazis in 1933 and the willingness of some SPD leaders to conciliate a dictator for the sake of preserving the well-organized machine which had taken so many years to build.[13] Perhaps this criticism is somewhat misdirected, since the party, by 1933, was organized not to fight, but rather simply to exist. In a way, the criticism was invited by the party through its own rhetoric, since it still employed the symbolism of "fighting" and "iron-clad" unity and radicalism in general, which seemed to promise that it was just waiting for the chance to use the strength it had developed. But "strength" and "well-organized" are highly ambiguous terms, and the only meaning they had for the SPD after the First World War, and prior to 1933, was in reference to the strength of the members' loyalties and the ability of the party to deliver sizable blocs of votes at each election. The party was better organized to secure satisfactions for the worker by creating a subculture of his own and winning a decent standard of living for him than to secure political democracy. Once the formalities of democracy had been achieved, the party did not seem to know where to turn next.

Twelve years of suppression under the Nazis cut the history short.

After 1945

There is no better evidence of the party's success in welding its members together with strong emotional ties than that provided in 1945 and 1946, when out of the ashes of defeated Germany the party reemerged with a membership equivalent to that of 1932 (adjusted to the changes in boundaries). Organizationally shattered in the Nazi years, the party rebuilt with relative ease, despite the opposition of the Occupation authorities to political

13. The literature is voluminous and includes just about everyone who has written on the fall of the Weimar Republic. Cf., for example, Arthur Rosenberg, *History of the German Republic* (London, 1936).

activity. By 1946 the SPD had 700,000 members in the Western part of Germany and by 1948 it numbered 800,000.

Right after the war the leadership was grouped in three locations—the remains of the exiled Executive Committee in London, the "Central Committee" in Berlin, and the *"Buro Schumacher"* founded in Hannover by Kurt Schumacher, the party veteran who had spent most of the period from 1933 to 1945 in Nazi concentration camps. The London group's influence was blunted by distance (the Allies would not allow the leaders to return to Germany until 1946) and by the twelve-year break in its connections with party members in Germany.

Berlin became the battleground of the first major party struggle, brought about by the pressure of the Communists and the occupying Soviet authorities for a unified party of the left. In a dramatic series of moves in the winter of 1945–46 amidst ruins, hunger, and the four occupying armies, the Berlin SPD organization, supported by a large majority of its members, refused amalgamation with the Communists. In no other part of occupied Germany was there such a direct test, though there was undoubtedly an undercurrent of feeling for "unity on the left" throughout the Western zones in those early days. Frustrated in their attempts to bring about a voluntary unification of the parties, the Soviets resorted to a forcible one in the Eastern Zone, creating the Socialist Unity Party (SED) in 1946. The KPD (which was refused permission to change its name to SED in the West) rapidly declined in power and influence as Soviet tactics, including the Berlin Blockade, made the KPD's eastern connections more and more a liability in West Germany.

Thus a totally new kind of situation evolved, in which the traditional division of the left in German politics became largely geographic, one more element of the developing Cold War rather than an internal fight among the organizations of the labor movement. This new situation for the SPD has taken a long time to affect party thinking.

Schumacher, strongly anticommunist from the start, and relatively free to carry on organizational activities in the West (although only relatively free for some time) and in addition possessing gifts of emotional rhetoric, became the unchallenged leader of the party, and his *Buro Schumacher* became, quickly, the equivalent of the party executive, a fact which was formalized at the first party convention in 1946 in Hannover.

The position the party took against the Communists was an extension of its policies from the period of the Weimar Republic, but it was not the only holdover. Much of the party's policy and organization was marked with the party's heritage.

With regard to policy, the SPD, in common with many Socialist parties in Western Europe, and even a good many "bourgeois" parties, appeared to feel that the end of the war was to coincide with the long-awaited triumph of socialism. Schumacher's *Aufruf* of 1945 declared that the economy would "of course" be organized along socialist lines, pointing out that the SPD constituted the only major anti-Nazi group in Germany that was really democratic. He repeated in essence the Marxist interpretation of Hitler's rise as the result of the policies of monopolistic business, and reiterated many of the unfulfilled demands of the party— equal educational opportunities, increased welfare provisions, etc.[14]

A 1946 proclamation of the first postwar party congress provided the following statements of principle and historical interpretation:

> In the period between the two world wars, the powers of high capitalism and reaction tried to escape the socialist consequences of democracy . . . as socialism is not possible without democracy, so in capitalism is democracy in constant danger . . . socialism is no longer a distant goal. It is the task of the day . . . [the SPD] . . . does not want to be one party among many. It wants to distinguish itself by the correctness of its perceptions, by the clarity of its policies and the reality of its measures . . . Today the class interests of the German workers coincide with the necessities of the

14. Kurt Schumacher, *Turmwächter der Demokratie* (Berlin, 1953), 2, *Reden und Schriften.*

whole German people and the insight and will of all progressive and free men.[15]

Schumacher sought to give the party new life, but he succeeded
chiefly in extending and emphasizing the old attitudes. He did
add an emphasis on nationalistic themes in party propaganda
(meaning, principally, attacks on the occupying powers and the
Oder-Niesse line), apparently to avoid being attacked from the
right as unpatriotic, as the party had been in 1919.

The formal organizational structure of the party was also carried over from the pre-1933 period. The organization statute
adopted at the 1946 party congress was in fact virtually a copy
of the statute in effect before the Nazis took power. So, too, were
the activities of the organization patterned on earlier examples.
The party immediately tried to establish its youth and women's
organizations, its party press, and the cultural organizations that
had been its hallmark before the war. Organization proceeded
largely from the ground up, because of the early hostility of the
Occupation authorities to national political activity. It was not,
however, the same kind of grass-roots movement that had characterized the party in the 1870s and '80s, but more the re-
establishment of familiar patterns by the older members.

These attempts to increase its strength by recreating its past
were doomed to failure, but the signs of that failure were only
slowly apparent. Electorally, the party was able to win again the
third of the popular vote that had become its average level in
the Weimar period, but it was not able to go beyond it, except
in those areas of the country that had always been strongholds
of the party: Berlin, Hamburg, Bremen, Hesse. In these areas
it elected Land governments regularly. This would have represented a passable success in terms of the Weimar Republic, but
as the Federal Republic was established and election after election passed, the situation changed, and the opposition to the

15. *Protokoll der Verhandlungen des Parteitages der Sozialdemokratischen
Partei Deutschlands, 1946.* Compare the statement in 1955: "the psychological
and political situation of socialism is as unfavorable as possible." Richard Freyh
in *Neue Gesellschaft*, Vol. 2, No. 6 (1955).

SPD coalesced gradually into the overwhelming electoral strength of the CDU:

Year	SPD % popular vote	CDU % popular vote
1949	29.2	31.0
1953	28.8	45.2
1957	31.8	50.2

The policies of the party were frustrated in part through the early hostility of the Occupation authorities to changes in the political or economic structure that would involve a concentration of power in a central government (as well as their own inability to unite on policies) and then later by the fact that the party was half forced, half induced to go into the opposition. Schumacher seems to have thought it would be possible to play the old Socialist game and let history provide the party with an electoral majority, but the party was overwhelmed with the neo-liberalism of Erhard and the CDU, which was able to capitalize on—if not independently bring about—the *Wirtschaftswunder* of rising living standards, which fostered distrust of Socialist economic policies and "experiments."

The nationalistic emphasis Schumacher gave to the party's policies became shot through with contradictions as a result of the emergence of the Communist threat on Germany's borders, the prestige Adenauer was able to win for Germany by accepting close ties with the West, and the wave of pacifist feeling, especially in the 1950–51 period (the era of *ohne Mich*) which penetrated the SPD itself, building on its traditional pacifism. The party's policy, which became more and more subtle and tortured as time went on, became intellectually unsound and electorally disastrous.[16]

As for the activity of the organization, a similar story of frustration of old goals is encountered. The membership began dropping off from almost 900,000 at the currency reform in 1948 and

16. The confusion and its dangers are illustrated by the fate of a poster the party prepared which simply showed Adenauer's close contacts with the United States. People apparently thought the CDU had put it up.

continued to fall until it reached around 600,000 in 1956. The party press, originally held back by limitations on paper and legal restrictions under the Occupation, had even greater difficulties when the party papers were thrown on the mercy of the readership, which no longer appeared to want political vituperation with its news, and the women's and youth organizations struggled along without making much headway among the people at whom they were aimed.

It is an open question whether any of this would have happened if the party had been just a bit more successful in the elections of 1949, when it was narrowly nosed out of responsibility and into opposition. Perhaps the infatuation with old forms and attitudes would have persisted more strongly, as they seem to be doing in the British Labor Party, which was once considered the most right wing of the European Socialist parties but now has the most virulent left wing. But the point here is that in the 1950s the party slowly awoke to find itself with only a shell of the old organization, held together by outdated ideological commitments, and this heritage was manifestly failing to provide the rewards of political patronage which is the essential minimum of the political needs of a major party.

Efforts to reform the party were gradually felt, and, reaching periodic peaks after each national election, have finally resulted in the symbolic changes cited at the beginning of this book. These have proceeded on many fronts—in the foreign policy of the party, in the personnel of the top leadership, in the style of the party's election campaigning, and in its broadest ideological pronouncements. The formal organization of the party has changed little, but informally the '50s have seen the growth of many new organizations designed to establish contact with groups in contemporary German society, such as professional people and religious groups, heretofore inaccessible to party propaganda and electoral appeals.

The discussion preceding these changes was not carried on in the standard terms of party disputes, i.e. Revisionists versus Radicals, or "politicians" versus "trade unionists." (The trade unions, in fact, have formally dissociated themselves from all political parties.) The changes just do not fit into Marxian or traditional socialist terms at all, a fact that many party members are having difficulty adjusting to.

What the results of these changes have been for the party structure will be discussed later. First, however, we will attempt, on the basis of some tentative generalizations about German political conditions and the basic possibilities for the SPD's development, to provide a framework for understanding the relations between party structure and the position of the party in the political system.

2. Choices Facing the SPD—
The Role of Parties in Political Systems

The SPD's Heritage and the Choices to be Made

The Social Democratic Party entered the 1950s with the loyalty of one-third of the German electorate, over half a million members, and a diffuse set of political ideas which, for purposes of analysis, can be said to have reflected a compromise between two traditional conceptions of party functioning and structure. On the one hand, there was the image of the revolutionary movement, whose ideal was a disciplined group of political activists striving (with peaceful methods) for drastic changes in social values, economic institutions, and political power in the name of, and for the benefit of, the working classes, or "producers." On the other hand, there was the image of the class movement, whose ideal was that of a mass organization devoted to promoting and defending the cause of labor by the party's direct services to labor and by pressure brought to bear on the government.[1]

With each postwar general election, high government office has seemed further and further away, and pressures for action

1. These two images of the movement are not exactly those that characterized the Revisionists and the Radicals in the early days of the party, although they are related to them. They are idealized and closer to the distinction Lenin made when he contrasted the revolutionary party with one that followed the desires of the workers rather than shaped their thinking. These two images are clearly not exhaustive of traditions in the party. Lassalle's image of the party and the one promoted by Social Democrats from southern Germany in the early days constituted two others.

within the party have become greater and greater. The most easily conceived programs for reform are those that reemphasize one or the other of the traditional images, renewing the party in one or the other of the old forms. However, behind the arguments of the '50s over reform of this or that particular phase of the party's organization and activity, there was a more basic disagreement concerning the priorities to be established between these traditions and the winning of power. The difficulty was that neither of the traditionally sanctioned forms of the party seemed to be compatible with hopes for winning major political office in the near future. Adopting a plan of "reemphasis" would in effect mean postponement of power for a considerable time.[2] The upshot was that the changes in the party structure that were actually carried out showed a gradual renunciation of the older images, and possibilities for a new role for the party began to emerge.

Power and Political Movements

Both traditionally sanctioned courses of action rely for the party's appeal on a more or less coherent set of interests which represent some relatively well-defined social group in the community. The ideologically oriented revolutionary party (especially in the socialist variant) emphasizes the logical coherence and historical validity of the demands put forward and their relation (in the typical case) to that group in the population which is either unjustly treated, or somehow the wave of the future, or both. The class-movement type of party emphasizes the unity of some specific group in the population, and may have a relatively unconnected or logically incoherent set of demands as its policy, as long as they relate to the expressed or obvious interests of that otherwise defined group. The success of either type of party in fulfilling its self-defined role, which may not include winning political office, depends on its ability to maximize the support of the group it represents.

2. The question of power was not thought crucial in the early days of the party, partly because of a strong belief that victory at the polls would come naturally rather than as the result of a special effort.

Assuming that the party's own definition of this group includes a majority of the population (which it usually does), the factors that limit the effectiveness of the tie between the party and the group are the ones that limit the ability of the party to win a majority mandate. Such factors have been present in the case of the SPD, in part because of the declining attraction of old-fashioned Marxist slogans, but, more fundamentally, because of changes in the structure of the German political system brought about by the Nazis, the prosperity of the postwar years, the development of the Cold War, and the unexpectedly pluralistic effects of the bureaucratization of society. The post-World War II changes can be grouped for convenience under three headings:

Changes in the issues that constitute the "agenda" of politics

Changes in the pattern of communications

Changes in the pattern (number and style of action) of organized political groups

These changes are as momentous as those that brought into being new parties such as the SPD in the nineteenth century. They would be bound to affect any modern major party.

Parties and the "Agenda" of Politics

A party that identifies itself with a movement, whether in terms of an ideology or a particular social class, depends for its appeal on the salience of some crucial issue in society that sharply divides its citizens and creates a serious clash of interests. In order to make a successful bid for power (which, in democratic regimes, means receiving the support of a large number of voters) the party must be able to convince "its" group that this divisive issue does in fact dominate the "agenda" of politics—that this issue, and the interests it brings into play, is the most crucial question facing the political system, and that the potential adherent should therefore make his calculation of advantages and disadvantages in supporting one party or another on the basis of this issue. The "movement party" must also, of course, convince the potential

23

supporter that his interests lie with the group supporting the party.

Distinguishing this kind of appeal from that of any political party which, at election time, praises itself and damns its opposition is the fact that its appeal is based on long-standing issues and is aimed at a group distinguished not only by its shared political ideals but also by some shared experience outside the political sphere, whether it be socioeconomic status, economic concerns, or a common historical experience such as participation in a war. A party with a very effective propaganda machine and excellent organization might be able significantly to affect the agenda of politics and the voters' group identification by forcing people to accept the party's definition of reality. In the long run, however, party propaganda is unlikely to convince people unless other experiences reinforce the message.

The possibility of any movement party achieving substantial success in Germany has been seriously undermined by changes in German society and politics which have (a) blurred the identification of individuals with particular social groups, and (b) dramatized issues that are not related to any socially reinforced group conflict. The type of political agenda that made possible the creation of the SPD has disappeared.

After German unity had been achieved in 1871 and the industrial growth of the country was under way, a great many of the issues demanding political action concerned the economic, social, and political role of a limited number of great social aggregates—the landowning class, the business community, and the working class, and, cutting across these, the two major religious communities and the regional blocs of the north, west, and south. The boundaries of the state were settled, but the roles and privileges of the groups were not. On questions of economic policy, colonial expansion, industrial regulation, foreign alliances, political forms (such as suffrage)—in fact, all major issues tackled by government and subject to conflict among political groups— the pattern of political forces could be explained largely by reference to the more or less obvious interests of these groups. Disputes over government policy chiefly concerned the fairly clear-cut effects it would have on the distribution among these groups of material benefits, social status, and constitutionally sanctioned political power.

In this situation, the working class held a special place. Recently created, growing rapidly, and subjected to the serious dislocations and insecurities characteristic of the early stages of industrial growth, its fragmented and demoralized position made possible the rejection of its claims to a reasonably just share of these benefits. Its grievances were serious, and its influence slight before the creation of trade unions and working-class parties, operating first outside and then within the dominant social and constitutional framework. The situation was made to order for the kind of political party referred to as a movement. In a pattern common to all Western Europe, parties arose that could articulate working-class interests and had some hope of finding a very large group (a) willing to accept the designation, (b) convinced that its most important political task was the improvement of its conditions as a group, and (c) aware that the agenda of politics included issues affecting its interests. None of these favorable elements could be exploited without effort, of course, but one could believe that intensive party actions would be effective. Neither World War I nor the events of 1918–19 changed the situation decisively. Although the empire and the emperor fell and a democratic constitution was adopted, no major group was destroyed and no acceptable pattern of cooperation was worked out. The chief difference from pre-World War I Germany appeared in the form of extremist groups competing for the allegiance of existing social groups, a result of the frustrations of losing the war, extreme economic fluctuations, and continued stratification.

After World War II, however, the situation changed dramatically, as did the character of the issues on the agenda of German politics. Certain political groups were destroyed and others modified their demands. The radical right and left were rendered politically impotent with the fall of the Nazis and the destruction of the Communist appeal brought about by Soviet tactics in East Germany. The division of Germany eliminated the Prussian landholders, the business community was weakened by wartime economic losses and postwar restrictions, and the military was chastened by complete defeat.

The political potential of the working class also underwent a transformation. Economic prosperity, which began in 1948 but did not really get under way until 1953, gave the worker, if not equality, at least an absolute standard of living and considerable security against the hazards of sickness, unemployment, and old age that removed him from the class of "proletarian." His social status remained subordinated, but his opportunities for rising above it were greater than before, especially in the postwar confusion of refugees and reconstruction.

These transformations did not erase all economic and social differences within German society, but they were sufficient to undermine the previous fragmentation of German politics and to reduce drastically the sense of urgency with which class interests had been asserted in the political sphere. The class struggle was not dead, the classless society was not achieved, but the struggle had been mitigated to the point where its presence no longer was able to dominate all issues facing the government. The bread-and-butter questions did not die out, by any means, but they became subordinate to other issues and lost their class character. Distributive issues assumed a diffused, bargaining aspect, in which the interested groups were no longer great social classes but particular interests engaged in political maneuvering over particular actions of government.

The information that supports these conclusions about the nature of class interest is complex and diffuse. It is unfortunately not given by general economic data, since it concerns attitudes. For the workers, some indications are included in information on class identification by working-class individuals, which shows an increasing tendency for workers to consider themselves as middle class—a trend noticeable in other Western countries. A pertinent bit of information with respect to working-class attitudes was contained in a study of Marxist attitudes among workers in a plant in West Germany, reported by *Neue Gesellschaft*,[3] a jour-

3. Hans Paul Bahrdt, "Marxistisches Denken in der deutschen Arbeiterschaft?" *Neue Gesellschaft*, Vol. 3, No. 6 (1956), p. 403.

nal closely associated with the SPD. This revealed that workers accepted the designation "worker" (*Arbeiter*), but not "proletarian," and that their use of Marxist ideas has been "instrumentalized," that is, has become a method of explaining the behavior of persons in different classes. This would seem to indicate a persistence of the "movement" attitudes, but in fact these workers had ceased to believe in the possibility of seriously affecting their situation through collective political action. Presumably influencing this attitude was the declining need for drastic action.

Also important for the agenda of the political system was the nature of the issues which were forced on it. The occupation, the division of Germany, the central position of Germany in the Cold War, the necessity of maintaining the recovery and expansion of the economy after 1953, and, from 1950 on, rearmament, became the central foci of attention. The dramatic political issues facing German politicians were no longer those of competing claims of classes but were rather the problems of guiding collective efforts in uncertain situations toward commonly held goals (national integrity, collective security, economic prosperity).

Aside from these changes in the interests of the classes and in the objective political situation, a concern with the practical business of material reconstruction and expansion fostered a decline in the tolerance by Germans of ideological attitudes and utopian hopes and probably independently affected the agenda of politics.

In this situation, which for some issues could be called pluralistic and for others tended toward consensus, the "movement's" hopes for immediate power were destroyed.

*The Movement and Changes
in Political Communication*

The appeal of a movement party has also been threatened by another kind of development. The pattern of communication—the means of establishing the link between leaders and supporters

27

—has changed in two ways. First, the media reaching large audiences have become more efficient in terms of speed of transmission, breadth of coverage, and accessibility. Secondly, popular reaction against partisan material and, in addition, Occupation policies encouraging nonpolitical journalism have fostered a new pattern of media independent of party.

These developments are linked to three changes in the structure of the political system: an increase in the autonomy of mass public opinion as a political force; a rise in the importance of professional technicians in groups (like parties) anxious to influence public opinion; and an increase in the prominence of party leaders. Now, in decisions involving the sensational issues that catch public attention, and even more so in the election of the top national executive, influences from the people are brought to bear directly on the decision makers through the press and occasionally through public opinion polls. The role of the party, a traditional link with the public, in articulating public opinion is limited because it no longer controls the media. The party's formal process of registering opinion by voting on resolutions, and even the more flexible informal communications through the ranks, are too cumbersome to compete with the media and polls in expressing current feeling. The most important, but not the only, example of such direct influence of relatively unregulated public attitudes is of course during elections.[4]

A second, and directly related consequence of the communications revolution has been the increasing role of technicians in the political process. This means not only, of course, the technicians needed to operate electronic communications but also the skills we have come to associate with advertising and public relations. The older skills of personal contact and public speaking are of reduced significance, and it is both possible and necessary to hire

4. For an analysis of a German election campaign which indicates the public relations aspects of the campaign, see Uwe Kitzinger, *German Electoral Politics* (Oxford, 1960). One reason why election time shows the influence of transitory public attitudes so sharply is that the voting process makes it possible for the citizen to influence the political system at the least cost (in time and effort) to himself.

experts to manipulate the media. It may be that politicians will in time become experts at such manipulation and be able to dispense with the "experts" who are accidentally available due to the earlier development of advertising. For the present, however, the increasing number of experts in this field is striking, especially of course during campaigns.

Another consequence of the revolution in communications has been the increasing importance of the small group of political leaders who alone have access to the media on a regular basis. Television, mass papers, and radio make possible a continuing and intensive exposure, but they tend to concentrate it on only a few people. The directness and intimacy of the media (coupled, unquestionably, with the decline of interest in purely political affairs for their own sake) leads to a heightened awareness of the personality of the leader. The Germans are a long way from the intense interest in the personal details of the lives of their public figures that characterizes American politics, but the record of past campaigns, and even past discussions of policy issues attracting public attention, shows that only a few top-level personalities from each of the parties receive almost all the publicity. Perhaps the personal character of politics will develop—certainly the parties in election campaigns have become concerned with projecting images involving not only the political attitudes of their candidates but also aspects of their personal lives and character.[5]

These consequences of changing communications patterns have a negative effect on the viability of the movement type of party. At an earlier stage in the development of mass communications this statement would have caused surprise, for in the 1920s and 1930s, when radio was being developed and the first practitioners of the art of mass propaganda were active, it was a widely held belief that they would produce demagogy and a strengthening of the absolute command of the leaders of increasingly mas-

5. Cf. Kitzinger. This trend seems to indicate a "repersonalization" of politics, in direct contradiction to the Weberian thesis about the rise of "rational–legal" relationships, although one might argue that the manipulation of these personalities has itself become bureaucratized.

sive parties.[6] Furthermore, the use of mass communications by Hitler seemed to confirm the worst fears of those whom Kornhauser, in *The Politics of Mass Society,* called the "aristocratic critics of democracy"[7]—those who feared that increasing the accessibility of the masses would have chaotic consequences. The techniques used by the Soviets to manipulate public opinion can also be cited to prove that mass media are the perfect tool of totalitarianism and aid the triumph of the mass party.[8] However, when many groups have free access to the media and are willing to employ them the effect is reversed. The emergence of a semi-autonomous channel of political pressure in the sphere of public opinion makes increasingly difficult any single party's efforts to maintain its close link with the social group whose support it seeks. Other agencies with access to the same people are able to interpret a range of issues in other terms. Unless the solidarity of the group is very great for reasons other than exposure to political opinions impinging on its interests, the link with the party leadership will be weakened.

It is likely, too, that the kinds of issues continually brought forward by the media are different from those that filter down through organized or informal channels. The standards of judgment emphasized in independent mass media tend to be of a more general kind, calling on general ethical principles and general principles of efficiency rather than standards held by narrow segments of society. This tendency, linked with the changing character of the issues mentioned above, also conflicts with the movement's desire to weld a particular social group to its leadership.[9]

6. Cf. for instance, Sigmund Neumann, *Modern Political Parties* (Chicago, 1956), p. 401.

7. William Kornhauser, *The Politics of Mass Society* (Glencoe, 1959).

8. The persistence of a variety of political regimes indicates, of course, that the form of communication is not a determining factor; evidence seems also to indicate that the quality of the voting choice is not particularly affected either. The voter seems just as immune or just as receptive to rational and irrational appeals whether they reach him through the mass media or in some other way.

9. One of the most prominent of the new German magazines is *Der Spiegel,* which publishes in the format of *Time.* It seems to contradict the tendency described here, since it specializes in the "inside-dopester" kind of information that

Finally, the nature of the movement, at least as it has developed in the past, is undermined by the attention given to individual leaders. In the past, the SPD has often had well-known and popular leaders, such as August Bebel and Kurt Schumacher, but their success and their popularity stemmed from their role as the servant and embodiment of the class or party point of view. The party has always, and by and large successfully, held that the personal characteristics of the leaders were less important than the policies or interests they represented. The impact of the new modes of communication have been to highlight the individual, personal characteristics of the leaders, rather than the policies; by exposing them continually to the light of publicity, in the eager search for attitudes on issues determined not by the party's actions but by political affairs of all kinds, the leaders' personal attitudes become more important than the party position. It is possible for the leader to become the embodiment of the group in a symbolic sense, and thus preserve the movement character of the party, as Schumacher did at least in part. But the sensitivity of the process of leadership recruitment to the very process of public opinion influence renders this increasingly difficult.

Interest Groups and the Movement

Another new element in the structure of the modern German political system which must be taken into account by would-be party reformers is the new pattern of organization brought about by the growth of independent, bureaucratized pressure groups, especially those that represent the interests of large groups of citizens.

Parties themselves underwent bureaucratization, as Weber and others have noted,[10] when the political system expanded through

---

exposes the groups and self-interests behind political actions. General values may still be reinforced by this kind of journal, however, to the extent that it encourages its readers to feel above the political fray.

10. H. H. Gerth and C. Wright Mills, *From Max Weber: Essays in Sociology* (New York, 1946), pp. 99 ff.

31

the extension of the suffrage and the development of a modern economy and society. Now many other political groups, varying greatly in complexity, size of clientele, importance, and permanence, have undergone the same process.[11]

The conditions for the emergence of pressure groups seem to include the existence of functionally specific interests, sufficient resources, a reasonable chance of success in winning concessions (involving access to the decision-making centers), and, relative to the size of their clientele, the technical means to establish a continuous communication among the members.[12] In all these respects, the conditions have been favorable, although not equally or simultaneously so, for all interests. The first great surge was no doubt among the business groups, which possessed all four requisites. As the nineteenth century progressed, the working classes, landholding groups, peasants, and others all acquired, in one way or another, some kind of group representation. The interests represented then became more specific and no longer were restricted to class boundaries. Nationalists, refugees, commercial interests, victims of past wars, ex-servicemen, all acquired representation in a criss-crossing pattern. The reasons for this growth and increasing complexity are probably to be found in the increasing prosperity of society (providing the material and communications resources) and the increasing involvement of the government in the affairs of society and the economy (providing both increased possibilities of, and motivations for, access).

The impact of this organizational revolution on the structure of the political process has been important.[13] First, pressure groups promote the bargaining pattern of policy making, especially for those issues that concern the distribution of the rewards

11. For a discussion of the various organized interest groups in West Germany, see Rupert Breitling, *Die Verbände in der Bundesrepublik* (Meisenheim, 1955).

12. The classic analysis of pressure groups from a general point of view is, of course, David Truman, *The Governmental Process* (New York, 1953). For a comparative analysis on a country-by-country basis, see H. Ehrmann, *Interest Groups on Four Continents* (Pittsburgh, 1958).

13. The importance can be indirectly measured by the increased attention which it is receiving in political science writings. But see the articles in *American Political Science Review, 54* (December 1960), for a discussion of the difficulties in this approach.

and deprivations flowing from government policy. They do so because the interests they represent are specific and negotiable, and the professionals who direct them are less anxious for victory at all costs than they are for the best deal possible. The number of groups, their independence of each other, and the flexibility of their resources also promote bargaining because different issues call forth different sets of groups, and they may be able to better their position by manipulating the number and size of groups involved in a particular situation. Both the motives for, and the means of, bargaining are present.

Secondly, pressure groups usually deal directly with the administrative agencies and the committees of the Bundestag, i.e., with agencies rather specialized and hidden from public view, instead of through the parliament, the parties, or the press, that is, relatively unspecialized institutions that maximize the publicity of political maneuvering. In Europe in general, this situation is emphasized by the fact that lobbying has always been directed toward the bureaucracy rather than the parliament. Again, a more or less autonomous arena or channel of decision making is created involving specialized institutions of government and specialized group interests.[14]

Thirdly, the "clientele" of pressure groups often overlaps, bringing about a multiplication of the lines of access for the politically interested individual. This tends to minimize the attachment of the voter or the potential political activist to any particular party or group and to maximize the detached, instrumental quality of affiliations.

All these factors undermine the ability to win power of a party devoted to the maximum organization of energies around some relatively homogenous and coherent set of interests relating to a fairly well-defined social group. The loyalty of actual or potential members declines when they come to feel that a particular interest group—for instance, one supporting pensions or benefits to

14. This trend seems particularly strong in British politics. See, for instance, S. E. Finer, *Anonymous Empire* (London, 1958). In general, see H. Ehrmann, "Les groupes d'interet et la bureaucratie dans les democraties occidentales," *Revue Française de Science Politique, 11* (September 1961), 541.

33

the disabled from the war—may provide a better way of realizing their objectives than the party. In the case of the SPD this has probably been an especially important factor, since the party has not held or shared national responsibility in the postwar period.

The preemption of the role of representation by pressure groups has forced parties, at least some of the time, for some issues, into the role of bargainer or broker for several groups or between the groups and government. In a political system such as the German one, however, the executive, the administration, and the governing party are the logical points of access for such groups and the opposition party tends to be isolated.[15] For the opposition party, if its goal is to govern, the task of winning elections requires finding policies that have not been preempted, or in which the clientele of special groups feels regularly deprived. If the pressure groups are normally effective, the opposition party must find dramatic issues impermanent enough to be free from preemption. Once again, the party is driven away from the close, permanent group-representation role.

Possible Roles for the Party
Based on Tradition

These diverse changes are not complete or irreversible, but they are sufficient to alter the conditions of short-run political success and specifically the effectiveness of the traditional variants of party strategy. Faced with these conditions the alternatives deriving from tradition appear to be the following.

First, the SPD might, without abandoning the objective of holding office with a majority mandate, subordinate it to a reinvigorated "revolutionary" ideology, content to wait for power until enough new converts had been won for the cause through intensive political propaganda and/or the inexorable march of events. The party would wait, in other words, until the return

---

15. For an interesting analysis of various factors that have worked against the viability of opposition parties, see Otto Kirchheimer, "The Waning of the Opposition in Parliamentary Regimes," *Social Research, 36* (Summer 1957), 127.

of a polarized political situation (polarized in its terms) had reversed the developments described above.

A second alternative would be to retain its class identification, redefine its power objective as only that which would assure it a position of influence with respect to questions affecting the working class rather than general political responsibility, and, in effect, become a political pressure group for organized labor.

As a third possibility, it might abandon both tradition and ambition and merely consolidate its position with respect to the government power it had already established on the local and regional levels. This would involve little change in the actual organization and practices of the party, since the party organization, as we shall see, has actually formed itself around these successful groups to a considerable extent. It would, however, require the greatest possible change in the attitudes of party members, in the mystique of the party, its basis of integration, and its hopes for the future. This alternative is not likely to be chosen, but it may perhaps be the fate of the party if a better alternative is not chosen.

Finally, if it allowed the traditionalist attitudes which are so strong in the party to determine its activities, it could become a kind of "expressive" party, announcing the aims and performing the rituals of European socialism for the satisfaction of the older members of the party. In this case, it would abandon altogether real hope of power, subordinating this objective to the preservation of traditional forms.

There are enough members of the party, however, who have come close to the locus of power at the national level (in the Bundestag and in the frustrating, but nevertheless important, experience of trying to promote party ideas and concerns in such fields as foreign policy and general economic policy) to constitute a strong group placing a very high value on the goal of winning national office. It is this group that has brought about many of the changes in the party in the last few years. Drawing on the natural desire of most party members to win elections, they have managed to bring about a number of changes that have begun a fundamental move away from the older conceptions.

35

Since there is no general philosopher of this change, these developments must be analyzed on the basis of some general conception of the party's potential roles and therefore of the system as a whole. The rest of this chapter is devoted to outlining such a frame of reference.

The Political System and the Role of Parties

The aspects of the changes in the German political system that have special relevance for an analysis of political parties are the changing patterns and the increasing diversification of the channels through which political demands are made and evaluated, and, partly as a consequence, the changing pattern of specialization of the groups and institutions involved in operating the system. A party (or any other politically involved group) can be located within this complex system by reference to the specialized activities it undertakes with respect to the different channels of influence. By outlining a set of categories indicating the major types of channels and broad distinctions between specialized activities we will have a scheme that will provide us with a tool both to describe changes in the political system and to describe important changes in a party's role.

Men and Policies

First we may distinguish between the two processes of policy formation and leadership recruitment. Although interrelated, in some political systems they become distinct and to some degree independent of each other. In other words, the election of top executives and legislators is carried out with relatively little impact on the policy issues, while, independently, pressures are brought to bear that control the policy outcome irrespective of the security of the incumbent's position in office. Such a situation comes about either when the executive is chosen through a nonpolitical mechanical means (e.g. royal primogeniture) or, in modern political systems, when elections are competitions between rival personalities.

36

The maximum blending of the two processes seems to be achieved in countries where a polarization of interests exists and the electoral choice therefore involves a maximum specification of policies to be followed by the successful candidate,[16] or in systems where the constitutional arrangements allow executive leadership a great deal of freedom, forcing those interested in the policy outcome to become necessarily interested in the orientation of the incumbent. The latter case appears to hold in modern cabinet forms of government operating with two disciplined parties. Even in this latter situation, however, the range of policies effectively decided by elections when parties have no fundamental cleavages may be limited to a few sensational ones.

The contemporary German situation is moving toward a two-party system based on a cabinet form of government, but at the same time to a differentiation between policy formation and leadership recruitment on all but a narrow range of foreign policy and broad economic issues. Although more difficult for opponents with fundamental differences, the process of decision making for most policies is carried on independently of the election.

It is sometimes felt that parties ought to be the link between the two processes, providing extensive policy commitments by candidates for high office. In fact, however, in a pluralized situation they are often simply involved in both processes independently, managing campaigns on the one hand and on the other serving as coordinating agencies for policy demands, for example in parliament. Party specialization may reach the point where parties become purely electoral (the American parties are the closest approximation to this type, at least in their stereotyped image) or purely policy-oriented, as in the case of the so-called third parties.

In conditions such as those outlined for present-day Germany, the demands on a party that wishes to participate influentially in both processes vary considerably. On the one hand, successful

16. The fact that voting decisions have results significant for both men and policies does not, of course, imply that the choice is any more "rational" or that the parties are more responsible, but simply that as a result of the vote certain policy consequences can be predicted.

37

campaigns require considerable attention to the mechanics of public relations, involving professional use of the means of mass communications and an ability to capitalize on the broad and sometimes transitory concerns of the public at election time. Influencing policy, on the other hand, demands the ability to deal with a variety of organized interest groups and to evolve some system to keep abreast of or contribute to the increasingly complex information that serves as the basis for decisions the responsible political elite has to make on questions of armaments, international strategy, and economic growth.

The Arenas of Politics

Modern political systems may also be characterized by relatively distinct arenas in which issues may be subjected to different kinds of discussion or conflict. The outcome of decisions in regard to men or policies may be influenced by pressures generated from one or more of three possible arenas, which require different sets of skills and allow for different roles on the part of the particular political organization.

The first of these arenas is within the political elite, where influential men (in government, administration, party leadership, and influential nonpolitical circles) interact on a more or less personal basis, using the resources generated by friendships, individual skills, policy agreements, personal favors and disfavors, and so forth.

At the other extreme, there is the arena of public opinion. Through mass media or other forms of communication, demands arise, are exposed and discussed, support for candidates or policies is mobilized, and conclusions are reached; "mass action" (in Weber's sense of unorganized action[17]) includes elections, referenda, opinions registered through polls, demonstrations, letters to editors or deputies, and changes in behavior, such as buying decisions. The public may show that it wants or does not want a particular candidate or policy (with varying success in determin-

17. Cf. Gerth and Mills, pp. 180 ff.

ing the outcome, of course) through failing to show up at speeches, refusing to obey existing laws, taking direct action to prevent the execution of policies, and so forth.

Between these two extremes lies a third arena of intergroup action and conflict in which representatives of important groups engage in a bargaining process, employing organizational weapons to alter the balance of bargaining advantages. They may bring about coalitions, engage in economic or other tests of strength, harangue, reason with or subvert each other, and thus affect the choice of candidates and policies.

All three arenas are interrelated, and it is clear that when a major issue is at stake (for example, a conflict between the main social groups in the society or a radical change in the constitutional structure of the society), all three will be involved. In conditions of polarization, all arenas may be coordinated through political parties which maximize the coherence of one set of leaders, one set of organized political groups (under the party itself), and one bloc of public opinion. This, of course, is the situation the movement party seeks to create and exploit. Given the kinds of issues facing the German public today, however, the relation of the three arenas is much more tenuous. Only when the issue is sensational—for example, the remilitarization of Germany—do all three arenas assume anything like equal importance, and even then they are not likely to be coordinated. Public opinion trends do not exactly parallel the attitudes of important political interest groups or groups within the elite. Much more often all three arenas seem to work in different directions.

The role of a political party can vary with the choice of the arena in which it participates. The Radical Socialist Party in France under the Fourth Republic seemed to limit its activities very much to regulating conflict within the elite. Deputies within the parliament were concerned with parliamentary maneuvering, especially when it dealt with the formation of governments. When the deputies faced the country, the party as an entity had minimal coherence.

However, most parties will become involved in more than one of these arenas, and in order to distinguish such parties one has to look at the different kinds of activities they undertake with respect to each arena.

The Functions of Politics

For the purpose of analyzing these different activities we can draw on the sevenfold classification of the functions of the political process suggested by Gabriel Almond.[18] These include:

1. Socialization and recruitment: the incorporation of individuals into the political process and the acquisition by such individuals of sets of values, goals, standards, and attitudes that define their individual roles and their political objectives;

2. Interest articulation: the formulation and advocacy of political goals;

3. Interest aggregation: the process whereby different interests are brought together and by some method are reconciled or compromised to produce a result acceptable to the various groups supporting them;

4. Political communication: the conveying of politically relevant information, attitudes, and goals;

5, 6, 7. And then, finally, the three government or "authoritative" functions of rule making, application, and adjudication, corresponding to the traditional legislative, executive, and judicial functions.

The crucial functions relevant to the potential roles of parties seem to be the first four, supplemented by an additional one which, in Almond's terminology, might be included under "articulation." This is the "intelligence process" (emphasized by Lasswell[19]) or the process of research and information gathering

18. Cf. G. A. Almond and James Coleman, *Politics of the Developing Areas* (Princeton, 1960), Introduction.
19. Harold Lasswell, *The Decision Process* (Bureau of Governmental Research, University of Maryland, 1956).

40

which constitutes an important and potentially separate task in an on-going political system.

These various functions have come to be performed in modern political systems by increasingly more specialized and professionalized agencies, but the development has by no means been uniform in the various arenas of politics. As noted above, in the arena of public opinion the mass media take over much of the communication once performed by political parties, allowing a greater flexibility in the presentation of issues. The interests represented demand for their articulation and aggregation a more personalized and more flexible tool than political party organizations. The role of the individual party leader or other prominent person takes on greater importance. On the other hand, in the intergroup arena increasing professionalism of group articulation and the search for the precise points of access where leverage may be greatest leads the process of aggregation to become increasingly the result of officially sponsored consultations[20] or committees, rather than public debate.

Intra-elite relationships are perhaps the most unstable of any of the political processes with respect to the functions performed. The demand for institutionalization is not as pressing since the number of actors is much smaller, and predictability can be achieved through mutual knowledge of personal characteristics rather than institutionalization of the relationships. In addition, the patterns tend to change with changes in elite personnel, and therefore do not become fixed. In almost every political system, for instance, the chief executive substantially rearranges the intra-elite relationships according to his prior commitments and his personal wishes.

One function that appears to take on extra importance in the intra-elite arena is that of "intelligence." The elite has the responsibility for dealing with problems of considerable complexity that face modern society. When the agenda is not dominated by class conflict, its principal task is to devise effective ways of meeting common problems and managing the bargaining that goes on

20. See especially Finer.

41

among interest groups. In either case, the job may require a considerable amount of technical knowledge.

The articulation of interests among the elite is flexible and is carried out by individuals or cliques, and changing circumstances may materially alter the pattern from week to week. The function of aggregation becomes something like a staff problem.

Party Structure and the Role of Parties

Turning to the analysis of party structure and its relation to these various patterns, we must proceed on a somewhat different basis from that characteristic of many studies in the past. The analysis of party ideologies, leadership, and organization has often begun with the assumption that the central function of parties could be described in terms of articulating interests and, perhaps, a special kind of socialization and recruitment. Analyses of this kind have therefore been preoccupied with such questions as the degree of democracy within the party (thus, the faithfulness with which interests are represented), the content of its ideology or program, and, finally, its strategy for satisfying interests. The analysis of Socialist parties has often focused, for example, on the revolutionary and reformist strategies and the elements of the party structure corresponding to each.[21] Such questions are, however, on the fringe of concern if the party's role is questioned rather than assumed. Instead of determining whether the workers' interests are being truly represented, we have to discover first whether any group is being directly represented, and, if so, how many such groups and in what arenas. We must determine what functions the party's decision apparatus performs before we can decide whether it is doing it well. Instead of analyzing the theoretical validity or philosophical significance of party ideology, we must first consider whether the ideas identified with the party are in ideological form and what significance they have for the party members and the party's decision making.

21. See the historical analyses by Gay, *The Dilemma of Democratic Socialism,* and Schorske, *German Social Democracy, 1905–1917.*

These problems have been discussed in the literature of political science. Stimulated by the efforts to understand the functions of the apparently amorphous American political parties and the differences in party roles in societies marked by class conflict, rapid socioeconomic change, and consensus-based stability, comparative political analysis has distinguished more and more often between different kinds of party systems on the basis of their ability to cope with different patterns of group representation, varying political traditions, and so forth. In an effort to understand the existence and appeal of extremist parties, analysts have even turned to a discussion of the psychological satisfactions derived by their members.[22]

Generally, however, the internal structure of the party has escaped detailed analysis from the new perspectives, perhaps because many parties have very loose and changeable structures (e.g., U.S. parties), others are walled off from view (e.g., Communist parties), and yet others appear still to be playing a predominantly representational role (e.g., the Socialist parties). As a result, the study of party structure still shows the influence of an implicit representational model.[23] Even the new emphasis given to the organizational aspect of parties in the work of Maurice Duverger does not escape it, as is shown by the Michelian emphasis he gives to the study of leadership in parties and to questions of representation in the final chapters of his book, *Political Parties*.[24]

The following chapters examine the structure of the party with specific attention to the way in which the SPD has realigned itself to the changing German political scene; they constitute therefore a step toward bringing analysis abreast of the suggestions of

22. For an analysis of the personal attitudes of Communist party members, see G. Almond, *The Appeals of Communism* (Princeton, 1955).

23. The influence of this model is evident in the analyses of European parties found in a variety of books. See, for example, the discussion of the distribution of power in R. McKenzie, *British Political Parties* (London, 1955), which assesses the power of parliamentary and extraparliamentary organs over the selection of the leadership, and, for German parties, R. Wildenmann, *Partei und Fraktion* (Meisenheim, 1955).

24. Maurice Duverger, *Political Parties*.

modern theorists. Before proceeding to this examination, however, an outline of some hypotheses indicating possible ways in which elements of party structure may be related to the role the party plays may help to sharpen the focus of the analysis and make us aware of the many subtly varied lines of development along which the SPD might travel.

Ideologies, Interests, and Political Functions

Perhaps the most obvious element of a party's structure is the complex of ideas, goals, and values identified with it—its ideology, policies, or whatever they may be called. The most evident distinction to be made is the familiar classification of ideological and nonideological parties. When parties formulate conceptions of the development of society supported by ethical theories and revealing historical objectives for some social group, this indicates not only a highly fragmented political system but also shows the party to be an actual or aspiring representative of a dissident subculture within the community.

As we move, figuratively speaking, toward the nonideological end of the spectrum, the programs and symbols take on a variety of patterns indicating different orientations of the party. The philosophical and semi-scientific elements may fall away, leaving a party firmly committed to one or a specified few groups and their interests, but in a secularized fashion, indicating a role for the party in articulating group interests and serving as a bargaining agent for the group.

Another role is taken on, however, if the party, so to speak, lets fall away the symbols of group identification and group demands, but retains some aspects of its *Weltanschauung*. This may seem improbable to those trained to think of ideas as associated with social groups. But in this age when societies are in crisis but without obvious class conflict, such parties are plausible. In terms of party political culture, this kind of pattern could be described as a focus on problems held to be facing society but not receiving adequate treatment by existing social agencies. Variations on this scheme occur depending on the elaborateness of the program offered to meet the problems. A programmatic party would bring it close to Burke's definition of a party as a "group of men united for promoting by their joint endeavors the national interest, upon some particular principle in which they are all agreed."[25] Parties concerned with disinterested reform might be considered of this type; parties emphasizing religious, social, or political values, including nationalism (when these are not linked with a particular group interest), are other variations. Although no clear role with respect to the process of group interaction would be indicated thereby, the value or problem focus might constitute part of an articulative function, especially with respect to the arena of public opinion, where the party may serve as a political spokesman for interests unable to find a more direct support because of the absence of an economic basis.

At the other extreme, the symbolic framework identified with a party may be virtually nonexistent, or highly variable over a period of time, indicating a high degree of agreement with the dominant social values and the priorities assigned to them. American parties viewed over any length of time fall into this category, although the party as formed around a presidential candidate at election time, especially in times of crisis, may border on the last-mentioned type, or, perhaps, on the group-interest type. The lack of a coherent program leads only to negative conclusions about the party's role, and our attention is directed to the way in which the short-term policies of the party, advocated in parliaments and during election campaigns, are formulated, i.e., to the way in which its decision-making process is organized.

Orientations Toward Power and Political Processes

Parties are usually striving to win or stay in power, and the norms they accept as controlling that effort and the way they define the power they seek are also important indications of the role they play. The broadest distinction (and the one often used to dis-

25. Edmund Burke, *Thoughts on the Causes of the Present Discontents.*

45

tinguish parties on the left) is that between revolutionary parties and ones that accept the rules of the game. Taking these as extremes, however, one will need categories for analyzing those that fall somewhere in between.

With respect to the character of the power the party strives to win (as a realistic short-term goal), a distinction should be made between parties that aim at winning top national office and those that are content to seek influence within the institutions of government (in coalition governments, seats in parliament, appointments to administrative office, etc.). When the latter power orientation is connected with a set of goals identified with a particular social group, the party most resembles a pressure group. A party that concentrates on winning the chief offices of government (president, a majority in parliament, etc.), will have established a ranking of priorities that will probably lead it toward compromise among competing interests, preoccupation with the public (which in a democracy controls access to these offices), and, perhaps, lead it to avoid the policy-making process entirely in order to concentrate its efforts and preserve its unity for elections.

There are clearly many variations here, and it is difficult to generalize since the aspect of the party being considered is roughly identical with party strategy, and strategy is obviously dependent to a great extent on the nature of the constitutional system in which the party operates.

Party Policy Processes
and Political Specialization

Turning away from the ideas and values of a party and to its organization, our attention is directed to the way it makes policy decisions. A basic variable in determining the role the party plays in the political system is the degree to which the party policy process is self-contained. At one extreme, the revolutionary party purposely rejects society and evolves its program and strategy independently, relying solely on its own intellectuals. At the other extreme, parliamentary delegates make party policy by simply

46

adopting draft legislation directly from pressure groups or administration sources. The rubber-stamp parties of the dictators fall into this category, as do many of the loose aggregations known as parties which are found in parliaments throughout the world.

Between these two extremes, a variety of possible patterns exists which is relevant to the party's role. One of the classic distinctions employed in analyzing party structure is between parties dominated by their parliamentary delegations and those in which power rests with the extraparliamentary organization.[26] This distinction has proved useful for analysis because the latter type of party could be assumed to be chiefly the spokesman for party militants most closely attached to the party ideology, while the former reflected the interests of constituents or, more exactly, served as the clearing house for a broad range of interests which normally found access to the loci of power through parliamentary deputies. This rule of thumb may break down, however, if variations in party structure occur that make the extraparliamentary organization as open to diverse pressures as are the deputies. The essential characteristic is not really the degree of power of one or the other institution, but rather the degree to which the party serves as a channel for policies formulated outside. In a sense, it is a question of the prevailing pattern of communications.

Seen from this broader point of view, there are at least two aspects of the party's policy-making apparatus the variations of which may distinguish parties in a manner important to their role in the political system. First of all, parties may vary by the degree to which they rely on the expressed interests of organized groups within the community, ranging from nationally organized groups to local organizations. A party that is the captive of a church hierarchy or a labor union, or, on the other hand, that represents a kind of conference committee or coalition of leaders of a few important organizations, will be engaged only in a high-level policy-making process of its own. In contrast, a party that

26. A recent textbook on political parties uses this variable as an important key to analyzing parties: Avery Leiserson, *Parties and Politics* (New York, 1958). The distinction has of course a long history.

maintains a large-scale grass-roots organization (unless member-ship in the party is conditional on acceptance of a set of political objectives) will be engaged in a more elaborate policy-making process. These differences influence not only the style of the party's aggregation, but also the arena in which it operates.

The second important variable differentiating the policy-making processes within parties, and associated with its "self-containment," concerns the degree to which the party itself en-gages in intelligence operations necessary to the formulation of policy for complex issues. Some parties have been able to call on expertise within the party, in the form of either experienced individuals or institutionalized agencies. One finds the rudiments of this process even in American parties, at least on an ad hoc basis, with the creation of policy committees and task forces dur-ing the 1960 presidential campaign. Recalling the hypothesis of-fered earlier concerning the emergence of complex issues not based on the clash of more or less obvious group interests, the importance of this function in parties may be on the increase. Also, in view of the near monopoly that bureaucratic agencies appear to have established over crucial sources of information, the presence or absence of such agencies, or at least the ability to draw on independent agencies, may have relevance for democracy in general and opposition parties in particular.

Party Leaders and the Arenas of Politics

The pattern of recruitment and socialization of the leaders, mem-bers, and adherents of a party also affects its role. With respect to the part the party plays in equipping its leaders with skills and attitudes, two important patterns are, first, what Max Weber called "parties of notables,"[27] in which candidates and party leaders are already prominent people, and, second, parties build-ing independent "counterelites."

But again, within these two extremes there are variations that are more relevant in discussing party roles in Western political

27. See Gerth and Mills, *From Max Weber*, pp. 99 ff.

systems. There are important differences, with respect to the way the party operates in the different arenas of politics, between parties that establish methods of testing their leaders' popularity (promoting, for example, only leaders who win elections) and parties that are organized in such a way that the election or cooption process rewards the ability of leaders to satisfy major interest groups and to hold coalitions together.

Party Militants: Technicians or Debaters

Looking at the party's activity in recruiting and training its active membership, a broad distinction can be made between parties that, with the help of an ideology and auxiliary organizations, absorb the member entirely and parties that demand from the members only helping hands to put up posters and ring doorbells.

In between, there are different patterns. Parties may promote activities among their members which provide them with the ability to handle relatively complicated policy questions, through training in party doctrine or continual discussion of major issues. Or they may provide members with some technical training, enabling them to run elections, conduct campaigns, influence public opinion, and organize meetings. The first of these patterns, if associated with a criterion of membership implying allegiance to some particular view of politics, would indicate that the party tended to produce a fragmentation of the political culture and a narrow interest articulation. If associated with a relatively open membership, however, it might indicate a role for the party in a low-level aggregation of interests, i.e., among a large number of politically interested individuals in the community. The second, more technically oriented pattern, would make the party a training ground for potential leaders.

The Party and the Public:
Blocs, Votes, and Pressure Groups

A party's efforts to influence the general public provide a final aspect of party structure that shows how the party's attitudes and organization influence its role in the political system. The extreme cases are those presented by the party that seeks to build a bloc behind its ideology and/or class demands, and, in contrast, the party that seeks merely to discover the most superficial, but temporarily determinant, aspects of public attitudes on the basis of which it makes a very limited effort to convince the public to vote for it.

Again, significant variations can be found between the two. Parties may choose to appeal to the public by securing the support of leaders of well-established social institutions, such as the church, business organizations, and labor unions, or, on the other hand, they may seek to reach the voter himself directly, winning him away from those leaders if necessary (and if possible). These patterns have a significant effect on the type of interests the party articulates, its ability to aggregate and bargain with existing social organizations, and the arena in which it operates.

The various aspects of party structure discussed above, along with hypotheses connecting them generally with characteristics of their potential role in the political system, do not, of course, constitute a theory of parties. Nevertheless, they show, I believe, some of the more important relationships involved, and thus are a beginning point for analysis. At the very least, they can serve as guideposts for studying the SPD which will help to avoid the somewhat sterile debates about the "iron law of oligarchy," and the party's fidelity to socialist ideals. It should help us to keep aware of the party's complex problem of adjusting to the changing German political system.

Types of Modern Parties

Having suggested ways of characterizing the present German political system and the resultant pressures on the SPD, and some categories to be used in analyzing the party, it will be appropriate to end this chapter with some suggestions about different types of parties that might emerge in a political system such as Germany's in order to indicate the alternatives at least theoretically open to the party. The four types put forward here all assume that the winning of national executive office is an important goal of the party. These are therefore to be added to the types listed above (pp. 34 ff.), which had assumed that the party preferred maintaining its traditions (or the status quo) to the attainment of office.

1. The modern party of notables: Originally, the "party of notables" was described as a loose alliance of individual members of the elite—an elite determined by means other than party membership. In modern times, it might still be possible to identify such parties, for example the parties of *ministrables* or the loose groups of deputies who formed for procedural purposes in the French Fourth Republic Assembly. The distinctive feature of such a party is its almost complete dependence on high-level brokerage between groups, and, perhaps, its influence on public opinion based on the status or personal attractiveness of its candidates and leaders. It is an unlikely choice for the SPD, since it would involve a total decay of the organization, which is strongly entrenched, but under exceptional circumstances it is a possibility.

2. The American electoral party: This kind of party can be characterized as an organization with highly developed techniques for the manipulation of public opinion and with only one goal— winning elections. In contrast to the "party of notables," it is highly professional, but in a narrowly party-political sense. As we shall see, this type has much in common with many aspects of the SPD, and it serves as a kind of horrible example (because of its apparent extreme opportunism) held up by critics of the current trend in the party.

3. The "corporate" party: In this type of party, major organizations or institutions are brought together in some form of regularized relationship. The CDU took on something of this shape in the first years of its existence, insofar as it was made up of representatives of the two major Christian religious communities in Germany.[28] The SPD itself, when the unifying elements of the

28. One of the most interesting examples of a corporate party is the Partido Revolucionario Institucional (PRI) in Mexico, which brings together the major

51

socialist ideology had weakened, leaving it a party built on massive organizations such as the trade unions, also approached this type. The role of such a party is to maintain a high-level aggregation process between the constituent groups and to articulate their common interests within the political system. One of the difficulties this type of party runs into in a modern political system is the reluctance of many major groups to make such a commitment to one party.

4. The "cadre" party: The fourth type of party retains an extensive but open membership. It avoids exclusive commitments to nationally organized interest groups, and instead builds up its organization as an extensive, professionalized communications network which makes contact with interest groups and the public at a fairly low level. It recruits and develops a technically trained active membership to accomplish the transformation of the raw information acquired into policy proposals. It plays an extensive role in aggregation of diverse interests, and, at the same time, is in a position to articulate unorganized public opinion. It requires as flexible a policy as an electoral party, while operating at the same time a regularized policy-making process within the mass organization. This last type of party represents an idealized end point of trends apparent in the SPD today.

---

groups—unions, agricultural workers, and a loose grouping dominated by government employees—under the banner of the revolution. Cf. Robert E. Scott, *Mexican Government in Transition* (Urbana, 1958).

3. The Style of SPD Goals—
Policy and Ideology

The Social Democratic Party of Germany is one of the relatively few modern parties with a written program meant to be more than a transitory platform of demands: its program is intended to express the fundamental commitment of all party members. Therefore, the rewriting of this program in the 1950s provides us with an opportunity to analyze the propositions the party uses to describe its fundamental objectives, the priorities among those objectives, and the kind of commitment desired from the members.

The new program clearly indicates that the party has ceased trying to incorporate a theoretical analysis of society (whether Marxist or not) into the program as a basis for its political demands. The contents, and perhaps even more the discussions which surrounded its adoption, indicate also that a pattern of commitment is emerging that differs considerably from that of the party in an earlier stage of its development. In an examination of the course of the discussion which preceded the final adoption of the program at Bad Godesberg on September 17, 1959, we can trace the development of the pattern.

The Postwar Program Debate

Before 1953

As noted in Chapter 1, the party developed a century ago amidst considerable debate on the purposes and proper organization of a working-class party. After the turn of the century, the ideological discussion hardened into relatively well-institutionalized factional disputes. At the same time the end goals became less and less significant in the normal activity of the membership and the working politicians. One could say that the ideological debates became ritualized, meaningful only to a relatively limited circle of high priests initiated into its esoteric symbolism. The simplified features of class-conflict, working-class identification, more or less revisionistic concern with bread-and-butter goals, and political democracy remained relatively fixed as a set of ideas commonly held by party members, unperturbed by the formalized debate that went on around them.

After the interruption of World War II, as indicated in Chapter 1, the party perpetuated many of its old forms and old policies. Largely absent, however, were the ideological disputes of the past. One has the impression that the disputants burnt themselves out in the sterile arguments that preoccupied the exile colonies or were snuffed out in the enforced silence of Nazi Germany.[1] Thinking of the old style of the party, a good number of respondents to my questions, as well as leaders of the party, noted the "lack of concern with fundamental or theoretical questions" in the immediate postwar period.[2]

Contributing factors were held to be (1) the extremely disorganized economic situation in the wake of the war, which gave people little time to think or worry about fundamental theoretical problems, and (2) the drastic limitations placed on publication by the paper shortage and the policies of the Occupation authorities. It appears, however, from later debates among party intellectuals, that a more basic reason lay in the fact that these in-

1. There are two books that deal in detail with these rather futile debates: Erich Matthias, *Sozialdemokratie und Nation* (Stuttgart, 1952) and Lewis Edinger, *German Exile Politics* (Berkeley, 1956).

2. This was the dominant theme of an informal paper shown to me by its author, who had left Germany in the late 1930s after having engaged in underground Socialist activities. Written for friends still in the United States when he returned to Germany in 1950, the paper verged on despair. In general, the interest in fundamental questions shown by the rank and file after 1957 seems to have come as a great surprise to party leaders.

tellectuals had, chameleon-like so to speak, blended into the background. It was, and still is, very difficult to distinguish the writings of Socialists from those of non-Socialists on such questions as automation, the basic problems of international politics, and social legislation.[3] As in other countries, Great Britain for example, there has been a convergence of opinion among intellectuals of all parties, especially in the important area of the government's participation in the economy. This was true in Germany in spite of Erhard's "free market economy."

The rank-and-file membership, or at least its representation at the first party congresses, appreciated that the old social analysis and political demands were no longer valid in the radically altered conditions of occupied Germany. Failing (it seemed) to notice that the intellectuals were no longer expressing a distinctive socialist theory, they insistently demanded of them that the old program be brought up to date. Willy Eichler, later chairman of the program commission,[4] noted in 1952 that:

> Since the beginning of the reconstruction of the Social Democratic Party of Germany immediately after the political and moral collapse of the Hitler empire, a new program was demanded by many party members, one could even say by almost all of them. Party activity should have a firmer foundation through revising and programmatically formulating the intellectual, political, and economic postulates of the political struggle for socialism. These demands seemed to all to be taken for granted.[5]

3. For example, see the book by Leo Brandt, *Die Zweite Industrielle Revolution* (Munich, 1957); although written by a prominent socialist, it contains very little that could be labeled distinctively socialist. The party itself sometimes acts as though the differences between socialist intellectuals and others in society are minimal. Albeit with a particular end in mind—winning favor among members of the Catholic Church—the party's continual quoting of Oswald Nell-Bruening, a Jesuit social theorist, is a case in point.

4. Eichler was actually *Feder-führender*, or secretary, of the commission. He was and is the member of the party executive concerned with cultural and educational questions. Cf. *SPD Jahrbuch, 1958–59*, p. 372.

5. *Protokoll der Verhandlungen des Parteitages der Sozialdemokratischen Partei Deutschlands, Vom 24. bis 28. September in Dortmund, 1952*, p. 103.

The demands were raised at almost every one of the postwar conventions and, at most of them, resolutions were passed calling for the formulation of such a program.[6]

Kurt Schumacher, leader of the party until 1952, was unconvinced that the time was right for such a reformulation. He said in 1946:

> We are in a period of transition, in a period in which the events have not yet taken shape, and as long as there is no clear tendency, programs will be senseless. One cannot give order to life with dogma, one must take lessons from life. One can have a morally and scientifically based desire, but one must steadily deal with reality. An action program which decided all questions today would be a dream.[7]

Schumacher noted, among other things, that the presence of the Occupation authorities and the division of Germany had injected uncertainties into the situation.

Despite the rank-and-file demands, and influenced by those who, like Schumacher, were fully involved in the immediate problems of rebuilding Germany along lines that many thought would "of course" be socialist, the party failed to produce any significant programmatic writings in traditional socialist form. Instead, a series of committees and weekend conferences produced reports and statements on particular policy questions, and some general statements about the role of socialist theory in the party. Some of the latter foreshadowed the formulations of the

---

Eichler was introducing the *Aktionsprogramm* at the time. (All party congress protocols will hereafter be referred to simply with the word *Protokoll* and the year in which the congress took place.)

6. A resolution from the 1948 congress reads: "The party congress instructs (*beauftragt*) the party executive to institute a program commission without delay. The draft of the program commission is to be distributed throughout the whole party for discussion before it is laid before the party congress for decision." *Protokoll, 1948,* p. 208.

7. Kurt Schumacher, *Turmwächter der Demokratie, 2,* 75. Note the extent to which Schumacher uses idealist or Hegelian language. This manner of speaking has steadily declined in popularity since his time.

1959 Godesberg Program. A meeting of the 1947 Ziegenhain Conference of the Cultural Policy Committee of the party executive declared, for instance:

> The results of Marxist methods [of analysis] are a source which the party cannot overlook. However, they are not the sole and absolute basis of all knowledge. The SPD considers the spiritual freedom of men and their ethical responsibility as formative factors even of the historical process. The SPD struggles for its ultimate political goals not alone in continuation of the tendencies of economic development, or from reasons of material expediency, but also for the dignity of man.[8]

Despite what one might call the pretension of this declaration, the intent of it is clearly to loosen the ties between the party and the more extreme Marxian ideological formulations. This, however, was not the kind of thing the militant members of the party wanted, and there seems to have been little enthusiasm among them. A leading party intellectual complained that the results of these conferences were "only brochures" which remained unread.[9]

In preparation for the 1953 elections, the party leaders decided to issue an *Aktionsprogramm,* listing the relatively specific demands that formed the basic policies of the party, but carefully distinguished from, and introduced as a temporary substitute for, a *Grundsatzprogramm* which would later provide the more basic analysis on which these demands would presumably be founded.[10]

There were no startling propositions in the program that distinguished it from the policies followed by the party in the years immediately preceding its adoption, and insofar as it did touch on fundamental questions at all its language was vague. It was prefaced by the last piece of writing Kurt Schumacher was to

8. Quoted from a report in the *Rhein-Neckar Zeitung,* November 10, 1947.
9. Gerhard Weisser, "Die Wissenschaftliche Grundlage des Berliner Programm der SPD und des Stuttgarter Entwurfs," *Kochel Briefe,* May–June 1959.
10. See the speeches of Ollenhauer and Eichler, *Protokoll, 1952,* esp. pp. 103 ff.

finish before his death. It bears the marks of the period in which it was written—disappointment that the workings of change had forced the party into opposition, but optimistic enough about the future (based on the tide of opposition to the Adenauer regime that had swept the country in 1950–51 as a reaction to the government's tentative steps toward rearmament) to maintain aggressively that it had been right all along:

> One acts today in Germany as if everything that has happened since 1945 is the result of the activity of the federal government. It must here be stated: in the years 1945–49 there was not yet a federal government, and in those times the decisive situation of Germany emerged. Almost always, it was the Social Democratic Party alone which took a clear position.[11]

There was little debate on the 1952 Aktionsprogramm either prior to the party convention at which it was adopted or at the convention itself. It was a project of the party leadership and a commission of experts, undertaken with an eye on the coming elections. It was a long document, however, and ill-suited for a widespread propaganda effort, and there were many voices later noting that not even the members of the party had absorbed its roughly 60 pages[12] or the explanatory handbook that followed it. The manner of drawing up the program evoked numerous complaints about the party's reliance on "experts," who usurped the members' right to make party decisions.

Before 1953, the party was compartmentalized into a variety of groups that seemed to have little communication with each

---

11. *Aktionsprogramm, 1952* (Foreword). I have in general not attempted to provide specific citations to the various fundamental programs of the party, since they have appeared in a variety of easily available forms, and being short would not give difficulty to someone who wishes to trace a citation. See Bibliography.

12. The need for drastic pruning was often declared, especially after the party executive submitted a draft program in 1958 that was 64 pages long. In the end, no synthesis of a slogan program and a program of detailed analysis was found possible, and the final program, which might be said to fail in both respects, was 19 pages long.

other. The intellectuals were a small group, impressed by the growing meaninglessness of Marxian conclusions (though often distinguishing them from his methods of analysis) and increasingly inclined to reject as inappropriate a revolutionary or even reformist program in the old style. They failed, however, to make a deep impression on the rank and file, who wanted the old revolutionary socialist analysis translated into terms that would apply to the contemporary scene. The central leadership was involved with practical problems and contented itself with postponing a showdown on a new program. The fourth and in later years decisive group consisted of relatively young leaders, together with the so-called *Bürgermeister-faktion*. These members were not party militants but were acquiring experience in politics in the administration of Länder and in the Bundestag. The name *Bürgermeister-faktion* comes from the fact that its leading members were the heads of the Social Democratic governments in the *Stadt-länder* of Bremen (Wilhelm Kaisen), Hamburg (Max Brauer), and Berlin (Ernst Reuter). Their strength may be partly explained by the fact that, in contrast to the national leadership, they were successful in winning public office.

In the period prior to 1953 this latter group had opposed a good many of Schumacher's policies—especially his foreign policies[13]—but had been relatively silent on questions of the basic structure of the party, including its ideological basis. Such general statements as they did issue on the subject came to the same conclusion Schumacher had supported—that a new program was undesirable. Their reasons, however, were quite different. They emphasized that a program in the old sense was impossible, while Schumacher insisted (at least publicly) that the time was simply not yet ripe.[14] These differences did not result

13. Kaisen, for example, had become involved in a group called the "German Section in the Socialist Movement for the Creation of a United States of Europe," which sought a more positive approach to the problems of European integration than the long opposition maintained by Schumacher.

14. Ernst Reuter, mayor of Berlin for many years and at one time widely considered the second most important personality in the SPD next to Schumacher, in fact proclaimed that the party could only carry on "successful politics . . . when it bases itself on a secure intellectual and moral basis . . . [and] when

in an open clash. A more typical approach of the Burgermeister-faktion to the program debate was to avoid it altogether. For example, a volume of speeches given by Max Brauer (mayor of Hamburg) throughout this period contains no speculation at all about the general nature of the party but deals only with the problems of reconstructing the city of Hamburg.

1953–1957

The 1953 electoral defeat of the SPD was a turning point in the party discussion. The election, influenced by the Russian threat, the suppression of the June 17 workers' uprising in Berlin less than three months before, and the relative economic prosperity in West Germany, led many to the conclusion that the party's "socialism," however distinct it was from Communism, was severely damaging to the party's electoral chances. More and more of the active party members decided that something had to be done to reverse a very unfavorable electoral trend. Immediately after the defeat, a series of reform documents appeared in Berlin, Hamm, the new "Süd-West" state, and elsewhere, sponsored chiefly by groups of younger Socialists. They included among their demanded reforms the need for a new program.[15]

I shall discuss their reasons for desiring a new program more systematically later, but it is sufficient to note here that their

---

these leading ideas spread out from the movement . . . and become the common property of the people." But in the same pamphlet, written in 1947, he emphasized the need to make the party the rallying point for the whole people, as a necessary step toward legitimizing the democratic regime. The latter is the primary goal. Ernst Reuter, *Grundsätze und Ziele der Sozialdemokratie* (Landesverband Berlin der SPD, 1947).

15. Representative documents are the following: *Beitrag zur Erneurung der Sozialdemokratischen Partei Deutschlands,* Vorgelegt von Jungen Sozialdemokraten des SPD Unterbezirk Hamm, 1953; "19 Thesen für die parteiinterne Diskussion," *Mitteilung,* published by SPD Süd-West, 1953 (mimeo.); *Ernst Reuter Briefe* (Berlin), which appeared irregularly seven times up to June 30, 1954; and *Die Linke: Sozialistische Informationen zur Aussprache und Kritik,* published twice (February and July 1954) by Georg Kahn-Ackermann and Dr. Gerhard Szczerny in Munich.

In 1954, the party executive outlined its own proposals as "Empfehlung des Parteivorstandes und des Parteiauschusses zur Partei Diskussion."

demands appeared to be motivated by a desire to bring the party back into contact with the tides of public opinion and to eliminate the inconsistencies in the party's policies and general political posture. They by no means wished to reinstate the purity of the older socialist doctrine or to rejuvenate the party's radical, revolutionary tendencies, which had been the staple elements of the rank-and-file demands for a new program up to that time.

In retrospect, 1953 seems to have been the crucial turning point—a point at which the uneasy coalition of the groups which (for differing reasons) were against efforts to write a new program was destroyed, and a new coalition in favor of a new program (again for differing reasons) emerged. It was to take six years before the *Godesbergerprogramm* was passed, and then only after the reformists had gained the strength to make their image of the new program acceptable to the majority of the party members—but it was in 1953 that the tide began to turn.

After the initial rash of reformist manifestos, the movement for reform disappeared once again behind the scenes in the form of a committee—although this time the committee really produced something. The first result was a new preamble added to the *Aktionsprogramm* in 1954 at the Berlin party congress. It sought both to maintain the radicalism and idealism of the party and to render it less objectionable by redefining it in more general terms than was common in prewar SPD programs. At the same time, they (rather self-consciously) carefully distinguished the party from the more extreme and rigid forms of that idealism which had become part of the party's public image.

The Social Democratic Party of Germany declares itself (*bekennt sich*) more decisively than ever for the great ideas of democracy and socialism—for the emancipation of men from unworthy dependence and spiritual serfdom, for a society of peace and justice.

In the previous century, Marx and Engels created the scientific basis for socialism. Since that time, the conditions for a fighting (*kämpfenden*) socialism have fundamentally

61

changed . . . The Social Democratic Party of Germany was always concerned to reexamine its policies [in the light of] social realities and spiritual development. It is conscious that it must realize its goals under the changed conditions of the present. It will, in the process, never deny its essence and its tradition . . .

The Social Democratic Party of Germany does not represent the special interests of single groups . . . A new society . . . does not come about by virtue of the inevitable (*gesetzmässigen*) course of history . . . Socialism will therefore always remain a mission.

Socialist ideas are not an *Ersatzreligion* . . . In Europe, Christianity, humanism, and classical philosophy are the ethical roots of the socialist body of thought . . .

Social Democracy has, from the party of the working class . . . become a party of the people.[16]

Although many of these phrases were incorporated into the *Godesbergerprogramm* five years later, this preamble was not presented to the members or the public as a substitute for a new program but rather as a temporary and provisional expression of certain general goals which would eventually be included in a more detailed program. Accordingly, the 1954 party congress formally directed the party executive to establish a committee, which, according to Eichler's report in 1958, it did by naming:

Thirty-four members, supported by advisors and consultants in a series of special areas, [who] formulated a draft for a fundamental program in about 40 meetings, above all in subcommittees.[17]

16. Ironically, this preamble contains the first mention of Marx in a major party program.

17. *Protokoll, 1959,* p. 333. The 1959 Protokoll is an unusually useful party document, containing both of the drafts of the program submitted by the party executive, a report of the debates at the meetings, and all of the changes proposed by party organizations. It is even indexed. I have cited this volume wherever possible, even for materials issued earlier in pamphlet form.

Although spread out over four years, this was undoubtedly the most extensive record of work that any program committee had shown.

Publicly, however, the party debates over the new program, and more generally over party reform, died down after 1954, especially with the approach of the 1957 elections. Despite the undercurrent of reformist activity, the leadership of the party was securely in the hands of Ollenhauer and others who were bred in the traditional movement and carried on Schumacher's attitudes and policies. Ollenhauer, whose 1959 resignation from the position as chief party candidate was celebrated in the party's internal journals by an editorial entitled, "Ollenhauer, Man of Compromise (*Ausgleich*),"[18] was (if the reports given to me retrospectively by party members in 1960 are valid) almost universally considered a representative of the status quo with regard to the party, and lumped by his many critics on both right and left among the members of the *Apparat*—the party bureaucracy.

Klaus-Peter Schulz, critic of virtually all tendencies within the party but identified more or less with the reformers, concluded that the post-1953 reformers attempted too much without sufficient foundation, that is, without prior organization. He felt that their plans for a spiritual renewal of the party scared the left into a temporary coalition with the tradition-minded party members and the *Apparat;* this coalition was able to control reform groups at the 1954 convention. By using the party leadership's insistence on "harmony,"[19] it succeeded in warding off any serious challenge to its preeminent position.

Except for the passing of the Berlin preamble to the *Aktionprogramm* and the establishment of a behind-the-scenes committee, there was little done in the way of fundamental reform of the party's program until after its defeat in 1957—when Adenauer gave the party its most serious setback by winning over 50 per

18. Cf. for example the 1959 Summer issues of *Der Sozialist* and *Der Sozialdemokrat*, papers published monthly for party members in Hamburg and Frankfurt respectively.

19. Klaus-Peter Schulz, *Opposition als Politisches Schicksal?* (Cologne, 1958), pp. 17 ff.

cent of the votes. The reformers were at that time moving to the offensive in another field: against the party's policy toward rearmament. In 1956, the party engaged in an acrimonious, though inconclusive, debate on the subject. Under the leadership of the "new men" such as Fritz Erler, the party's defense expert, some headway was made, however, in bringing the party around to accepting an expanded army with close Western ties. Also in that year, the party convention in Munich had as its theme the challenge of the "second industrial revolution" (automation and atomic energy), through which the leadership tried to redirect the members' attention to modern social problems instead of old-fashioned problems of class conflict. With respect to the program itself, however, this period saw only the by then conventional demands that a new party program be written as soon as possible.

1957 and After—The New Program

After the disastrous 1957 elections, reformist efforts for a new program shifted into high gear. At the same time, changes were made in the party's parliamentary leadership, and these were followed closely by a change in the leadership of the party organization itself.[20] These changes left Ollenhauer as the leader of the party, apparently only as a concession to the old guard—though chiefly a symbolic one.[21] The 1958 party congress finally saw the submission by the party executive of a draft for a *Grundsatzprogramm,* an event that touched off a surprising amount of interest among the rank and file. Actually it contained nothing dramatically new that could not have been found, in

20. See also Ch. 6. Carlo Schmid's speech, "Die SPD vor der geistige Situation dieser Zeit," before the 1950 party congress, *Protokoll, 1950,* pp. 225 ff., could be considered one of the first reformist speeches by a major party leader in the postwar period. Significantly, Schmid was one of the few leaders who survived the change-over in 1957 with enhanced prestige. His contributions have been almost exclusively in the field of the underlying intellectual liberalization of party dogma and not the programmatic declarations or the party structure.

21. This is probably a good example of satisfying a group with a symbol when its fundamental demands have in fact been rejected. See the interesting elaboration of this practice in Murray Edelman, "Symbols and Political Quiescence," *American Political Science Review, 54* (September 1960).

germ, in the previous documents noted, but, spelled out for final commitment by the party, these ideas stimulated much more controversy than ever before. It was a long document—64 pages in length—rambling and repetitive. The draft included a *Bild der Zeit* (analysis of the contemporary situation), a section on the "fundamental values of socialism," general statements of party policy in a variety of particular fields, and it ended with a section on "The Only Way," which reviewed the history of the party and issued a general inspirational call for support from the German people.

Virtually everyone criticized its length and diffuseness; intellectuals criticized its conceptual sloppiness and its lack of fundamental analysis in the Marxian spirit of critical analysis.[22] By far the most vocal criticism came from those who, for one reason or another, objected to the abandonment of certain traditional socialist aims and formulations, which, although they had not really been a working part of the party's policy making in the previous decade, had not been so dramatically rejected before: attitudes toward nationalization and private property (which were now rejected and accepted respectively), toward the churches (tentatively embraced), and toward military defense (now affirmed as a necessity, in spite of somewhat pacifistic objections). Criticism of these provisions of the new program came, as might be expected, from both the tradition-minded rank and file and a vocal group of younger actives who, by and large, had not followed the steps of men like Erler (the defense expert) or Heinrich Deist (the economic expert of the party) into public office but had made their name in the party organizations and thus had not found it necessary to alter their more militant radical beliefs.

In the year and a half between the submission of the 1958 draft and the Godesberg congress, there were many conferences, special lecture courses, debates, and speeches concerning the new program throughout the party organization, which resulted in the submission of a total of 86 amendments. Later, in response to the second or revised draft submitted by the executive in 1959,

22. *Protokoll, 1958,* pp. 359 ff.

an additional 172 proposals flowed in, making a total of 258 separate initiatives from party organizations, including 6 completely new programs. The discussions continued right up to the calling of the Godesberg congress, which was dedicated exclusively to the passage of the program.[23]

The convention itself was expertly managed, as all the SPD's conventions are, but proposals to reinstate more radical formulations on the economic, religious, and defense issues nevertheless managed to win the votes of up to one-third of the delegates (who were indirectly elected to participate in the congress by lower party organizations). However, the bulk of the party membership appeared to support the efforts of the leadership to make clear the party's new moderate position. The program finally passed with only 16 negative votes from a total of 340 voting delegates, and in almost exactly the form proposed by the party executive in the second draft, which was, in turn, little more than a condensation of the original 1958 draft.[24]

The victory of the reformists was virtually complete. The formulas of the Berlin preamble, which had been worked out by the intellectuals in the postwar years, now became the official doctrine of the party. Through the device of debates, and given the prestige of a fundamental program, the reforms were brought home finally to the rank-and-file membership. So far, at any rate, there has been no significant revolt against them, although one attempt was made in 1960 to form a leftist party out of the small group of members who had resigned because of their opposition to the tendencies expressed in the new program or had been expelled because of contacts with the East German Communist regime. This splinter movement, one of whose leaders was Victor Agartz, ex-SPD economic expert and leading intellectual in the labor unions, appeared to be so thoroughly compromised by its

23. The 1958 party congress instructed the executive to have the program ready for passage "no later than 1960" and to meet in 1959 to decide whether a special congress should be called in that year (which was an off-year in the biennial cycle of congresses). The executive met in January 1959 and called an "Extraordinary Congress" for November. The second draft of the program was not circulated until six weeks before that congress.

24. Both are included in *Protokoll, 1959*.

inclination to think well of the Communist regime in the East that it had no chance of succeeding among the sizable group that was hostile to the line taken at Godesberg but at the same time anti-Communist. This larger group has made no move. Many of its members appear to be taking the position that one must wait and see.

From the point of view of our study, however, the significance of the *Godesbergerprogramm* is that it has no ideology. The party has changed enough so that an ideological program is no longer appropriate.

Ideology in the New SPD

Those who demanded a new fundamental program after World War II commonly assumed that the party would simply reanalyze society in the light of socialist principles, objectives, and standards and that these would—with enough excogitation—produce a new theoretical analysis of the present historical stage of social development, which would in turn justify and enlighten the party's tactics and recreate the kind of intellectual unity and clarity obviously lacking. The Godesberg Program contains virtually no such theoretical analysis, a fact attested to by defenders and critics alike. The program itself declares: "The Social Democratic Party . . . is a community of men holding different beliefs and ideas. Their agreement is based on the moral principles and political aims they have in common."[25] Willy Birkelbach, one of the leading spokesmen for the critics of the program at the Godesberg party congress and party chairman of the Hessen-Süd Bezirk, opened his remarks on the program by saying: "I call this a . . . part of a program . . . a fragment. It lacks the grounding . . . in the historical situation."[26]

The program is "fundamental" only in its declarations of very general ethical principles (e.g., "freedom, justice, and solidarity"), and although there are some generalizations about historical development (e.g., "an important characteristic of the modern

25. *Protokoll, 1959*, p. 13.
26. Ibid., p. 78.

economy is that steadily strengthening process of concentration") they are not cast in the Marxian mold that projects the trends into the future. They very often remain so general that it is impossible to deduce even a general policy direction from them. An example might be drawn from the section dealing with the developing countries:

> More than half the world's population still lives in deepest poverty and ignorance (*Unwissenheit*). As long as the riches of the world are not newly distributed and the productivity of the developing countries is not considerably increased, democratic development and peace remain threatened.

This is given simply as a fact, and there is no theoretical analysis of why this should be so or the conditions under which the "generous and unselfish help" which the program then recommends will be successful, unless this can be read into the rather vague conclusion that the developing countries will only avoid "new forms of oppression" if their development is accomplished with the "ideas of democratic socialism."

It may seem to be going far afield to draw examples from the situation of underdeveloped countries and the party's policy toward them to illustrate the lack of social theory in the Godesberg Program, but it shows most clearly, perhaps, the theoretical inadequacy of the program and is by no means untypical.

An attempt was made to evolve a new general theory in the opening section of the first draft of the program submitted by the party executive in 1958—Das Bild unserer Zeit—but this was later dropped from the final program. Its rejection was not based on disagreement; because it failed to give anything like the basis for political action that Marxism and reformism had provided, it was cut out to make the program shorter (and more likely to be read).[27] The central theme of the piece is man's lack of autonomy in modern society. According to the analysis, his attainment of autonomy is threatened from two sides—by the "in-

27. Ibid., pp. 335–47. Unless otherwise noted, the following pages contain quotations from this document only.

security and fear" of the modern world and by the unequal opportunities for individual development.

> Two world wars with their catastrophic results, a world economic crisis which man faced helplessly, the rise of systems of government using methods of repression of frightful gruesomeness, inflation, which destroys the confidence of the people in the legitimacy of the state, the pitiless expulsion of many millions from their homeland—all this has given mankind a serious moral injury. The old system of values is shaken to the core. The guiding images of men and their tasks are shattered.

The result is the "widespread pessimism of our days, which seems to give no more opportunity for freedom and *Kultur*." Threatened by the possibility of war and by the obviously growing capacity of man to destroy himself, man has lost the confidence necessary to master his environment, partly because of his legitimate distrust of the panaceas which have been offered him in the past: "The cure for pessimism can no longer be faith in progress, since, of course, science has taught us that the . . . optimistic belief in the unavoidable progress of man . . . finds no verification in experience." But if history has not been able to provide a solution, then neither has the automatic working of the economy advocated by classical economists nor the economic policies of modern governments: "Although economic policy is today in a position to limit economic crises and long-lasting unemployment, the social insecurity of men is a basic fact of our life."

The threat from outside—in the form of war—is traced by the party to the existence of two power blocs in the world and (in a final parenthesis) to the division of Germany, which is considered a special contributing factor. The party notes that here too existing solutions—international organizations like the U.N.—have so far failed to fulfill their task and provide security.

This analysis does little more than set up the problem around a question generally similar to the Marxian one of alienation. But whereas Marx goes on to analyze the causes of alienation in

69

the relationships of men to their work and the economic relationships of society, the document discussed here strikes off tentatively in another direction. Private property, far from being the bête noire, is part of the solution to the ills of society. For the small factory owners, handworkers, farmers, and small businessmen, "property is an important foundation of their independence and freedom." In fact, "all men have a right to property."

Having turned away from economic determinism, the party turns to a political analysis of man's difficulty. The key is not property, but organization. This leads to the conclusion that it is not the owners, but the managers who have accumulated excessive power, though there is a tendency to generalize the argument beyond this relatively simple proposition. There are two broad forms of the argument, which are not clearly distinguished from one another. The first is that the existence of massive organizations (benefiting from the administrative "economies of scale" they have been assumed to have ever since Max Weber analyzed modern bureaucracy) means that those not so benefiting start with a disadvantage. The second is that within any one organization the leaders tend to arrogate to themselves the power and privileges provided and to undermine democracy.

The appearance of this last argument is interesting because it represents the effort of the party to turn the weapon of the theory of the "iron law of oligarchy" on society in much the same way that Michels developed it as a criticism of the SPD in his book on political parties written fifty years ago.[28] The document states:

> All organizations, whose influence has unavoidably displaced the individual, have the tendency to develop their own lives. For an organization is not only determined by the ordering or founding principles on which it is based, but above all by the men who lead it. Once the organization has reached a certain power and intensity, it is difficult to control them. Thus the servants can easily become the masters.

28. Robert Michels, *Political Parties* (New York, 1959).

This danger of bureaucratization [sic] threatens not only the state today but the whole of social life.

The new dependencies that develop out of the growing organization of social life are the central problems of our society. They come about independently of the class division and will in no way disappear when it is possible to dispose of class rule.

But it appears that the "law of oligarchy" is not confined to particular organizations but to society in general: "The democratic parliamentary state, whose purpose it is to secure equal rights and freedom, is subject to the same tendencies as every large-scale organization in society." The problems generated by these tendencies include the decline of the legislature in the face of executive power and the power of business organizations over government policy and elections as well as their economic power over the market and even science.

The omission of the section of the draft program that included the analysis of the world as a universal oligarchy was justified because it could not have constituted a new ideology. To do this, it would have had to explain and justify a large part of the party's policy objectives. But the program takes up problems of inequality of income, maldistribution of educational and other resources, international organization, and so forth, without relating them to the "iron law."

In addition, the "iron law" theory does not qualify as a social theory because the conditions under which oligarchical tendencies become manifest or the means of reversing them where they do occur are not discussed in the writings of party intellectuals, much less in the program. The so-called theory is really a condemnation of special interests and of organizational elites as opposed to the "general will" of the people. In fact, it does little more than present the bare form of a problem and its solution—where inequality of political power and economic reward are found, steps should be taken to equalize them, usually through the device of establishing a "democratic" collective decision-making

71

process. This covers everything from codetermination in industry and increased power to the Bundestag to the creation of PTAs, and is therefore almost completely indeterminate. It provides no guide to action.

One might interpret the absence of a valid and comprehensive social theory as simply the result of an intellectual decline, but before jumping to this conclusion let us analyze the purposes a theory might serve in order to see whether they are still appropriate to the party in its present situation. The purposes can be summed up under three headings: the role of a theory in policy decisions, its role in ensuring unity in the party, and, finally, its role in mobilizing public support.

Theory in Policy Making and the Party

An old slogan of the party reads *Wissen ist Macht*—knowledge is power. As heirs to the tradition of rationalism stemming from the Enlightenment, and decisively influenced by perhaps the most rationalistic of all ideologists—Karl Marx—socialists have had and still have a strong belief that successful political action requires a thorough knowledge of the general trends of historical development and of the essential factors that influence the structure of society. For socialists this has not only meant the desirability of theoretically informed individual behavior (as it has meant for many others) but also collective behavior. Collective rationalism is perhaps the hallmark of socialistic movements in the twentieth century, and one can still find innumerable quotations from writings of party members of all shades and varieties that echo this ideal. For example, the reformer Fritz Erler was quoted as saying that the party needed a "comprehensive analysis of society" and a "new outline of society" in order to determine the extent to which party policies "lead toward or away from an order that ends privileges and brings about the abolition of societal conflicts of interest."[29]

29. Quoted in *Hamburger Echo*, November 25, 1953.

Otto Stammer, sociologist and intellectual closely affiliated with the party, uses the typical political language that identifies desirable characteristics with real ones in saying, "Social Democratic policies are distinguished from [those] of other parties in that [the party] tries always to hold the total interrelation of social and political events in its view."[30] Or going back to Schumacher, "the problem for a political party is . . . not to have been right in the past, but to have a great new political conception of events, how they should happen and how they must happen."[31]

The fact that these three quotations are found in different contexts—the first as part of the post-1953 reformist drive to reshape the party, the second in a reaction against the course these reforms seemed to have taken, and the third in the typically Schumacherian self-conscious mixture of apology and arrogance —illustrates the common attachment to the rationalistic norm.

In one of the clearest departures from tradition, the party's leaders have now rejected the Marxian doctrine of historical inevitability still found in the statement quoted above from Schumacher. One can reasonably argue that a belief in such inevitability is not really rational; nevertheless the conception of how things must happen has always been an important element of Marxist thinking. Scientifically, Marx's predictions have been a failure and are so recognized by most socialists. Marx failed not so much in predicting the impoverishment of the middle and working classes (about which there can be, and is, argument), but much more importantly in showing the way to overcome such "contradictions" and cope with the major political issues in society, such as the rise of Nazism and the impact of the Bolshevik Revolution.

In short, although some developments may be predictable, and therefore appear inevitable, no sure guide is provided to answers to the problems the party faces, nor is the party (and the citizenry) relieved of responsibility for independent attempts to understand and solve social problems. This line of reasoning lies back of the statement in the *Godesbergerprogramm* that "We are called on

30. Otto Stammer, *Die Freiheit des Menschen in der industriellen Gesellschaft* (Munich, SPD Landesverband Bayern, n.d., probably 1958).
31. Schumacher, *Turmwächter der Demokratie*, 2, 323.

to solve these contradictions. In our hands lies the responsibility for a happy future or for the self-destruction of humanity."

Erler's demand, noted above, is for a model of utopia, though this does not imply belief in history's inevitable progress toward it. Such a utopia would apparently serve as a yardstick by which the party could measure its policies. Although the party has often been called utopian, a model such as Erler suggests would be a radical change. The well-known absence in Marx's writing of descriptions of the socialist society is a true reflection of the party's emphasis on the historical movement rather than the end goal. The utopian element in socialist thinking has been largely emotional and symbolic rather than rational.

However, explicit rejection of a theoretical base for party programs is also made by some party members, who seem to feel that perhaps a unified rational picture of the world, translated into terms simple enough to be communicated to the voting public and the membership, is perhaps not the best way to guarantee rational behavior. This attitude was often implied in the attacks on "dogma" by the defenders of the Godesberg Program, but they were somewhat ambiguous, since they could apply either to those who wished to retain old principles or to those who wished the party to identify with a single theoretical conception of reality.

The point has been more clearly made in connection with the ineffectiveness of the party in 1933 when, it has been held, the party member with stereotyped ideas about reality was unable to assert himself effectively against the threat of Nazism.[32] Dissenters from this point of view assert, on the other hand, that the "ideological parties"—the Catholic Center Party and the SPD— were the only ones that managed substantially to maintain their voting strength against the inroads of Nazi appeals up to the end of the Weimar Republic.[33] This argument, however, goes

32. For example, an unsigned note written by a party member in exile in the early 1930s, on file at the Institute of Social History in Amsterdam, bitterly complained that the party had not prepared the working classes to think for themselves.

33. See, for example, Wolfgang Abendroth, "Warum Parteiprogramm?" *Neue Gesellschaft*, 3 (1956).

even beyond the Marxian notion of equipping the workers with an understanding of their world in order to protect them from the ideologies of the bourgeoisie; dogma is here considered good in itself no matter what the content, which seems to have been too great a step for most socialists since it finds little echo in the writings of leading members of the party.

The clinching argument against the adoption of a theoretical view of society in a party program, however, has been the obvious one that there is no theory that commands universal or even widespread support in the party. Following Schumacher's lead (p. 56 above), Eichler in 1952 considered the problem of finding a fundamental theory as contingent upon getting modern science to establish a unified theory, and concluded that both tasks were for the present too great.

> The scientific methods in psychology, mass psychology, sociology, and also economics, not to speak of the natural sciences, have been so refined, the results of research in these sciences have brought so much new knowledge about man himself, his personal and his social reactions, relations, and capacities, that no one today can maintain that everything has been worked through enough to make our picture of the world and our intellectual and politico-technical programs as scientifically grounded as is possible in principle, and will be possible in the foreseeable future.[34]

In the ten years or so since that speech, the party may be said to have become either tired of waiting for social science or more and more convinced that what it was waiting for was never to come. In any case, by 1959 the emphasis was not on the temporary insufficiencies of science or the fluidity of current events but rather on the impossibility of creating a binding theory. The insistent demands of critics of the program (such as Birkelbach at the Godesberg convention and other "radical" intellectuals throughout the party) for a "new theory" seem only to emphasize

34. *Protokoll, 1952*, p. 103.

the impossibility of fulfilling their demands, since none of their speeches or conversations offers such a theory, and there is a tendency simply to revert to Marxian formulations. The commonly demanded change in the nature of property relationships, for example, has never been elaborated. There was a tendency at the Godesberg congress to fall back on nationalization as a solution even when questions as far apart as distribution of income and competing with the Russians were being discussed. Without a new theory and/or a dramatic personality, the radicals appear to be limited to Marxian-sounding formulas, since these are the only ones with any chance of appealing to a wide group. There is a traditionalist bloc among the members which always seems willing to applaud and vote for the old symbolic demands —but few who will support their implementation.

If a theory is not to be made part of the structure of the party, the question then arises of the role played by the process of theorizing or research. Some Social Democratic leaders have made statements recently that suggest a more flexible conception of theorizing as an on-going intelligence operation. In 1956 Fritz Erler, writing in the *Neue Gesellschaft,* the semi-official theoretical organ of the party, suggested for example that the party should realize that the rank and file have neither the interest nor the capacity to deal with problems of social theory. He proposed that the party transform itself into an arena for the discussion of serious social problems, especially the consequences of industrialization and economic development.[35] Willy Eichler has suggested:

> Socialists are not relieved of their tasks through the development [of history]. They are lasting tasks, which demand continual investigation of the real situation and a continual proved readiness for struggle . . . here lies the necessary connection of science, politics, and education.[36]

35. Fritz Erler, "Eine Partei unter vielen?" *Neue Gesellschaft, 3,* No. 3 (1956), p. 200.
36. Willy Eichler, *Lebendige Demokratie: vom Wesen und Wirken der SPD* (Bonn, 1957), p. 10.

And Ulrich Lohmar, editor of *Neue Gesellschaft,* has written:

> We cannot conceive of a socialist theory . . . as a perma-
> nently binding and stable model. It must be the result of a
> continual comparison of empirical analysis with the values
> suited to our practical work. This comparison allows us to
> determine at the time the ways and means that lead to the
> realization of socialist goals . . . science is the connecting
> link between the goals and methods of socialist politics.[37]

Finally, the 1958 draft program itself asserted that:

> Out of the historical conditions of social life, the basic values
> of freedom, justice, and the dignity of man, and fundamental
> judgments about the order of social life, a standard is pro-
> duced for the democratic socialist, who will take into ac-
> count every new development of the society in an un-
> doctrinaire fashion, but will persevere in those things that
> count.[38]

Although these comments are vague and ambiguous, they
indicate a new self-image of the party. Structurally, the emphasis
shifts from ideas to thinking, from fixed interpretations to research. It makes the cognitive apparatus a process rather than a
fixed element. The decision-making structure of the party reflects
this change by its use of experts.[39]

Social Theory and the
Integration of the Party

A theoretical interpretation of society can also serve to bring
about or maintain unity within the party. During the course of
the program debate, many of the proponents of a new program

37. Ulrich Lohmar, *Neue Gesellschaft, 2,* No. 6 (1955), Editor's Note.
38. *Protokoll, 1959,* p. 351.
39. Cf. Ch. 5.

argued that it would reestablish agreement on policy which had suffered major shocks from opportunistic machinations in short-term election activities and/or the influx of members who did not know what there was to agree to. Especially in the early stages of the debate, the problem was cast in terms of conflict between militants and politicians.[40] The following statement by Erich Arp, speaking in 1948 in favor of the formulation of a new program, illustrates this point of view:

> we find ourselves in a stage in which the real revolutionary will of the active members and functionaries finds less expression in the practical policies of our party than . . . an independent activity of the *Parteiapparat* on the one hand and the *Ministerialismus* on the other . . . [which results] all too often in only empirical-opportunistic politics.[41]

To their way of thinking, an explicit social theory in a party program allows the active members and functionaries to make their own judgments about the appropriate political strategy to be undertaken in any particular situation. They are able to use the tools of analysis provided in their common program to come to their own understanding of appropriate action and to measure the behavior of the deputies and party leaders. This system presumably prevents the politicians from succumbing to the temptations of opportunism or the blandishments of pressure groups. Klaus Schütz, rising young member of the party, MdB and political scientist from Berlin, credited the party's independently formulated ideas (along with independent financing) with preventing it after the war from becoming, as other parties had, the creature of nonparty groups such as the Occupation powers, the Catholic Church, or business.[42]

---

40. One of the striking features about much socialist writing about the party is the assumption that the "real" party is a combination of ideas and the people who are most dedicated to them—the militants. This image underlies even Robert Michels' work on the early Socialist party.

41. *Protokoll, 1948*, p. 65.

42. Max Gustav Lange et al., *Parteien in der Bundesrepublik* (Stuttgart, 1955), pp. 166 ff.

As years went by, and the demand for a new program was taken up by the reformist wing in the party, the same argument was used against the *Apparat* to prevent continued public pronouncements by older party secretaries and functionaries who still talked in the language of the Weimar Republic. At least that was the public line of argument. But here as elsewhere the attack on the party bureaucrats was really an attack on the radicals and left wingers in the party. A substantial number of the party members with whom I talked expressed the opinion privately that the Godesberg Program could be used to silence the radicals or oust them if necessary, although this was not openly declared. One can surmise that the reformist leaders were unwilling to proceed further than they already had against the party militants, who could muster significant voting strength in party congresses at many levels. The passage of the Godesberg Program was enough—and the proper political tactic was then to award the left a share of the rhetoric. Consequently, both before and after adoption of the program, party speeches were filled with compliments to the organization, the functionaries, and the active members of the party organization, employing the standard image outlined above of their function and failing to mention that the passage of the program had cut out its core. The Godesberg Program could henceforth be the basis of independent judgment by party militants who were not necessarily in a position to be informed about the technicalities of the legislation that would be necessary to transform extremely vague generalities into policies. The use of the program as an integrator was important, therefore, not as a theoretical basis for each to judge independently the actions of all, but, on a completely different level, as a tool to discipline the few who damaged the party's public image.

It would be tempting to argue from these developments that, for whatever reason, modern political parties in pluralist systems such as the German are no longer viable if they identify themselves with political theories about social realities and development. The problem facing the SPD, however, has not been a clear-cut question whether it should be an ideological or a non-ideological party, but rather whether, in its particular circum-

79

stances, it could find, elaborate, and accept a new programmatic social theory in place of an older one which could no longer receive a majority vote in the party and which large numbers of party leaders were very much opposed to on the basis of political expediency as well as intellectual disagreement. The problem of evolving a new program was summed up most bluntly by one of my respondents, a member of the Bundestag and prominent party leader on the Land level: "An analysis [of society as a basis for party policy] was abandoned because it could not be made the subject of a democratic vote." A debate of considerable intellectual proportions would have been required, but even the little that occurred often stirred resentment. Attempts to air fundamental issues in journals and magazines met with apathy or even hostility since, especially in reformist hands, they were usually critical of the leadership.[43] Even in committees, progress was difficult. The subcommittee that was to draw up a fundamental philosophical statement of socialist principles failed to find sufficient basis of agreement to submit a draft. When an attempt was made to shorten the *Bild unserer Zeit* section of the original party executive draft of 1958 (discussed above) there too the "experts" failed to agree to a shortened and more unified version. The idealism of party members who desired a reorientation to society was not sufficient to make up for the diversity of existing ideas or the lack of a dramatic leader or situation who could impress a new vision on the members.

Party Theory and the Public

The demands for a new program also referred to benefits the program would produce in winning support for the party among the public. Perhaps the most common assertion of this kind in the early years of the party's debate after the war was that without some kind of well-founded idealism, such as the party pro-

43. In the second issue of *Die Linke* (cf. note 15), Gerhard Szczerny complains that the reaction to the first issue from party members had been to accuse the editors of violating party discipline by publishing public criticisms of the party. The most sensitive issue was apparently the leadership.

vided (or thought it provided) in the early years of the century, the youth of the nation would never be attracted to the party and the intellectuals would never be convinced that political activity was a worthwhile arena for their special talents. The following quotation from the 1958 party congress debate is representative of many statements of this kind:

> In my opinion, this program must put the following line of thinking in the foreground, and only with this . . . will we win [*erobern*] the students, the intellectuals, and the youth. First, that the present economic structure is not working, and second, that it cannot be fixed by minor corrections, and third that we are not giving up the vision of a new economic order in freedom and democracy.[44]

Or another: "We must give to man the feeling that the world is comprehensible, that it can be changed, and that [one] can do so with and through us."[45]

Another view holds that a fundamental program is essential for the "organization of the propaganda of the party,"[46] and this is linked with a constantly reiterated objective of the party to instruct as well as to secure the simple act of voting for the party. For this a program is necessary—a fundamental program:

> What is successful politics? A party which, as a mere party of interests, does not pretend to give society a specific meaning and a specific form needs no program. A socialist party, which wants to act politically and pedagogically . . . must know in advance . . . what is most useful to this goal of freeing men internally and externally.[47]

It is believed that the public tests the party on the depth of its vision. "Only with extensive, clear ideas of society . . . can we

44. Joseph Neuberger from Dusseldorf. *Protokoll, 1958*, p. 395.
45. Wolfgang Jansen. Ibid., p. 440.
46. Eichler. Ibid., p. 361.
47. Ibid.

avoid the practice of appealing to isolated single groups in the society and become a real party of the people."[48] And "Such isolated appeals condemn the party to being considered unworthy of trust [*Unglaubwürdig*]."[49]

It is interesting to observe that the emphasis on renewed idealism referred to in the first of these quotations and the many others like it stems usually from the early stages of the debate or from the wing of the party that sharply criticized the Godesberg Program. In contrast, the emphasis on the *Glaubwürdigkeit* of the party and on the organization of propaganda stem from the later periods and from the defenders of the program. There was a slow change, therefore, from the ideal of making the program the rallying cry of the revolutionary center to the need for a program to correct the impression that the party was still living in the '20s. The program became less and less a new conception and more and more an up-to-date statement of goals. One justification for abandoning the effort to find the new conception is frequently evident in the party discussions, where the "youth of today" is described as somehow "different," somehow less accessible to the kind of revolutionary idealism characteristic of the past. A number of older socialists with whom I talked seemed to despair of this new youth and often wrote it off as materialistic or egotistic. In contrast, Klaus Schütz, the young party member and political scientist cited above, interprets youth's dissatisfactions with revolutionary conceptions more positively. The following quotation is from a 1952 speech of his (and is, incidentally, the only place where the conclusion is openly drawn that the party should abandon its tradition of fundamental programs):

the party must understand that one must speak to the youth and probably to other parts of the population with more seriousness and genuine realistic conviction . . . for this reason, I wish to speak out expressly against a Grundsatzprogramm . . . with beautiful words, however holy they are

48. "19 Thesen." (Cf. note 15.)
49. "Beitrag zur Erneurung." (Cf. note 15.)

to us still, we will accomplish absolutely nothing with the younger generation.[50]

The sentiment against a revolutionary theory later became even stronger, although with the publication of the draft program in 1958 there was no need to inveigh against the idea of a Grundsatz-programm, since the abandonment of theory had been accomplished without abandoning the formality of a fundamental program. Besides criticizing "dogma" in the abstract—a favorite word of abuse used in the Godesberg party congress to attack the leftists—many of my respondents insisted that the party had to avoid giving the impression of knowing everything or of dictating the shape of the future. Asked whether the party should now go to work to evolve a new theoretical conception of society, one man threw up his hands and said, "No, no more theory. The people are tired of *Zukunftsmusik!*" This attitude was, not surprisingly, especially common among the party members active in responsible local positions.

An important segment of party members no longer seems to view the public as a great thinking being which has to be rationally convinced with sophisticated arguments or inspired by the vision of a new society. More and more, the tendency is to see the party's essential role vis-à-vis the public as offering a series of well-founded, concrete plans, which can be accepted or rejected depending on the voter's interests and conviction that the party can accomplish the objectives he desires. In the "theoryless" Godesberg Program, global theory has been abandoned.

The Objectives of Political Action: From Revolution to Problem Solving

Except for Socialist parties, theories of society are not commonly found in party programs, but policy objectives are. Objectives vary, however, from party to party in their "style." The demands of an African nationalist party for "Freedom now!," of Demo-

50. *Protokoll, 1952,* p. 163.

crats in the United States for 90 or 100 per cent parity for farmers, and of particularistic parties in many countries for protection of their ethnic groups differ in the degree to which their demands can be realized, the priorities with which they are held, and so forth. These differences can imply fundamental differences in methods of action.

From Goals to Values

The SPD asserts in the Godesberg Program that it is a party united on "moral principles and political aims." This is, of course, a very vague statement, but it contains an important element of truth. For the fixed programmatic objectives the party has today are in fact a series of values or abstract moral criteria that purport to control its actions in all policy areas, flexibly and without specific reference. On a different level, party policy is a changing array of plans and programs that express proposed methods of tackling current social problems, without elevating those programs to absolutes or specifying any single problem as of such earth-shaking preeminence as to demand absolute priority.

The writing of any statement of goals and principles, such as the Godesberg Program or an election platform or a parliamentary policy statement, is of course a complex process of adjustment and bargaining, of reconciling the views of the politician needing a specific demand to appeal symbolically to a particular group wavering on the edge of support with the views of the more or less professional mass psychologist trying to achieve the right tone for the particular document. The result is that such documents do not often fit into neat conceptual categories. The Godesberg Program, for instance, is a mixture of general and specific demands.[51] On the whole, however, party leaders tried to preserve the fundamental character of the program by confining its statements to ones of general purpose and intent, leaving more specific policies to the various plans the party has

51. The proposed amendments at Godesberg were about equally divided between points of literary style and attempts to strengthen party statements on particular subjects, especially cultural and social policy.

published and to electoral programs. The intent was to put into the program only those demands the party expected would continue to be valid for at least the next decade or so.

The result is instructive. The program contains principally objectives which (a) pertain to no particular group, (b) are for all practical purposes unrealizable, and (c) are purposely vague about the steps the party might take to achieve them. Such is the case in the initial section of the program, which sets out the "hopes of our time":

> Make [man's] life easier . . . free him from anxiety and distress and create prosperity for all . . . secure world peace . . . [establish] the rule of international law . . . [reduce] mistrust between peoples and [stop] the arms race . . . For the first time in history it will then be possible for everyone to develop his personality in a securely founded democracy and to broaden his cultural outlook free from want and fear.[52]

These generalized objectives are naturally also characteristic of the sections on the "Fundamental Values of Socialism" and the "Basic Demands for a Society Worthy of Man":

> Freedom, justice and solidarity, the mutual obligations which arise out of the common bonds [of men] are the basic values of socialism . . . the Social Democratic Party strives for a way of life in accordance with these basic values. Socialism is a lasting task . . . All people must submit to the rule of international law . . . all peoples must have an equal chance to share in the world's wealth . . . we are fighting for democracy. Democracy must become the universal form of state organization and way of life . . . all privileged access to educational institutions must be abolished.

This vagueness is all the more significant, however, in the following sections, which deal with separate topics. In the section

52. The translations of passages from the program are a synthesis of those provided by the party executive and my own, which are supplied when the others, which appear to have been hurriedly prepared, become extremely loose.

dealing with the "Order of the State," for example, the party demands:

> the unity of Germany in secured freedom . . . freedom of belief and conscience . . . the rights of minorities [must be] protected along with the rights of the majority . . . the division of the public authority into federal, state, and local should distribute power, secure freedom, and give citizens manifold access by means of codetermination and coresponsibility to the institutions of democracy . . . the freedom of local communities [*Gemeindefreiheit*] should be further expanded and financially secured . . . Associations . . . should have a democratic structure.

and so on.

In contrast to earlier programs, the party minimizes its demands on behalf of particular groups—there are neither the specific demands such as suffrage for the working class nor the general ones for the economic emancipation of the workers which characterized the old programs. Where groups are mentioned, they are usually defined in role terms, that is, in terms of all who enter into particular relations—such as "consumer," or "citizens," "families," and even "workers" and "employers," who are not treated so much as classes in the population as parts of a particular social relationship.

There are exceptions—for instance a demand is made for pensions for those disabled in the war—but these do not fit the general pattern, and there are many goals that are simply enunciated without reference to groups at all, declaring in effect that any persons found to be ill-treated within the terms of the general standard deserve the right of Social Democratic protection and representation.

Correlatively, the goals enunciated are not cast in terms that emphasize realization, but instead, as the program says, set out "lasting tasks." Very few of the demands pose specific objectives such as universal suffrage, nationalization or socialization of all industry, or other classic goals which, however difficult, could at

86

least be accomplished in the imagination. Values such as "just distribution of income" and "equal opportunities to develop one's personality" are not set forth as goals to be accomplished but as permanent standards with which to judge recurring situations.

The absence of detail regarding methods to be used to accomplish the goals is conspicuous and is perhaps most dramatically evident in the party's pronouncements on economic policy.

> Totalitarian control of the economy destroys freedom. The Social Democratic Party therefore favors a free market wherever free competition really exists. Where a market is dominated by individuals or groups, however, all manner of steps must be taken to protect freedom in the economic sphere. As much competition as possible—as much planning as necessary!

This statement is of course mainly significant for its clear implication that nationalization of industry is not considered the most important or even, in some cases, an appropriate method of achieving the party's economic objectives. The effect is to make the section on economic policy like all the others—imprecise as to methods. The party avoids declarations that commit it to any particular act and confines itself to a statement of standards under which action will presumably be taken.

This change in the style of goal setting met with both approval and disapproval among the SPD members to whom I spoke in the course of my interviewing. Many referred with satisfaction to the party's "pragmatic" orientation and to the importance of applying the basic principles of the party—economic equality and justice, equal opportunities in education, etc.—to society and discovering where society fails to live up to them. When questioned as to groups to whom they felt this approach would appeal, the majority again—especially among the *Kommunalpolitiker*—simply used the injustices to identify them, by speaking of the "socially or economically weak" as the group which could most benefit from the party's activities. However, members who had hoped for a more meaningful program complained that the program had "fine ideals" but no concrete demands and no indication of how the ideals would be realized.

The reasons for this change in emphasis from goals to values seem to be pretty clear—it is based on a desire to appeal to as large a number of potential voters as possible, and the party leaders seem to have concluded that a far greater consensus can be found on these general values than on specific proposals. The party seems to be in the process of changing its focus from specific goals to problem areas. It is beginning to see itself as the vehicle for concentrating political activity on the long-range solution of rather well-defined problems, which are not prematurely petrified by insistence on particular analyses or particular solutions, and thereby to define the party's position and distinguish it from its competitors who treat problems individually and out of their historical context.

A party oriented toward problem solving but chiefly characterized by vagueness in analysis and proposed solution may seem to be exhibiting nothing more than opportunism dressed up with a noncommittal moral tone. There is, however, potentially more involved. A problem-solving approach can represent a positive contrast with the idealistic party in the older sense in that it may imply that the party has established institutions and a pattern of activity which brings competent men into contact with responsible leaders for a continual review of developments to produce measures, if not solutions, to alleviate continuing problems. This means that the party has become pragmatic and that its pragmatism does not rely on the individual responses of party leaders to isolated issues. It means that a pattern might develop to make "collective pragmatism" possible.

Problem Orientation

In turning to the particular problem areas that actually interest party members it is apparent that there are several. The fragmentation of the SPD's present problem orientation can be explained in part by the fact that different groups within the party have had radically different experiences and have therefore formed different ideas concerning what constitutes the main threat or challenge to German society. All share, however, pro-democratic goals and attitudes. Democracy, as a matter of fact, has become a better term than socialism to describe broadly all types of SPD goals.

The first problem area is economic and social inequality among classes. Two groups have taken different interpretations of this problem as the focus of their concern. The first still holds to the Marxian analysis, which finds the cause of injustice within the system of property and the form of economic production. Curi-ously enough this group, which thinks of its main task as the overthrow of the system of property, is not made up of the oldest members of the party, but rather one segment of the youngest. Certainly the most radical Marxist sentiments I heard were among the members of the *Jungsozialisten* (Young Socialists) and young socialist students, plus a few of the slightly older members whose occupations were closely involved with the labor movement in organizations such as the unions. They are not a majority, but they are often the most vocal, especially in the Frankfurt area. The other group, and on the basis of my interviews the dominant one among the party members holding local political office, can best be described as preoccupied with goals aimed at bringing about the welfare state. Essentially, for them, the threat to Ger-many lies in the political domination of the CDU. Their solutions lie in legislation—to achieve better distribution of income, better health insurance, better security for old age, and so forth.

The second problem area, one clearly generated by the his-torical circumstances of the Weimar Republic and the immediate postwar period, is the threat to democracy from organized ex-tremist movements of the right and the left, operating *within* the political system. Except for a few small right-wing parties, this no longer involves a competition for votes, since the Communist Party was outlawed in 1952. The Communists and their allies, however, still force the party into competitive organizing in the factories and in pacifistic organizations. The immediate threat is seen as infiltration and loss of control of major organizations, and the conclusion is that countermeasures should consist of the greatest possible mobilization of persons into the party and the greatest internal solidarity.

I was very much struck in the course of my interviews with the degree to which the latter problem preoccupied the older members of the party, especially those most closely connected with the unions, cooperatives, and other subsidiary organizations of the labor movement. It was sometimes but not always combined with the "anti-system" attitude mentioned above. Perhaps the most firmly convinced organization fighter I met, who emphasized most strongly, for instance, the need for absolute unity in the party and lived in an almost romantic world of conspiracy, had spent several years in a Siberian concentration camp.

A third set of experiences which dictated and dictate a particular definition of a problem area was the struggle against the Nazis —not the struggle against the emergent Nazi party of the Weimar Republic but the seemingly hopeless struggle against the armed might of the Nazi regime in power, supported as it seems to have been by a considerable degree of consensus among the German people. Those who were and are preoccupied with this situation have become involved with the question of the psychological characteristics of the German people and their level of political education. This third group, many of whose members engaged as young men in hopeless underground conspiratorial activities against the Nazis, is very important in the SPD today, especially in the present leadership. Herbert Wehner, for example, is fond of quoting Kurt Schumacher's opening words to the preface for the 1952 Aktionsprogramm: "The Social Democratic Party of Germany emerged after 1945 with the intent of creating a Germany which would exclude (*ausschliesst*) the repetition of the horrors of the past."[53] Wehner himself, a Communist until 1942, actually represents something of a synthesis of the second and third orientations I have discussed. However, in his role as chief defender of the Godesberg Program against the criticisms of the left, which he assumed at the Godesberg party congress, he has

53. Cf. for example, *Die Arbeiterfrage im Grundsatzprogramm der SPD* (Bonn, n.d., probably 1960), speech before functionaries of the party working in the factories in early 1960.

been inclined to defend the necessity to reform the Germans rather than fight the radical movements. This third orientation has been especially significant in recent years in the party as a lever for changing its style, since it commits the party to seeking a position of responsibility within the country and not contenting itself with the organizational contests characteristic of the second orientation. This is a potent idealistic argument for winning elections and making the concessions necessary to that end.

A fourth problem area has emerged in the past decade, born out of the experience of the Cold War. It might be called "anti-Communism—new style," that familiar feature of virtually all Western politics. It is "new style" because it involves not the organizational in-fighting of the 1920s (or late 1940s in the Eastern Zone) but rather the Realpolitik of international affairs, armaments, economic competition, and propaganda competition which is by now so familiar. This orientation has been relatively long in emerging, probably as much because of the division of Germany as because of the tradition of SPD–KPD hostility, which tended to blur the fact that a new situation had arisen.

Party members who think in these terms seem to be on the increase, but as yet I would judge that it is the dominant concern among only a relatively few members and leaders of the party, chiefly those associated with the formulation of defense and foreign policy in the party's parliamentary delegation. The outstanding example in the leadership is Fritz Erler, the defense expert. Another example of this modern concern, and the modern definition of the problems facing democracy today, was evident at a lecture given by Helmut Schmidt, MdB from Hamburg, who spoke on the complicated problems of military strategy in terms of missiles and bombers, retaliation capacities and deterrents, and all the rest of the all-too-familiar jargon of the military expert.

These four are not the only interests of party members, but they do provide a basic framework within which more particular problems are thrashed out, and they guide such fundamental thinking as there is in the party today.

To understand the historical significance of the minor drama which the passing of the Godesberg Program presented, with its rejection of many old socialist shibboleths, it is important to realize that the older demands, long identified as peculiarly "socialist"—for instance, the nationalization of basic industries—had always been considered solutions to the whole range of problems outlined above, or at least the myth was maintained that this was so. To socialize the means of production would, by traditional Marxian analysis, solve the problem of alienation and inequality, undermine the extremist movements—to put it crudely —by entrenching social justice in the operation of the state, defeat the tendencies to authoritarianism among the Germans by habituating them to collective, democratic decision making (perhaps most importantly, with respect to the last two problems, it would undermine the large capitalists who were considered the chief support of right radicalism and Nazism[54]), and even fight communism by encouraging economic growth and a strong economy.[55] The last-mentioned was, of course, by far the weakest link, and a belief in the opposite effect of socialization has become common, i.e. that socialization sometimes produces—as "proved" by the lessons of the Soviet experience—the very dangers the party is anxious to guard against. Thus one finds the otherwise difficult to explain statement in the Godesberg Program that "totalitarian control of the economy destroys freedom . . . The Social Democratic Party therefore favors a free market wherever free competition really exists." It is this breakdown of the all-purpose solution that exposes the fragmented quality of the party's concerns.

The problem orientation of the party is also seen in its effort to implement its general moral goals· with relatively detailed plans dealing with problems such as education, welfare policy, and even certain aspects of foreign policy. Perhaps the Aktionsprogramm of 1952 should be considered the first of such plans. It was, however, in the old style—a bastard fundamental pro-

54. The interpretation of the fall of the Weimar Republic and the rise of the Nazis as the last gasp of capitalism (or what they thought was the last gasp), evidenced by the businessmen's support of Hitler in the late 1920s and early 1930s, is common among socialists.

55. Cf. for instance, the arguments of Willy Birkelbach in *Protokoll, 1959*, pp. 77 ff.

gram, too diffuse to be effective. It was not until the years 1956–59 that the party took the significant step of publishing a variety of these special plans, not as fundamental programs but more as invitations to open discussion, also showing of course, the general line of policy the party would take once in power. They are, significantly, plans rather than demands. The most important were the *Sozialplan für Deutschland* and *"Plan Z"* (or *Die Zunkunft Meistern*) on education policy, and the *Deutschlandplan.*

One of the reasons for their publication in that period was the impatience of some leaders with the endless discussions of "fundamentals," which they found too vague. Herbert Wehner, for instance, wrote in an internal party newspaper in 1958:

> One should not have too great expectations for the effects of a *Grundsatzprogramm* . . . we would be considerably further if we could succeed in clarifying our action program with figures and, with the help of a comprehensible social plan and precise demands in the fields of tax and finance policy, make clear what the Social Democrats want in the interest of the broadest strata [of the population].[56]

Many also felt the need to overcome the negative image the party had acquired in its years of opposition[57] and to counteract the impression of SPD recklessness Adenauer had managed to convey with his 1957 slogan, "No experiments!" For whatever reason, and despite some setbacks, the party continued to make relatively specific proposals, not to bring about a realization of general principles but rather to stimulate rational attacks on current problems.[58]

56. *Der Sozialist* (Hamburg), January 1958.
57. See Klaus-Peter Schulz, *Sorge um die deutschen Linke* (Cologne, 1954). Concern for the party's negative image has been considerable. The party has taken to publishing party votes on all bills in the Bundestag—most of which are of course uncontroversial and receive the "Ja!" of the SPD.
58. In the 1961 campaign the party produced a "Governing Program" complete with a detailed budget intended to destroy the impression that Social Democrats are spenders.

However, the party learned somewhat painfully that not all problems are susceptible to this kind of treatment. The *Deutschlandplan* of 1959 is a case in point. It envisaged a series of steps leading to reunification of Germany through a negotiated integration of various institutions with the East German regime. The process of promoting this plan was something like the process of "marginal differentiation" in marketing and advertising. Although on a different scale, the party was comparable to a toothpaste manufacturer adding a "secret ingredient" to his product to provide the slight differentiation that will lead the consumer to his rather than his competitor's toothpaste. The party tried in the Deutschlandplan to differentiate its "product" from Adenauer's by suggesting particular concrete steps that would lead to reunification—universally desired—presumably faster than the "position of strength" from which Adenauer wished to wrench East Germany away from the Russians. The plan rested on the assumption, common to much of the SPD's Eastern policy in the 1950s, that there was something to gain from trying to sit down and talk with Khrushchev to work out a scheme for reunification. Whatever the validity of the plan, the basic reason for its negative reception and ultimate withdrawal by its chief author, Herbert Wehner, seems to have been that it gave the CDU propaganda mills something they could translate into the old attack—that the SPD, once in power, would be "soft on communism." The party had picked the wrong policy, it seems, to differentiate itself. A year later, the Deutschlandplan was dropped, and during the 1961 election campaign Willy Brandt, the SPD candidate for chancellor, prominently asserted the fundamental agreement of the party with the government in matters of foreign policy, attempting thereby to withdraw that unfortunate ingredient from the market.

The problem-solving approach thus failed to work when the specific proposals ran up against emotional reactions evoking an already negative evaluation of the party. The lesson seems to be that the problem-solving orientation produces satisfactory results only when it deals with unemotional, i.e., noncontroversial topics. In any case, there are clearly limits to its application.

94

The withdrawal of the Deutschlandplan ended—at least temporarily—the pattern of offering initiative in foreign policy (which began with Kurt Schumacher's leadership in the 1940s), and the party's more traditional concern with internal policy— welfare, education, cultural, social, and communal—seems to have come once again to the fore.

4. Party Objectives—
Power and the Means to Achieve It

Disputes over the means of bringing about a socialist society were common in the early days of the socialist movement and were in part responsible for the split that occurred at the beginning of this century between the democratic socialists and what are now the communists. With the emphatic public abandonment of the ideological and more radical elements of the party program in the last few years, discussions about means and ends have now taken on a different character. In view of the generality and vagueness of the program goals of the present SPD, the older questions of what power is adequate to carry out a social transformation have died out, and the discussion of means and ends turns around more technical questions concerning the position the party can hope to win in the German political system and the strategy it should adopt in order to win this position. It is now possible, perhaps even necessary, to consider these last questions separately from the party's program problems—something that would have been impossible thirty to fifty years ago.

This is not to say that since broad ideological goals are no longer at stake the problem of means is simply one of how to run an effective election campaign. Elections are the obvious means to power in a constitutional democratic system such as Germany's, and, for the SPD, the problem of winning "five million voters who have never voted for the party before"[1] is a

1. *eilt: Sozialdemokratischer Brief,* September 1960, p. 7.

crucial one. But, as we shall see, this goal cannot be achieved without prior attention to the party's relations with pressure groups, the existing elites in many fields, and, in general, its alignment with the whole social and political system. The SPD cannot assume the social acceptance enjoyed by the Democrats or Republicans in the United States for example, and therefore its concern with means is a basic one. The scope of the problems facing the SPD is, in fact, what lends significance to a study of the SPD in general and its perspectives on power in particular.

The Meanings of "Power"

The party has always sought to gain the influence that is attached to the legitimate authority of the "state," to use a conventional but ambiguous term often employed by Germans.[2] Brief reflection on the evolution of socialist aims will show, however, the variety of meanings this proposition may have.

In the earliest days of the party, the variety of ideas and tactics was so great that it is difficult to make any firm generalization. In any case, the major occupation of socialists seems to have been to wring concessions from the government, either by mandates or by indirectly influencing public opinion. The state was the target for both Lassalleans and Marxians. Their disputes concerned the extent of the transformation of society necessary to achieve socialist goals.[3] In this early period no one seems to have thought (in contrast to some other countries) that reformation of the system could come from below in the sense of direct pressure on, say, the industrialists and landowners. Only one power could be effective—the power of the state. Trade unions grew up in Germany as adjuncts to the party in its effort to win political power. The "radicalization" of the party in the 1880s and 1890s

2. When the word *Staat* is used by a German politician, it is sometimes difficult to determine whether he means the governmental apparatus as such or the whole political society.

3. Cf. Peter Gay, *The Dilemma of Democratic Socialism*, pp. 17 ff., where the author contrasts the Marxists and the Lassalleans with respect to their evaluations of parliamentary and nonparliamentary methods as tools for winning power.

consisted in a growing feeling among a segment of the movement that the party had to command the whole power of government in order to accomplish its goals, coupled with disbelief that the existing formal means of winning power would ever enable the party to win such control.

As noted earlier,[4] the radical ideological goals froze at this point; the practice of the party and its affiliated organizations tended to become moderate as the party extended its efforts into wider and wider fields of direct, independent social action. Although the real impulse for this change seems to have come from what socialists call the "trade unionists," the famous text of Revisionist Eduard Bernstein will give an indication of the attitudes involved.

> [I have] little interest . . . in the final goal of socialism . . . this aim . . . is nothing to me, the movement is everything . . . And by movement . . . I understand not only the general movement of society, that is, social progress, but political and economic agitation and organization for effecting this progress.[5]

Believing in the inevitability of progress, the SPD in the pre-World War I years had a relatively modest immediate power objective: the influence that could be gained through increased representation in the Reichstag. It attempted to influence directly the factors affecting the lives of workers through its activity in large trade union organizations and cultural, social, and educational organizations. For all practical purposes in this period, the SPD was a tremendous pressure group.[6]

The establishment of the Weimar Republic was not marked by significant changes in the power aspirations of the SPD, despite the opportunity the party had (very briefly) to form the govern-

---

4. Cf. Ch. 1.
5. Gay, p. 62.
6. The Leninist strain in socialist thought and party structure moved in the opposite direction. It discarded attempts to become a pressure group and abandoned efforts to alter society except through the exercise of political power.

ment and later to participate in coalition governments, but rather by the evolution of new threats and competition. Although in a somewhat better position to influence government policy, the party never had a chance, or did not seem to be willing to exploit its chances, to establish itself in a ruling position. In nongovernmental spheres, the party continued, through the trade unions and other organizations, to influence society directly, but it was faced with challenges from competing mass organizations, which forced it into a two-front war with left and right. The party had to fight both Communists and Nazis for the right to represent the workers in this direct action.

After World War II, the situation changed considerably, for a variety of reasons. The party's hopes for power in the normal way, as the dominant element of a legitimate government, were at first very high, and despite setbacks in its hopes there has been no significant radicalization or return to direct action in society.

The history of the SPD therefore shows three attitudes toward power:

First, with respect to influence over the executive power, the party's realistic short-run goals have evolved from those of a pressure group seeking to influence but not to control the state to the present objective of forming a government.

Secondly, with respect to the degree to which it relies on executive power to fulfill its goals, the party originally emerged as an organization devoted almost exclusively to influencing the state, and then passed through a stage in which it sought in addition to achieve its goals through direct influence on society. It has now returned to an exclusive concentration on the state.

Finally, with respect to the character of the executive power itself, the party originally did not think any power other than that inherent in the imperial government was necessary—understandably, because that power was great. Later, the ideas now thought of as characteristically socialist—nationalization and planning—took hold and the party came to consider a transformation of state power necessary to achievement of its ultimate goals, although in what seemed to be its chance to carry out such a change—1918–19—it failed to act, being more concerned with democratic forms and "republican defense." It has now returned once again to an acceptance of state power as it is.

Along with the underlying changes in the general orientation of party members and the changing patterns of politics in Germany which are discussed elsewhere, there is one reason for the changing attitudes of the most influential party members toward the executive power which deserves special attention here. That is the increased power and prestige the executive now has in the Bonn Republic, due both to constitutional provisions and to the activities of its recent incumbent, Konrad Adenauer.[7]

Despite the desire of the Allies (especially the United States and France) for some kind of federal government and a general reaction against the extreme concentration of power in the Nazi period, the German authors of the Basic Law for the Bonn Republic placed considerable power in the hands of the chancellor. Reflecting the lessons learned from the collapse of the Weimar Republic, one of their major objectives was to strengthen the executive, in the hands of the chancellor, against possible threats to his authority from either a recalcitrant multiparty parliament or from the president. The chancellorship became one of the most powerful offices of its kind, buttressed first by the so-called "constructive vote of confidence," which made it extremely difficult for him to be overthrown between elections, and, secondly, by his complete authority over the cabinet. The federal provisions of the constitution, put in at the behest of the Allies and of regional blocs, proved to be no significant brake on the power of the central government or of the chancellor.[8]

Other factors made this power even greater—Adenauer's personality, the importance of international decisions (which require the greatest executive initiative), and the political success of the government in riding the wave of prosperity that has swept Europe, and most dramatically Germany, since the end of the war.

The increase in the power of the chancellorship has been

7. Cf. Arnold Heidenheimer, *Adenauer and the CDU* (The Hague, 1961).
8. See John F. Golay, *The Founding of the Federal Republic of Germany* (Chicago, 1958), for details concerning the constitutional debates.

especially important for the party because of the decline in the number of parties from 11 in 1949 to 3 in 1961 (no doubt in large degree brought about by that increase in power). It has become increasingly possible for power to be in the hands of a single party, as it has been in fact, if not always in form, in recent years under Adenauer and the CDU.

This particular pressure toward centralization of power would probably be mitigated should a situation arise in which the SPD formed a coalition government. It is also possible that with Adenauer's departure the trend toward concentration of power in the hands of the chancellor may be reversed. In any event, the perspectives of the present SPD leaders seem to be conditioned more by the recent past than by possible future developments.[9] The party's concentration on winning the top executive office has thus been conditioned by the increasingly attractive quality of that office.

This orientation of the party may seem conventional enough to an American observer. The present aspirations of the party are those of a major party in any democratic two-party regime. The party simply seeks to win the offices of the legitimate government and to exercise their powers without greatly changing their character. Fritz Erler, member of the party presidium and deputy leader of the party's parliamentary delegation, however, found it necessary to remind party members shortly before the passing of the Godesberg Program that:

> The electorate will only award the Social Democratic Party the responsibility for this state and its policies when [the party], in all its elements, shows the capacity and the will to shape *this* state in which we live, and not some state in the distant future.[10]

9. Party spokesmen have only occasionally mentioned the possibility of a coalition, although in the 1961 campaign, and especially after it when there seemed some chance that Adenauer would not be able to win the FDP's support for a new government coalition with the CDU, the question again became important.

10. *Vorwärts,* October 30, 1959.

Or again, as he said later in the course of the Godesberg debates:

> This state, which in many things does not please us, in which there are many things which we want to change, we observe not from the outside, *Genossen,* but rather we observe it from within. We are fighting not the state, but a false policy of the government and its majority . . . we are fighting not against the state, but for the state, and, in fact, not the state of the distant future, not the state only in a reunified Germany, but the state in this Federal Republic, which we want to govern.[11]

Still left to be convinced, it seemed, was the CDU. After the passage of the program, the party was attacked by Dr. Bruno Heck, a leading CDU figure, as having made a "claim of totality" (*Totalitätsanspruch*) by declaring that democracy could only be fulfilled through socialism. In response, an editorial writer for the party newspaper disclaimed the implication of radicalism or radical changes in the government and its power by insisting that the party sought only to exercise the "government function" on the basis of the mandate, and he went on to say that it would treat the opposition better than the CDU had done.[12]

The Means to Power

Two accurate but not very useful descriptions of the party's present attitudes would be that it renounces any violent or revolutionary methods and that it adheres to the rules of the game. The first is not useful because no significant group within the party has ever advocated violence as a means to power. With regard to the second statement, the party has always supported formal democratic rules and has changed its adherence to existing rules as they became more democratic.

The "rules," however, cover only a narrow range of political

11. *Protokoll, 1959*, p. 153.
12. Paul Meyer in *Vorwärts*, January 8, 1960.

activity: elections, behavior in parliaments, and so forth. Other more pertinent characteristics of the party's perspectives on winning power can be found by examining the ways in which it has sought to win support among the elements of the political system discussed in Chapter 2: the elite, the political interest groups, and the public.

The SPD and the Political Elite

The attitudes of the SPD have undergone radical change from its early days with respect to other elites. Following Lassalle's failure to establish a working relationship with Bismarck, it was clear that close relations between party and government leaders were impossible. Marxist ideology held that no satisfaction could be gained from the existing elite, and the party leaders for a while constituted a kind of counterelite in opposition to the military–bourgeois–Junker ruling class. The First World War lessened hostilities for a while under the conditions of the *Burgfrieden* (peace between parties), and, much to the disgust of many radicals, party leaders began to develop some status within the elite structure of the community. Cooperation broke down in the Weimar period, when Germany was divided as much by competing, conflicting elites as by the clash of parties and mass organizations.

Postwar developments have, through the growth of the CDU and the longevity of the chancellor, reunified the elites in Germany to a very great degree. Catholics, industrialists, the bureaucracy, the military, and to some extent the trade unions—all have learned to live together. Through the mechanism of the CDU, the political conflicts between these groups have been mitigated.

There is, of course, one significant exception—the SPD. Fritz Erler wrote in 1958:

Only in . . . Germany are those who have other opinions than the federal government curtly denied the right to be concerned for the security of the nation . . . That is Chan-

103

cellor Adenauer's inclination . . . he wants to eject the Social Democrats and their supporters from the state.[13]

Once again, the party found itself on the outside, especially at the national level. Schumacher's decision to go into the opposition in the bizonal government in Frankfurt as early as 1948, even before the Republic was established, began a period of isolation. The situation conformed so exactly to Marxist analysis that one might assume the party would produce a more and more radical counterelite as a result.

In fact, the opposite developed. The party is presently engaged in a campaign to make its leaders acceptable to the ruling class. The party encourages its experts in various fields of policy, taking every opportunity to extol their capabilities. The party press and propaganda always note occasions when party leaders have found a "good response" or "attentive audience" among important nonsocialist groups,[14] and Brandt, in a pre-election speech, promised that he would "mobilize the experts (*Sachverstand*) independent of party and other affiliations," if elected.[15]

Aside from tactical considerations, this new emphasis on the respectability of party leaders among their would-be peers has arisen as the natural result of the fact that many of the most powerful leaders of the party after Schumacher are, or have been, leaders on the Land and local level who have been able to win power and take an active part in the political life of the community. In my interviews it was clear that the *Kommunalpolitiker* were by far the most interested in gaining acceptance among the powerful within their range of action. They have had considerable experience working with the leading members of other parties or other (including official) groups. Their perception of the need for good working relations with influential men, together with

13. Quoted in *Der Sozialist* (Hamburg), November 1958.

14. *eilt*, for example, a party magazine for a party audience, eagerly reports invitations by nonparty groups to Social Democrats.

15. Quoted in *eilt*, May 1961. In an article written before the 1957 election, Brandt emphasized the necessity of making it possible for the Social Democrats to form coalitions with other parties.

personal desires they probably have of peer group acceptance, has led them to lend their support to the campaign for better integration of the party elite with others.

At the national level, as the quotation from Fritz Erler shows, there is some bitterness among the members of the Bundestag at the coldness with which their ideas and suggestions have been received in the highest circles of government. This attitude can be found in the reports the Bundestag delegation writes for the biennial party yearbooks. Their bitterness has not discouraged them, however, but has led instead to increased efforts to gain acceptance. The broader basis in society that could maintain an opposition on principle is not present. The SPD has therefore attempted to build up an elite within the party that can win the respect and confidence of at least those influential members of society who are not so closely tied to the CDU or so antisocialist that rapprochement is impossible.

The style of the party's action with regard to the elite has been, for reasons of future working relations, to emphasize differences between the SPD and the CDU and not between the SPD and "the system."

Influence Among Interest Groups

The style of Social Democratic politics has traditionally been dominated by concern with the group arena of politics. The working class was perhaps initially a purely abstract designation, referring only to social categories of persons distinguished by their position in the rather rigid social stratification of the empire and by their relation to the economic process. The party and the unions, however, became the organized group representation of that class. The distinction between organized groups and social categories was obliterated, and the political system became, for the party, an arena in which organized groups clashed.

In the postwar period, the disappearance of many of the party's affiliated organizations and the development of looser ties with the trade unions have made a change in style inevitable, although it took several years before it began in earnest. The drive to break down exclusive attention to particular organizations was, in fact, one of the major points of attack of the reformers of the mid-fifties. One document read: "The [party] should be represented everywhere that politically interested people congregate, and should represent its standpoint there. We are far behind the government parties in this field."[16]

Herbert Wehner, deputy chairman of the party, now in charge of organizational questions, has been one of the most active advocates of a more concentrated effort to establish contact with other groups, especially by mobilizing Social Democrats who hold positions in these groups.

> We must help the Social Democrats who have positions of trust in their professional organizations, in order that they may there acquit themselves as Social Democrats. That follows if the political activity is going to be more than merely talking in the parliaments. For there in the organizations something decisive is shaped. Our political opponent speaks of the "anteroom of politics." There are a great many such anterooms, in which Social Democrats earlier knew how to work, if not in those which have become more and more important in the postwar years.[17]

This quotation is taken from a speech given by Wehner before a meeting of the *Arbeitsgemeinschaft selbständig Schaffender* (Working Group of Independent Producers), one of the middle-class organizations the party has sponsored in the past decade.[18] The contrast between this group, composed of Social Democrats important for the role they play independently of their party connections or for their expertise, and the youth, women's, cultural, and other traditional groups of the SPD is a good example of the party's efforts at a more open approach.

16. "19 Thesen." (Cf. note 15, Ch. 3.)

17. Herbert Wehner, "Selbständig Schaffende und Sozialdemokratische Politik," in a pamphlet of the same name, issued in 1959 by the SPD. The pamphlet contains Wehner's and Heinrich Deist's speeches to the national congress of the Arbeitsgemeinschaft selbständige Schaffenden in Hamburg, April 1959.

18. Cf. Ch. 7 for a more detailed analysis of this group.

The party has tried to make contact with groups that are not normally supporters of Social Democratic policies—that is, groups that have no traditional ties with the party because of its role as the working-class party—middle-class groups such as the one mentioned above, refugee organizations, professional organizations, and so forth. Their distinguishing characteristic is their influence. One party expert in public relations has referred to the party's efforts as organizing the opinion leaders of society.[19]

Among the members I interviewed there was a considerable difference of opinion concerning this objective. In Hamburg, where the interconnections between the party organization and the local administration were closest, there was strong approval for the practice of establishing good relations with such locally important groups as civic groups, local welfare organizations, organizations of small businessmen, and groups involved with development of housing.[20] In Frankfurt, especially among members whose major connections were with unions, doubt was often expressed that profitable relations could be established, and my respondents tended to look upon the effort as opportunistic even if they approved it. There were even a few who opposed the appeal to influential groups altogether. For them the alternative was to reinvigorate working-class commitments and to work more closely with the unions. The pessimists and dissenters seem to perceive the goal of the party with respect to other groups to be the integration of these organizations into the movement—and on that basis the pessimist is probably more than justified. This objective is unrealistic in the eyes of professionals in the interest groups. A member of the executive of one of the larger organizations promoting the welfare of people who had suffered in the war brought out the point that these organizations, whose leaders depended on their ability to bring returns in the form of favorable

19. Heinrich Braune, *Mittel und Methoden der Meinungsbildung* (mimeo.), reprint of a speech given by the author, an editor of a newspaper in Hamburg and member of the party's committee on recruitment and propaganda, to the South-Hesse Bezirk party congress in Offenbach/Main, April 1960.

20. In Hamburg, three of my respondents suggested that the party needed particularly to establish such connections to avoid possible domination by labor interests!

legislation from any government, could not identify themselves with the party even when they were generally favorable to the party's policies in the area of their special concern. Therefore, the party's objective in the new style is to cultivate good contacts and remain *Zuverlässig* ("reliable" or "trustworthy") with key groups without demanding too much.

The SPD's new orientation is marked not only by an attempt to make contact with the new strata of notables, but also (perhaps necessarily) by fragmentation and flexibility of appeal. Party rhetoric and tradition emphasize winning people and groups for the cause by creating general sympathy and by marshaling support for specific proposals for legislation or for specific policy declarations. There is an extremely tenuous connection between "the cause" and remedies sought for fishermen who complain of water pollution by industry in the rivers in North Germany (one of the examples Wehner cites of a problem in which he was able to be of assistance[21]). The efforts of the party with respect to groups having particular interests or representing particular occupational categories, aimed perhaps ultimately at winning support for the more general policies of the party, do in fact constitute a separate sphere of policy interaction in which the party serves as a kind of broker of interests. Because the party is dealing with highly articulated interests, it is drawn into forming loose coalitions in which both the coalition and the party's performance are continually tested. In the name of national responsibility and in its search for wider support, the party has sought to create a new framework of instrumentalized relationships with these organized groups.

The Party and the Public

An early style of the party's propaganda aimed to force people to choose sides. To do this, it identified the enemies of the group it sought to influence and justified its own claim to leadership. This kind of sharp, emotional dichotomy has long been the stock

21. "Selbständig Schaffende und Sozialdemokratische Politik."

in trade of socialist propaganda. It was designed to mobilize the working class against the ruling class. To make its appeal effective, it sought to shape the basic orientation of the workers to the existing social system. It tried to raise their aspirations in terms of prestige, material welfare, opportunities for education, and so forth, and to convince them that these higher aspirations could be fulfilled through political action by the party. In the Weimar period this theme was augmented by the effort to mobilize the workers as defenders of the Republic against political extremists.

All party propaganda shares something of this friends–enemies approach, since it must be based to some extent on the idea of "throwing the rascals out" and some kind of promise that things will be better if the "antirascal" party is elected. But the possible variations of this theme are great, and the party has modified its approach considerably. The shift came about chiefly in the '50s. Schumacher, the first postwar leader, had considerable talent in holding audiences with his speeches; his attractiveness, which was especially great for the radically minded rank and file within the party, lay partly in his willingness to invoke the old style of political vituperation. Ollenhauer, who followed Schumacher as leader and chief spokesman of the party, was a much more mild-mannered speaker, and though he might use the same words they never seemed to have the same effect. In general, the tone of the speeches of leading Social Democrats has undergone a change since Schumacher, more marked than can be indicated by the milder manner of Ollenhauer.

Basically the party has reacted to an increasingly serious negative image of it in public attitudes. Even Schumacher noted that "The Social Democrats have never suffered so much from what [the party] really was, as from what the deceiving propaganda of the propertied (*die Besitzes*) made of it in the eyes of those without judgment."[22]

This false picture—Herbert Wehner has called it the *Goebbelschen Zerrbilder* (Goebbels' distorted images)—was not felt to be an important problem in the early days after the war. Party

22. *Turmwächter der Demokratie*, 2, 39.

leaders believed that the decisive majority of the German people had a basic disposition (*Grundhaltung*) in favor of socialism and democracy.[23] Ten years later the situation had reversed itself. An intellectual writing in a party journal expressed the general sentiment with the words: "the psychological and political situation is as unfavorable as possible to socialism."[24]

For the many Americans who, judging from their public reactions to European affairs, have had a hard time distinguishing between democratic socialism and communistic socialism, the negative image that developed will probably not seem surprising. The problem of making the distinction clear to Germans has been a major one for the SPD. Wehner noted that "[Our enemies] . . . use against the SPD the prevalent feeling against the 'SED' [the East German party] . . . [and] socialist conceptions."[25]

The fear among the German people that an SPD victory would cause the country to move closer to the Communist system or perhaps even into the Communist orbit has been exploited both by Adenauer, who came close to asserting it for a fact in his campaign speeches, and by the SPD itself, in its support of an ambiguous and subtle policy of negotiation for reunification. The SPD has also gained disfavor by its generally admitted lack of clarity on basic ideas (at least before the Godesberg Program), which has occasionally allowed speakers for the party, especially on the lower level, to use radical language hardly distinguishable from a mild form of Communist propaganda.[26] CDU propaganda has been able to exploit this situation by evoking the German bourgeoisie's old fears of the "Reds."

Confidence in the party reached such a low ebb that party organizations in the Ruhr were able to report that many working-

---

23. See Ernst Reuter, *Grundsätze und Ziele der Sozialdemokratie.*
24. Richard Freyh, "Sozialismus Heute," *Neue Gesellschaft, 2,* No. 6 (November–December 1956).
25. *Der Sozialist* (Hamburg), January 1958.
26. The party's confused position on foreign policy is said by some to have caused confusion within the ranks, prompting pro-Soviet statements not reflecting the intentions of the leaders. It has also been said that the party is so sensitive to this issue that it has branded as a Communist anyone who has spoken independently for a militant, worker-oriented policy.

class voters deserted the SPD in the 1957 election because of a rumor that the policies of the SPD would lead to unemployment![27] The reaction of the party leaders, aside from righteous indignation, has been a long-drawn-out effort to let the people know what the party really is and to reestablish its *Glaubwürdigkeit* (trustworthiness).

Speaking on foreign policy at the 1956 congress, Fritz Erler noted, apropos of recurring instances of slander against SPD leaders during the campaign:

> legal proceedings against defamation have no influence on elections . . . therefore our policies must create a climate in Germany and in the world that assumes public confidence (*Glaubwürdigkeit*) from the beginning, in spite of the expected defamation.[28]

Speaking to the Social Democratic Working Group of Independent Producers, Wehner sets out as their first task:

> making the members of the middle classes so aware of Social Democratic goals that the false images (*Zerrbilder*) that are spread about us will, insofar as possible, lose their effect. That is a modest task, but one can't avoid it if one wants to get under way at all.[29]

The elements of the ideal image the party is trying to project will be discussed in Chapter 8; the important fact about such a campaign is that the party seeks to establish a basic groundwork of sympathy and respect for itself among the people. The party has not approached the task of winning support from the public by mobilizing one bloc against another, but has rather sought to convince the public that the SPD members, too, are honorable men and should be listened to with respect. Appeals can then be made to broad and shifting segments of public opinion on specific issues.

27. Cf. *Jahrbuch SPD Bezirk Östliches Westfalen, 1957.*
28. *Protokoll, 1956*, p. 114.
29. "Selbständig Schaffende."

This procedure is, of course, a far cry from the creation of workers' *Klassenbewusstsein* (class consciousness), and there is again a minority which feels that the party has failed to fulfill its mission by failing to develop such consciousness. One may cite, as an articulate representative, Wolfgang Abendroth, a professor of law at the University of Marburg and member of several committees of the party executive; he was so opposed to the Godesberg Program that he submitted a complete substitute draft that followed the older programs very closely. In 1957 he argued that "the only chance" for the party was to "recreate a social consciousness":

> A large section of the German workers have taken over the ideology of the classless character of the present society which was sponsored by the ruling classes . . . and have not developed their own. So long as that is lacking, the workers can be manipulated through the usual advertising offensives . . . [the party] must be the opinion-forming center and leading cadre of the employed in their political–social opposition (*Gegensatz*) to finance capital.[30]

These voices, which have become uneasy about the trend of socialist propaganda, are however scattered and ineffective. It is the advocates of the new style who are in full command.

30. *Der Sozialdemokrat* (Frankfurt), November 1957.

5. Policy Making

So far our analysis has dealt with the varying kinds of goals and standards the party has set for itself. In this and the following three chapters, we shall turn to an examination of the organization the party leaders have at their disposal to help achieve these goals. In contrast to the recent policy changes, developments in the organization have not been sensational, rarely causing open controversy in the party press or congresses. But if less dramatic, they are in the long run just as significant.

There are several reasons why they have been carried out so quietly. First, developments such as the introduction of specialists in public relations or advertising seem to be the result not of any basic change in the party's orientation but rather of changes in the technology of communications. They could be justified by the universal desire to keep up to date.

Secondly, party practices that have served as symbols of the democratic character of the movement, such as free speech within the party congresses, election of party officials and candidates, and supremacy of the party organization over the parliamentary delegations, have not been directly attacked, although the effect of the new patterns of activity in the organization has often been to alter fundamentally the significance of these institutions. Since they have not been directly attacked, however, the opposition has been deprived of ready symbols on which to fix its discontent and to mobilize that of others.

One traditional rallying cry of militant party members did appear briefly in the debates of the '50s—when the influence of the bureaucratic *Apparat* was protested. This served the advocates of the new style as well as the more traditionally leftist members, however. The focal point of the reformers' attack was Ollenhauer's colorlessness as a candidate (in public relations terms). The Apparat label could be used because he and his close associates on the executive had risen in the party through paid positions as party secretaries. The militants used the slogan generally to attack the dominance of the more conservative party secretaries throughout the party. They wanted to see a more vigorous "radical" leadership, symbolized by Schumacher. However, in 1959, once Ollenhauer had been dropped as a candidate, the militants were unable to use the Apparat as a rallying symbol to attack the new leaders of the party, although these leaders were even further from the militant leadership they wanted. A ready symbol for mobilizing opposition to organizational changes had disappeared, and the opposition became unfocused.

In any case, for these or other reasons the question of the organization of the party never became as dramatic a subject of dispute as the party's military policy or its abandonment of traditional Marxian goals. Discussion in the party was lively, especially after each defeat, but not organized into factions, and in the absence of organized opposition changes were instituted either through simple action of the party executive, or, more subtly, through changes in emphasis given to different kinds of activity already going on.

A crucial area of change has been the policy-making process. As we have seen, the party has abandoned its traditional practice of committing itself to particular policies in its long-range program. This makes the distribution of power within the party, the pattern of negotiation, the flow of information, the access of interest groups, and the methods of binding members to decisions taken—in short, the policy-making process—even more important than it was when the fundamental program set limits on its flexibility.

"Policy making" refers to a wide range of behavior. As a "policy producer," a party clearly has many kinds of "products." Not everything said by party leaders can be called policy. One might define party policy as any stated course of action to which the party publicly commits itself and which is therefore binding in some important way on party members. Among such policies there are many variations depending on the immediate purpose and the context in which the policy is proclaimed.

Most obvious are the more sensational demands and principles announced by top party leaders in the full light of mass publicity, sometimes touching on fundamental or crucial questions but usually relating to current crises and popular moods. There are also the legislative policies—proposals and judgments—made in the course of routine parliamentary work. And there are the tactical decisions that involve parliamentary maneuvers, formation of governments, presentation of candidates, and so forth.

An important feature distinguishing the SPD from most other major Western parties is that there is a great deal of "party policy," as defined here. That is, declarations in parliament and to the press, and published plans, programs, and platform planks on subjects ranging from child allotments to atomic armaments, are more often announced as the policy of the party, *and* considered binding on members' actions in public, than is usually the case, except for totalitarian parties.[1]

For American parties, only a political analyst can describe a "Republican" or "Democratic" policy—and even then the result is dubious and its meaning limited. Despite the present lack of an intellectually respectable and cohesive ideology, and vague as it often is, SPD policy is usually identifiable.

The Party Organs Responsible for Policy

The two most important bodies charged with declaring policy are the *Fraktion* (parliamentary delegation) and the executive.[2] The

1. A reverse indication of the extent to which policy is considered as party policy and binding on the members is a resolution passed at the 1958 party congress, which asserted, "All comrades are obligated to designate as their private opinion all statements which are in opposition to the official statements of the party." *Protokoll, 1958*, p. 506.

2. Technically, the party congress is the highest court (*Oberste Instanz*) according to the organization statute, Article 10. It meets only once every two

115

division of labor between them is important, though it is not as clear as their superficially obvious fields of action seem to indicate.

The Fraktion is the parliamentary party of the Bundestag. There are similar Fraktions in the Landtage and local parliaments and councils. At the national level it included in 1960 the 181 SPD members of the Bundestag (which had a total of 519 members). It elected its own 23-member Fraktion executive, including a chairman (Ollenhauer), three deputies (Carlo Schmid, Fritz Erler, and Dr. Heinrich Deist) and three "whips" or "managers" (*Geschäftsführer*). As in the past, party voting discipline is almost always enforced. There are regular caucuses as well as special working committees (*Arbeitskreise*) in special policy areas.

As is normal for parliamentary delegations the Fraktion presents bills, formulates policy on bills put forward by other parties, and questions (criticizes) the government. The forms this activity takes range from quiet work in committees to occasional dramatic sessions concerning controversial bills or periodic debates on, for instance, foreign policy, in which top party leaders cross oratorical swords with the government with maximum publicity, including occasional television coverage.

The executive (*Parteivorstand*), according to the party organization statute, "has the responsibility for the leadership of the party" (*Die Leitung der Partei obliegt dem Parteivorstand*[3]). Its organization has recently undergone changes. Prior to 1958 it was composed of about 25 members elected by the party congress, seven of which were paid members. These seven, including the chairman (Ollenhauer), his deputy, and five others, were both the chief leaders of the organization and the core of party leaders in residence in the German capital. Many of the others lived and worked throughout the country; meetings of the executive were held roughly once a month.

In 1958 a general reorganization of the major organs of the party was initiated after deliberation by a special committee set

years, however, and is very rarely involved in formulating policy. For a discussion of its functions see pp. 133 ff.

3. Article 17.

up by the executive itself as a result of the 1957 election defeat.[4] The executive was expanded to 33 and a smaller group of 9 members was formed which was called the "party presidium." The presidium consisted entirely of members whose principal occupations kept them in Bonn, either as permanent paid officials of the party (in 1960 four members: Ollenhauer, Wehner, Von Knoeringen, and Nau), or as important members of the Bundestag (in 1960 five members: Erler, Deist, Schmid, Schanzenbach, and Schoettle). It was thus able to meet about once a week.

The fact that the leadership of the executive and the Fraktion is united in the presidium makes the latter clearly supreme in the party. The presidium takes a hand in all important business of the party whether in the parliament or in the party organization. Judging from the reports of its work in the yearbook[5] and in the internal party magazine, *eilt,* the presidium lays down general lines of policy for the Fraktion, sets the agenda for the larger executive, and, when important occasions arise that require immediate action, issues policy statements itself.[6] Formally, the presidium may be overruled by the executive but not the Fraktion. The different functions of the party organization and the Fraktion are thus bridged by the presidium.

It is difficult to distinguish the executive's policy responsibility in practice from the Fraktion's. My respondents in interviews said in general something like "the executive lays down general policies and the Fraktion the particular ones that implement them." To be a bit more illuminating, one can perhaps best say,

4. This committee, called the Committee for the Reorganization of the Top of the Party (*Parteispitze*) had as members: Ollenhauer, Mellies, Erler, Wehner, Nau, Von Knoeringen, and Carlo Schmid—a compromise between new and old leaders. Another committee set up at the same time to suggest changes for the "activation of the organization" was composed of Karl Vittinghoff, Willy Birkelbach, Fritz Heine, Luis Albertz, Franz Bogler, Fritz Ohlig, Egon Franke, and Max Kukil, bringing together about equal numbers of party organization leaders from the central office and from the Bezirke.

5. Cf., for example, *Jahrbuch der SPD, 1958–59,* p. 234.

6. One such instance is reported in *eilt,* November 1960, when a party member was convicted of spying for the Soviets. The presidium immediately condemned him and defended the party from expected attacks.

after examining the regular reports of the executive's monthly deliberations as published in *eilt,* that it is chiefly concerned with three types of party policy: (a) electoral platforms and detailed and extensive outlines of party policy in particular fields (recently the Godesberg Program); (b) party reactions to crises, dramatic events, and issues commanding a high degree of publicity— especially where a major criticism of the government is involved (for example, atomic armaments, government television policy), and (c) organizational questions. The breadth of the policies dealt with by the executive appears to extend from the coordination of policies and their declaration in general form to questions that emerge in a particular political context—in the arena of public opinion.

The different functions of party and parliamentary organs are more apparent when one looks at the lower levels. At the Land level, there is a partial lack of correspondence between the party and parliamentary organizations. There are 20 Bezirke (the next level below the national party organization) and only ten Länder (see chart, p. 119). Bezirk executives therefore have responsibility for an entire Land only in some areas, principally in the smaller Länder. In the '40s there was some agitation to make the units coincide,[7] but the only result was the creation of coordinating bodies called *Länderausschusse* or *Länderkonferenzen* which meet approximately four times a year under rules established by the national executive. Their functions are limited, relating principally to elections. The efforts to make the Bezirke coincide with the Länder were attempts on the part of lower party organs to gain control of the important Land governments and Fraktions. The opposition to the change seems to have come from the national leadership, although it is hard to say whether this opposition stemmed from a desire to maintain national control over these governments, or, what seems on the whole more likely, a desire to maintain control of channels to the lower party organization without the interference of strong party members in office at lower levels.

7. Cf. Klaus Schütz in Max Lange et al., *Parteien in der Bundesrepublik.*

Regional Organization of the Government and the SPD

Land	Party Bezirk
Schleswig-Holstein	Schleswig-Holstein
Hamburg Bremen (and part of Niedersachsen)	Hamburg-Nordwest (which has *Landesorganisationen*—structured as Bezirke—in Bremen and Hamburg)
Niedersachsen	Weser-Ems Hannover Braunschweig (and part of Hamburg-Nordwest)
Nordrhein-Westfalen	Östliches Westfalen Westliches Westfalen Niederrhein Mittelrhein
Hesse	Hessen-Nord Hessen-Süd
Baden-Württemberg	Süd-West
Bayern	Niederbayern-Oberpfalz Franken Südbayern
Rheinland-Pfalz	Rheinland/Hessen-Nassau Pfalz Rheinhessen
Berlin	Berlin
Saar	Saar

Where there is no correspondence, it is especially clear that although local executives have a general responsibility for policy in local areas, their public role is confined chiefly to organizing elections within the area and giving support to the national party on controversial policies commanding wide publicity—as, for example, during the party's campaign against nuclear weapons.

119

In my observations of party meetings and party media at the Bezirk and Unterbezirk level, concern for policy was confined to dramatic questions of foreign policy, occasional prominent issues of social policy, and the broadest program questions. The abundance of policy problems facing parliamentary delegates are either ignored or cursorily treated by the lower party organizations unless they become the momentary object of public controversy.

The contrast between the two types of organs, then, appears to be related to the visibility of the issues involved. The executives are charged with general policy, but this very often means that they are concerned chiefly with those aspects of party policy that receive, or that the party hopes will receive, the most attention from the public. The parliamentary delegations, on the other hand, are typically occupied with policy that receives comparatively little publicity and involves disputes between rival interest groups. The line is blurred, of course, and there are many exceptions. The issues that come up in the parliaments sometimes claim widespread attention and the executives are sometimes concerned with relatively dry organizational problems.

The Organization of Information and Access

The responsibility of the top organs, the party executive and the Fraktion, for the formulation of policy covers a very large number of fields. If we look at the organizations and personnel charged with transmitting demands and providing information to the policy makers we find a complex set of institutions.

Attached to and appointed by the executive are special committees whose number rose from 11 to 22 in 13 years.[8] As of

8. The growth has been steady, as the following figures show:

Year	Committees on policy	Committees on organization	Total
1947	8	3	11
1948–49	8	5	13
1952–53	13	5	18
1954–55	16	4	20
1956–57	17	4	21
1958–59	18	4	22

1960, 18 were concerned particularly with policy problems covering the following topics:[9]

1. Agricultural policy
2. Foreign policy
3. Factory and labor union questions
4. Reunification and policy toward the "Soviet Zone"
5. Interior and constitutional policy
6. Questions concerning victims of the war
7. Security questions (i.e. defense policy)
8. Refugee questions
9. Science and research
10. Finance policy
11. Questions relating to youth
12. Municipal and local policy
13. Cultural policy
14. Legal policy
15. Radiobroadcasting policy
16. Social policy
17. Economic policy
18. Housing policy

In addition, there were committees dealing with organizational questions:

19. Dues
20. Women
21. Organization
22. Recruitment and propaganda

Each of these committees was headed by a member of the executive.[10]

In the Fraktion, in addition to the specialization that comes about from individual membership on the Bundestag's 26 com-

9. *Jahrbuch der SPD, 1958–59,* pp. 242–45. The committees on youth and women were concerned with both legislative questions and organization.

10. See ibid., p. 473.

mittees, there have been created eight *Arbeitskreise* devoted to the following policy areas:

1. Foreign policy
2. Internal policy
3. Economic policy
4. Social policy
5. Budget and finance
6. Refugees
7. Law
8. Security[11]

The staffs of the various committees are exceedingly small. When the full complement is on hand, there is one assistant (*Referat*) in the Fraktion attached to each Arbeitskreis. In the party headquarters, there are assistants in charge of the secretarial and organizational work for the committees. They are, however, often responsible for several committees, and therefore several policy areas. In general, the whole party seems to have access to less *technical* assistance than is available to the members of one party in the United States Congress. The number of individuals specializing in a particular field of policy is, however, very high. One may think, for any particular policy area, of a set of concentric circles made up of increasingly large numbers of persons who have some special competence in that field. Let us take the field of social policy as an example.

At the top, one finds a few key figures who are the experts and the spokesmen for the party. In the field of social policy, chief among these in 1960 was Professor Dr. Ernst Schellenberg, who was chairman of the Fraktion Arbeitskreis for Social Policy, chairman of the Bundestag Committee on Social Policy, and member of the Executive Committee of the Fraktion. Also involved with various aspects of social policy was Marta Schanzenbach, member of the party presidium, chairman of the party executive Committee on Social Policy, and also a member of the Fraktion executive.

11. Ibid., p. 11.

At the next level come the members of the Fraktion Arbeits-kreis, apparently of varying number, meeting relatively often, and working together in Bonn, having the help—limited and probably overburdened as it is—of at least one technical assistant and some office help. At the next level comes the party executive Committee on Social Policy, of 22 members, including some who are already involved in parliamentary activities and others drawn from various regions, including members of Social Democratic Land governments and social policy specialists in Land parlia-mentary delegations. The committee met several times in the course of the period covered by the 1958–59 yearbook and in addition was broken down into five subcommittees dealing on an ad hoc basis with specific problems, chiefly important current legislation. The committee also considered during this period the social policy section of the new Godesberg Program.

The secretariat (*Referat*) of the committee, which in this case was the same as the Fraktion social policy Referat, apparently dealt chiefly with organizational questions for the committee, as well as questions sent to the executive from interested groups and individuals.

One final circle in this case was drawn in by means of a two-day conference on health insurance, a lively issue at the time. This kind of semi-public conference, attended by invited guests and other interested people, is organized around speeches by leading Social Democrats, followed by discussion. It serves as a hearing on the topic and a propaganda rally as well.

The elaboration of specialized organs for social policy is actual-ly even greater than this outline indicates, since there are other committees in the Fraktion and the executive concerned with closely related topics such as war victims, refugees, youth, women, and family and housing policy.

The elaborateness of the organizational devices by which the party draws larger and larger numbers of people into the decision-making process with respect to particular policy areas, and the way these devices are built into both the executive and the Frak-tion, indicate an extensive fragmentation of the informational aspects of policy making at the national level, which cuts across the conventional division of parliamentary and extraparliamentary organs. The party has apparently decided to continue, and if possible improve and strengthen, this system of committees.[12]

The development of channels of information does not occur only at the top, but extends throughout the whole party. The committees of the executive serve to connect the central decision process with experts in Land governments and in the Bezirke, the next level in the party organization. In some cases, too, there are parallel committees at the Bezirk level[13] that deal with similar problems, although chiefly with respect to locally significant issues. Finally, there are the newly emphasized *Arbeitsgemeinschaften*,[14] which are distributed unevenly through the party organization but which serve occasionally as a channel for drawing in interested professional men (doctors, lawyers, teachers) or men in particular economic groups.[15] Another, more irregular channel of information lies in the "contact conversations" (*Kontaktgespräche*) which the presidium carries on from time to time, involving direct contacts between party leaders and the leadership of influential groups. So far these seem to have been carried on chiefly with the representatives of the refugee organizations.[16]

Since they usually do not require party membership of participants, the Arbeitsgemeinschaften, the occasional conferences mentioned above, and the Kontaktgespräche represent attempts to extend the organizational basis of the network of information beyond the range of the party organization proper. Herbert

12. Cf. *Jahrbuch der SPD, 1958–59*, pp. 234 ff.

13. The most elaborate system of committees exists in Berlin. *Jahrbuch der Landesverband Berlin, 1957* lists 15.

14. *Arbeitsgemeinschaft* means literally "working community" and is applied loosely to any special group formed to undertake a special task. It refers here to the relatively formal groups established on a wide basis and regulated by central party organs. These are permanent, in contrast to the occasional ad hoc groups which may also use the name. I shall use the German term, since the English translation is so vague as to cause confusion.

15. Cf. Ch. 7.

16. The presidium obtained special permission from the executive to carry out these Kontaktgespräche on its own. Cf. *Jahrbuch der SPD, 1958–59*, Organization Report.

Wehner once outlined the objectives of the Arbeitsgemeinschaften in a speech to one of them:

> you should be an admonisher (*Mahner*) of the party, and we must strive for your recognition in this direction . . . you should be further a gatherer of as much expertise as possible in this area, and also a place for exchange of thinking and experience . . . We should make conversations with . . . Social Democrats, who hold and exercise office in their occupational organizations . . . into an institution of the party.[17]

Although originally an organizational tool to win party members and sympathy for party goals among special groups, the Arbeitsgemeinschaften now represent also the opening up of channels through which policy suggestions are sought as well as disseminated.

These organizational and rather formal means by which the party seeks to reach people throughout the country, both within and outside the party, do not of course exhaust the party's sources of opinion or expert assistance. Many members of the party leadership are, after all, elected politicians who depend in part on the informal, personal contacts they are able to establish with the groups on whose support they depend. These contacts are by no means absent even in "party-ridden" German politics. The contact between the deputy and his constituents, according to Kitzinger,[18] has been regularized to the point where constituencies that do not elect Social Democratic representatives are assigned to party members in order to provide constituents with points of access.

Several observations can be made concerning this organizational pattern. First, although strong centralization is manifest in the presidium, which unites the leading figures of virtually all of the specialized channels in the party, there is great fragmentation of policy-making channels just below the top rank, where the

17. "Selbständig Schaffende," pp. 17 ff.
18. *German Electoral Politics*, p. 183.

day-to-day, nonsensational activities of policy making are carried on. Various groups in society that seek to have their voice given weight in party policy have, according to their specific needs, fairly definite and distinct channels to which they can appeal, and where they presumably can be heard.

Secondly, the trend toward specialization reflects not only the complicated nature of the problems of modern society but also the changing party style. The party develops policy not only on its own initiative but also in response to the need for government decision on issues whether they are relevant to party goals or not. The party pattern of specialization follows closely normal parliamentary specialization.

Thirdly, these specialized channels of information are closely tied to the regular party organization but are not identical with it. In discussing particular policy areas, it is not necessary to refer to the regular party organizations at all unless highly controversial problems are involved. The idealized form of policy formulation, which consists in an interchange between the party leadership and party members at large, simply does not correspond with the facts.

There has been criticism of this specialization among the members of the party, especially those who reflect the older style and feel that too large a gulf has been created between the common party member and policy-making apparatus.[19] However, indications are that the great majority of the party's middle-range leaders accept this development either as inevitable or as positively desirable. The latter are, understandably, those most concerned with the activities of a particular group in society, such as the representative of an organization of war victims, the young director of a small shipping company in Hamburg interested in port affairs, and a local mayor. Thus criticism is perhaps valid insofar as it applies to the breakdown of direct contact between the regular member and the responsible party policy maker, but

19. Cf., for instance, Wolfgang Abendroth, "Warum Parteiprogramm?" published by Willy Birkelbach (SPD Bezirk chairman in South-Hesse) as a "contribution to the discussion" following a series of essays by Birkelbach entitled *Die Grosse Chance* (Frankfurt, 1956).

contacts have apparently been greatly improved with people interested in a particular policy being formulated. Despite the abandonment of ideology and specific long-term program goals, the party does not intend to play a diminishing role in the national decision-making process, but a greater one, and it is a part played by the organization as a whole, not just the parliamentary delegation.[20]

Largely absent from the policy process, incidentally, is an institution serving as a general platform for party intellectuals. In the past, the most important examples of such institutions were party journals (such as the *Neue Zeit* and the *Gesellschaft*) and the newspapers. The postwar period has not produced these outlets. At present there is one significant journal, the *Neue Gesellschaft,* but while it proclaimed at the end of its first year of publication that its circulation was already greater than that of its namesake, it also noted that the largest group of its readers were government officials.[21] A general look at its contents reveals that it is a platform for the leading specialists and officials of the party rather than for party intellectuals. It has no ideological focal point nor is it identified, as were its predecessors, with any particular point of view.

Since there have been demands for some kind of central research organization in the party at almost every party convention since the war, I included in my questionnaire an item concerning the desirability and functions of such an agency. Very few respondents urged that this would be a useful institution in the broad policy-making sense or indeed had any clear idea what its functions would be. The few who did specify a function significantly hoped for a counterweight to the current trend, a center of research that would prove the correctness of their faith in a stronger working-class orientation. One respondent, on the other hand, suggested that if such a body had been created

20. Wehner in "Selbständig Schaffende," puts the problem of activation of the organization in just these terms: "Political activity must be more than talking in the parliaments . . . this present-day variety of politics, which consists in talk among experts, upsets me . . . it must come to this: daily activity of Social Democrats in their organizations in the various social areas and strata."

21. Cf. Ulrich Lohmar in *Neue Gesellschaft, 2,* No. 6 (1955).

earlier it might have helped prove the opposite, i.e. the failure of socialist ideas. More common were those who thought such an institution might be useful for carrying out the kind of voting study familiar in the literature of social science, as a kind of adjunct to the electoral mechanism. Most significantly, the majority seemed to have no particular fear of bias that might be found in the normal sources of basic research available to the party—the universities, the unions, and government agencies.[22]

Party Democracy and Party Unity

Turning from the sources of information and the organizational channels through which the policies of the party are processed to the mechanisms for coordination and conflict resolution, one is faced with a long tradition of academic analysis and partisan debate. The question of whether the SPD, the grandfather of all mass parties, is in fact democratic or not received its first well-known analysis by Robert Michels, who influenced all later analysts. The Social Democrats themselves are oblivious to or contemptuous of the negative conclusions to which these investigations usually lead, and are very proud (and a bit self-righteous) about the democratic structure of their party.

An objective answer to the question depends on what range of interests and what range of members are made the basis of judgment. If formal membership in traditional party organizations gives an equal right to representation and participation, then in present circumstances the party is not very democratic. On the other hand, if right is relative to saliency of interest and involvement, then the effective organizations are the specialized ones described above, and "democratic" is a more accurate description.[23]

22. One respondent, however, complained of small but steady distortion from one of these agencies—the unions!

23. A sliding scale of "right to participate in a political decision" based on degree of involvement in the issue presents a sort of paradox. Members of parties (the agencies for popular decision making) are very often, unless they are active members, a very poor sample of those interested in the issue. Their interest is abstract and general. A different way of measuring democracy within parties must be found.

The evaluation of party democracy also depends on the kinds of policies considered important. Two German analysts of the SPD, for instance, came to opposite conclusions, the negative judgment resulting from observation of the rank-and-file role in the making of policies dealing with foreign affairs and broad national issues, the positive one from observation of its role in local and organizational issues.[24]

Instead of plunging into this mass of confusing issues and misunderstandings it is perhaps more pertinent to avoid casting the question in terms of democracy and simply consider the various ways in which the party structure is shaped to meet the requirements placed on it by the basic orientations of the members and the political situation. The basic question is not whether members' attitudes and interests are accurately reflected, but rather in what way and to what extent the party achieves unity on political questions.[25] The German word *Meinungsbildung* (opinion formation), which means decision making of and by a collectivity, admirably expresses this concept.

Party unity is a relative matter, that is, different parties expect and seek unity of different kinds on different issues. Politicians and party leaders everywhere (unless they are leaders of an opposition faction within a party) call for, and often claim the existence of, an extreme kind of party unity. Such "ideal" unity has two aspects: a high degree of awareness of party policy by all party members and the absence of open disagreement. Party leaders perhaps try most often to promote (in fact or in the minds of their opposition) not only this kind of unity, but also two slightly different things—solidarity and discipline. Solidarity involves an emotional element of identification with the party and placement of a high value on the existence of the party as such. Discipline involves obedience to orders handed down from the

24. See R. Wildenmann, *Partei und Fraktion*, who generally judges the party nondemocratic, and Klaus Schütz in Max Lange et al., *Parteien in der Bundesrepublik*, who inclines to a more positive evaluation.

25. A third common focus for the analysis of organizations, which is not usually applied and will not be applied here, is the efficiency of the operation of the organization.

party leadership, including at least the acceptance of leadership policies.

In common with virtually all socialist and labor organizations, the SPD has traditionally placed a high value on all three forms of integration—unity, solidarity, and discipline. Michels, in his famous analysis, notes the need for discipline and the atmosphere and terminology of military action that was characteristic of Socialist parties.[26] For example, the desire to maximize the party's effect in the Reichstag (or, more accurately, to dramatize the lack of effect) led to strict parliamentary discipline, which still persists.

Most important, however, was the early insistence on party unity, on the common awareness and commitment to party goals and social theory. In the effort to organize the working class, great emphasis was placed on raising the worker's level of political consciousness in order to secure rationally based adherence to party principles. A high level was thought necessary to secure the individual against temptations from other elements in his environment, such as the church, his family, and the paternalistic and/or authoritarian employer. Put in Weberian terms, the party depended to a great extent on mass action and the individual responses of a large number of people, and this required the highest degree of unity possible.[27]

As for solidarity, the party's concern was, similarly, to secure the member to the movement. The very high level of solidarity achieved can be seen in the countless references in party literature to the higher worth of the movement over individual decision and judgment and, most dramatically, in the swift reconstruction of the party in 1945 after twelve years of suppression.

Organs for Securing Agreement

The formal party structure is a product of these early basic demands and the democratic ideals of its ideology. It has been approximately the same since 1890, built hierarchically on a series

26. *Political Parties*, Ch. 3, pp. 41 ff., and all of Pt. I, section A.
27. Cf. Gerth and Mills, *From Max Weber*, pp. 180 ff.

of regional organizations in which the responsibility of the higher organs to the lower is maintained formally through elections and, less effectively, through votes taken directly on policy. Below the national level are the 20 regional Bezirke, each of which subdivides into Unterbezirke. Then there are the local organizations, or *Ortsvereine*. In large cities the Ortsvereine are broken down into smaller units with varying designations.[28] There is considerable difference in the complexity of the institutions found at different levels of the party, but the pattern of organization at the national level is substantially repeated at lower levels.

The responsibility for making policy and issuing it, lies primarily with the executive, as we have seen. There are two other major organs, the council (*Parteirat*) and the congress (*Parteitag*) which in different ways serve in shaping party policy. According to the organization statute, they differ in their functions, their composition, and the timing of their meetings.[29]

The Party Council

The party council, according to the new (1958) version of the statute, must be consulted on "basic foreign and domestic decisions, basic organizational questions, establishment of central party institutions that will represent a continuing cost to the party, [and] the preparation of Bundestag elections." In addition, it is charged with coordinating policies at the federal and Land levels. That this may be its most important function is shown from the fact that since 1958 its membership has included the following:

Chairmen of the Bezirke, plus one or two more delegates depending on the size of the Bezirk

Chairmen of the Land committee, when such is created where more than one Bezirk forms a Land

28. They are called, for instance, *Distrikten* in Frankfurt and, confusingly, *Bezirke* in Hamburg. The general name used by the yearbook for such organizations is *Stadtteilorganisationen*.
29. Articles 10–25.

Chairmen of the delegations to the Land parliaments

Minister-presidents or deputy minister-presidents of the Länder, when such exist[30]

These offices are all ex officio, except for the extra delegates from the Bezirke, who are elected by the Bezirk executives. It meets "as a rule" four times a year.

The requirements that the council be consulted before policy decisions are made appears to be a difficult one to enforce, since the timing of party decisions is not as clear-cut as, for example, the passage and promulgation of laws by the government. In one instance (the nomination of Willy Brandt as the chief candidate for the party) the decision was common knowledge in the press before the meeting of the council was called. In other cases, the requirement was ignored because swiftly breaking events necessitated immediate decisions (or immediate statements) that could not await a council meeting.[31] No doubt anticipation by party leaders of the wishes of the members of the council (a common phenomenon that confounds the political scientist seeking to specify relative degrees of power) goes far to cancel out these difficulties.

In changing the party committee (*Parteiausschuss*) into the party council, the 1958 reform brought into it a much higher proportion of parliamentarians and responsible government officials than had been the case previously when it was composed solely of representatives from the Bezirk party organizations. The council's members have expertise in party-political questions and local political backing that gives weight to its opinions. It is developing into the body through which the party leadership is able to convey its decisions to the outlying party organizations and as a place where conflicts with regard to party strategy, nominations, and electoral tactics can be thrashed out, although conflicts over details of parliamentary policy (unless, of course, they happen to figure in an election) are unlikely to be dealt with

30. Organization statute, Article 22.
31. Cf. *Jahrbuch der SPD, 1958–59*, p. 235.

132

here. It should also serve to prevent the emergence of the kind of split between the Bonn leadership and the Länder leadership that occurred under Schumacher and Ollenhauer.[32]

The Party Congress

The party congress is the "highest" organ of the party, according to the statute. Its functions are to hear reports of the activity of the executive, the *Bundestagsfraktion,* and the *Kontrollkommission* (a small body that reviews the party's finances and serves as a grievance organ). In addition, the congress elects the executive and the Kontrollkommission and passes resolutions on any question of party policy or organization it chooses.

It is composed of the members of the executive and the Kontrollkommission and 300 delegates elected proportionately by a variety of means (but always indirectly) from the Bezirke. Members of the council, a tenth of the Fraktion, and a few others attend but do not vote.

The congress meets once every two years, for about a week. In practice, its chief business is to hear speeches from a few leading members of the party concerning important policy issues and business matters, to discuss them briefly, and to vote on resolutions submitted by the executive and by lower party organs. The agenda is largely controlled by the executive but anyone may speak by submitting his name to the chairman of the meeting, and any regular organization may submit resolutions.

The party congress resolutions usually comprise general statements of policy on the topics discussed. Important resolutions are usually passed in substantially the form proposed by the party executive. These are binding when passed, but they are usually either vague or echo statements party leaders have made earlier. Many resolutions dealing with organizational questions, with suggested improvements in party activity, or with untested or unworkable but fine-sounding policy declarations are turned over

32. See also above, pp. 59 ff.

to the executive or the Fraktion for their information, rather than formally passed.

Although discussion of the resolutions takes up most of the congress' time, equally and sometimes more important is the election of the executive by secret ballot from a list of candidates submitted by the outgoing executive, plus any other nominations made from the floor which have the signatures of 30 delegates from at least four Bezirke.

The party congress plays a very small role in ironing out differences and resolving conflicts relating to the party's most important policy making, i.e. legislation to be presented to the Bundestag, plans for specialized policy areas, and even the dramatic questions of foreign policy and military affairs. It devotes itself almost exclusively to making already decided policies known to the delegates.[33]

The reasons for the unimportance of the role of the congress in these complicated fields are clear. The time allowed for debate is too short, the occasion too public, and the delegates are not organized in such a way as to make extended discussion possible. A further reason lies in the character of the delegates themselves. They are a cross-section of party functionaries, men who have been elected in the regional party organizations; they represent, by and large, regional groupings within the party. Since regional interests as such play a minor part in national politics, the groups that elect them are not especially identified with different points of view on national issues. The delegates are more concerned with questions of party organization and electoral campaigns than with legislation and national policy making.

The congress, then, tends to become a place where the national policy elite (in the form of delegates from the Fraktion and the executive) confronts the party organization. The delegates to the congress take on somewhat the character of a pressure group of local leaders and party bureaucrats. Their common concern is not with legislative policies (except to inform themselves about them) but most often with party solidarity. The congresses thus

33. Cf. Wildenmann, *Partei und Fraktion*, p. 24, and Schütz, in Max Lange et al., *Parteien in der Bundesrepublik*, pp. 181 f.

134

often turn into rituals in which party symbols are prominently displayed and emotional ties to the party reaffirmed.[34]

Given this pattern of representation, one might expect that the one set of issues regarding which the congress might perform a real function would be the changing style of the party, which is the subject of this study. Most policy questions concern details outside the range of most delegates' interests, but the ideology and the character of the leadership determine the general nature of the party and its ability to compete at the polls. These are questions directly relevant to the delegates' interests, and one might expect the congresses not only to generate considerable heated discussion but to provide the method through which conflicting views could be ironed out, or majority decisions taken and changes brought about.

An analysis of the congresses of the 1950s shows however that even here the role of the congress was limited to the ratification of changes in policy, candidates, leadership, and organization after key decisions had already been taken elsewhere. The reformers, in particular, were unwilling, it seemed, to challenge the existing practices at party congresses until they had achieved success elsewhere and a large majority vote in the congress was assured.[35] This was true for the decision to support some form of German army, to replace the top leadership, and even to write the new program. The congresses were by no means unconcerned with these issues, but they became important only after the fact, when the task was to enforce party discipline concerning changes that had already been made.

This situation might be explained in a variety of ways. It might be taken as proof of the Michelian thesis that the rank and file are powerless before the party oligarchy. This conclusion, how-

34. Schütz notes (ibid.), "the party congress serves as a periodically repeated self-pledging of the delegates and therefore of the party membership to the policies of the party."

35. Erler, summing up the executive's position on a foreign policy resolution which had met determined minority opposition from the left, called for "clarity through a majority decision, because that is better than indecision (*Verwaschenheit*) with unanimity." *Protokoll, 1956*, p. 167. In this case he was sure of his majority.

ever, would ignore the fact that the leadership of the party changed considerably in the postwar period, and its policies changed even more. If it is an oligarchy, then it is such a flexible one that the term is meaningless.

A more likely explanation is that the reformers deliberately avoided challenging in the party congresses those resisting change or advocating a more radical character for the party because they would have been selecting as a battlefield the enemy's stronghold. In any case, they had available to them other channels of influence. Prominent among them were members of the Bundestag and of the SPD governments in various Länder. From these positions they were able to bring pressure to bear directly on the executives, the Fraktion, and the committees. The issues were also not forced in the congresses because the reforms took the form of a series of relatively minor changes, and not until very late did they clearly involve ideological questions that could serve as a basis for debate in the congresses.

The failure of the left to make a significant last stand against the changes and thereby force the congress to become an arena for decision making must be explained, of course, by its weakness, astonishing as this may seem in view of the very great traditional sentiments of the members of the SPD.

Quite a contrast is presented by the much greater success which the left wing of the British Labor Party has had in blocking the same kind of change, despite that party's reputation for being on the right wing of international socialism. In the British Labor Party, the party congresses do seem to have served as the locus of controversy.

There are many differences between the two parties,[36] but one that seems to be of considerable importance is the respective positions of the labor unions. The SPD has become independent of them, while they are still closely tied to the Labor Party. In both countries the unions have traditionally been associated with moderate revisionist tendencies, in contrast to the more political

36. For example, the relative freedom of the Labor Party from any pressing need to dissociate itself from Communism, and, secondly, the partial successes of socialist programs the Labor Party was able to put through when in power.

group, which includes the intellectuals. One might expect, then, that the British Labor Party would have become the more moderate of the two. In the 1950s, however, both the British and German labor unions seemed to be strongholds of leftist socialist thinking. Aneurin Bevan and Frank Cousins were prominent British leftists closely associated with the unions. Spokesmen for the German left are not found among leaders of the German Union Federation, but they do include some of the leaders of the more important industrial unions, such as Otto Brenner of IG Metal,[37] and, more particularly, many of the staff members in these industrial unions. It may be, therefore, that the separation of the SPD from the unions has diminished a basis of leftist influence in the party.

In any case, the pattern of disputes within the SPD has not included clashes within party congresses. By and large, the mechanisms of conflict resolution must thus be those already discussed —the fragmented and specialized channels of committees and conferences leading to the party parliamentary delegations and the party executives. The resolution of conflict therefore seems to have fragmented just as the channels for information have. The organs of the party formally intended for this purpose, the congress in particular, actually serve party unity in another way, by conveying information about the policies of the leadership to the organizers, campaigners, and functionaries of the party throughout the country and by reinforcing their emotional solidarity with the party.

Party policy making has therefore become the province of specialists who are relatively unrestrained except by others who are directly concerned with the same policy area. The coordination of party policy in the normal course of events is undertaken with respect neither to ideology nor the long-run impact of policies

37. Cf. the uncomplimentary portrait of Brenner in *Der Spiegel*, November 4, 1959. *Der Spiegel* overdramatized the left-wing militancy of Brenner, yet there is no doubt that if he had a position in the party as strong as that of many union leaders in the British Labor Party he would have to be reckoned with as a left-wing threat to the "new style."

on each other but rather with regard to the tactics of the party within the framework of elections and to the ever-present problem of the image of the party. The exercise of discipline within the party takes place only when there is some issue involved, some kind of behavior that would seriously compromise the party. The chief worries of the decision maker are usually not focused on the membership at large as represented in the congresses but on the interest groups and on public opinion at large.[38]

The policy-making apparatus of the SPD is, despite the decline of fixed policies enshrined in programs, still extensive and active. In fact, this activity is increasing, apparently, by way of Kontaktgespräche, Arbeitsgemeinschaften, and the policy conferences, bringing together party secretaries and party delegates to the parliaments in the Länder. All of these organizations are composed of men who have escaped the exclusiveness of the traditional party forms and who may become the party's listening posts and propagandists. They provide an unexampled framework for integrating the party into the national decision-making system, while retaining their formal organization in the party. It would seem that the party might become much more of an aggregating party than is possible for the party with a less extensive organization, for it need not rely only on the top representatives of pressure groups and mass media to make its contact with the people, but may reach down deeper and become a more sensitive barometer for the many-layered, rapidly shifting trends of public opinion.

38. This conforms with the results of studies made of the British Labor Party. See, for example, R. McKenzie, *British Political Parties*. The existence of the extensive network of committees and specialized agencies to regularize the processes involved seems, however, to be unique in the SPD.

6. The Leadership

The leaders of a party are sensitive indicators of party attitudes and behavior patterns. Leadership and individual leaders have functions determined by the party's structure, its immediate goals, and the context in which it operates. The adequacy of the leaders may vary greatly and may have a significant effect on the success of the party in achieving its intended goals, but over the long run the leadership is more usefully considered as an "intervening variable" than as a cause of party structure and action. It is in this sense, as a reflection of—one could equally well say as a part of—the structure of the party as its new style emerges, that I wish to consider the leadership of the SPD.

There are two kinds of leaders important for our purposes. First of all there are the highly visible top men (or top man) in the party, who inevitably become symbols as well as decision makers. Secondly, there are the leaders at the next rank who are visible to the public in varying degrees but whose significance for party behavior lies in the skills and predispositions they bring to their jobs.

From Schumacher to Brandt— Changing the Top Leadership

Taking the very highest leaders first, it appears that the party's new style of political action has reemphasized their importance, but in respect to a completely different set of needs than existed in the days when the party could be considered a movement.

The abandonment of the ideology, the fragmentation of the policy-making process, and the pattern of contact with the public through mass media has led the SPD to rely on the personal qualities of individual leaders to establish a well-focused, unified character—unified in this sense referring to the clarity and "wholeness" of the public image of the party. The traditions of the SPD, by contrast, have always deemphasized the role of individual leaders. To achieve maximum dramatic impact, party lore calls for the closed ranks of the united party. Harking back to this tradition, a member wrote in a party journal apropos of the reformist criticisms of the leadership in 1958:

> in a party in which the majority decisions, taken on a democratic basis, are the highest law, it is in the last analysis a matter of no consequence who is the party chairman. We want no cult of personality in our party.[1]

Such faith in majority decisions is now clearly misplaced, with the fragmentation of the decision-making process. But even in the past, the party has often relied on dramatic political personalities.

The Background

In its first organized form, the party was the personal creation of Ferdinand Lassalle. In the early years, he, August Bebel, and Wilhelm Liebknecht played an important role in welding the party together and establishing contact with the working masses. In the Weimar Republic, however, there were no important leaders distinguished by their personal appeal. Frederick Ebert and Hermann Müller were thrust into prominence, but they did not achieve it by means of propaganda skills or charisma. The party seems to have chosen its leaders for their faithfulness to the ideology and their administrative skills, with little regard for their impact on party members or the public. But after World

1. *Der Sozialist* (Hamburg), February 1958.

War II, the party once again had a strong personality as a chairman. Kurt Schumacher was similar in many ways to the earlier style of Socialist party leaders. A dramatic speaker inspiring strong loyalty, he performed the same kinds of tasks as earlier leaders in reestablishing the party and maintaining its unity against the onslaughts of the KPD and the distractions of the fight for existence in a disorganized and temporarily impoverished country. He commanded the loyalty of party members, especially those who, like himself, had suffered under the Nazis and/or belonged to the tradition of intellectual militancy of the Weimar period. He appealed, as no other leader of the party had since World War I, to the class-conscious, dedicated socialist. He had, in fact, destroyed the alliance of the leadership with conservative elements in the party which had become characteristic of the Weimar period.

There was, however, an irony in Schumacher's success. After 1948, he was an old-style leader in a party that needed a new style. Although initially the problem was to achieve solidarity, after 1948 it was to establish better relations with traditionally nonsocialist sectors of the population. Schumacher himself advocated many times the "broadening of the party base." But except possibly in the period right after the war when there existed a certain popular receptiveness to socialist ideas, Schumacher's style worked against his goals. After the party narrowly lost the opportunity to share responsibility in 1948 and 1949 the discrepancy became increasingly apparent.

Schumacher's abilities were useful within the framework of a movement. His capacity to establish communication with the militants strengthened their ties to the party and probably increased their discipline. But the base could not be broadened by binding larger and larger numbers of people to a common goal, especially in the face of latent suspicion among the German people of disciplined party functionaries, radical attitudes, and "socialist experiments."

Schumacher died unexpectedly in August 1952 from the accumulated effects of his ten years in a concentration camp. One month later the Dortmund party congress elected his deputy,

Erich Ollenhauer, to replace him as chairman and chief candidate of the SPD. The choice was made quickly and with no overt opposition. Ollenhauer was in the line of succession, as it were, and had proved his loyalty and his ability to keep on good terms with conflicting political factions by his long service to the party as head of the youth organization in the '20s, member of the dwindling party executive in exile and as deputy chairman since 1946. In choosing him, the party followed the precedent of the Weimar period. For seven years he combined the offices of chairman, *Kanzlerkandidat,* and chairman of the Fraktion, and stood for two elections. His special concern was foreign policy, as was Schumacher's. He made no dramatic changes in the line laid down by his predecessor nor did he make important changes in the organization of the party or its style of action. True to his past, he managed to find ways to prevent the simmering revolt of the party reformers from openly splitting the party, while curbing the enthusiasm of the militants. Ollenhauer, *der Mann des Ausgleichs* ("the compromiser," as he was called in his political "obituary" printed in party publications when he stepped down as Kanzlerkandidat in 1959) proved to be a transition leader rather than the forerunner of other Weimarian types—or so the rise of Willy Brandt seems to indicate. The criticisms of the previous leadership and the circumstances surrounding the changes made in the years 1957–60 put the qualities of the new Kanzlerkandidat, Willy Brandt, in perspective.

The party's silence, in public at least, concerning Ollenhauer's election to party leadership was broken immediately after the 1953 elections. In the scattered manifestos from groups of younger members that appeared after the defeat,[2] a common theme was the criticism of the leadership and the basis on which it was apparently chosen. For example, a group from Hamm urged that:

> one must finally get free of the idea that mediocre men, if they are deserving, can replace exceptional people through sufficient length of membership and good character traits.[3]

2. Cf. Ch. 3, note 15.
3. *Beitrag zur Erneurung.* (Cf. note 15, Ch. 3.)

The leadership's task was:

> to formulate the [party's] ideas and to convey it to those
> outside the party . . . Achievement and character are alone
> decisive. Responsibility is a task and not a compensation.

All of these criticisms veiled their references to Ollenhauer. Only several years later, after the second electoral defeat, were specific suggestions made public that entailed Ollenhauer's replacement. Personal criticism seems to have been taboo. One group in Baden-Wurttenburg went so far as to delete its criticisms of the leadership in the published copy of its proposals although they appeared in a copy privately circulated.

In any case, these criticisms shared the fate of most of the suggested reforms: they had little noticeable effect before the 1957 election. Once again, numerous proposals for change or improvement of the *Parteispitzen* ("party peaks") appeared, but only after the party executive made an initial concession by appointing a seven-man committee to propose changes. The committee included Ollenhauer, Wilhelm Mellies (deputy chairman), and Alfred Nau (party treasurer), as representatives of the old guard, and Carlo Schmid, Herbert Wehner, Fritz Erler, and Waldemar von Knoeringen, who were identified as reformers although by that time they were all members of the executive.[4] Significantly, all of the latter formed the core of the new top leadership. The obvious conclusion is that the decisions that shaped the new leadership were made by the leadership itself and resulted from behind-the-scenes maneuvering.

The first formal change came not in the party organization itself but in Fraktion leadership in the new Bundestag. Mellies and Erwin Schoettle, co-chairmen with Ollenhauer, were replaced

4. Carlo Schmid, as was noted earlier, had long been an important member of the top leadership of the party, in contrast to the other three who had only slowly won themselves places on the executive after the war—Von Knoeringen in 1948, Wehner in 1952, and Erler in 1956. Von Knoeringen and Wehner were both on the Fraktion executive in the first Bundestag in 1949, at which time Wehner assumed the post of chairman of the Bundestag Committee for All-German Questions. Von Knoeringen did not become a candidate for the second Bundestag. Erler became a member of the Fraktion executive in 1953.

by Erler, Schmid, and Wehner in October 1957. The reasons for this timing seem to be twofold. First, there was the simple question of mechanics—the Fraktion was forced to reorganize at the first meeting of the new Bundestag, which occurred considerably before the next party congress when the party leadership could be formally changed. Secondly, the Fraktion leadership could be changed by the elite of the party directly—by a simple vote of the members of the Bundestag delegation. A change in party leadership required broader approval, from the delegates to the congress elected by the various regional party organizations.

Between this change in October 1957 and the party convention in Stuttgart in May 1958, a running debate on the character of the party leadership took place in party publications. Among the many particular suggestions two general themes predominated among the reformers. First, they called for the creation of a group leadership reflecting the "outstanding variety of men the SPD has had at its disposal,"[5] and showing the *Geistiger Spann* (intellectual diversity) which, it was asserted, characterized the party. The second and related theme advocated the separation of the political leadership from the *Apparat* (the bureaucracy); the objective here was to reduce the number of paid party officials holding important posts in the party executive.

At the May congress in Stuttgart, Wehner and Von Knoeringen replaced Mellies (who had died unexpectedly), thus surrounding Ollenhauer, who remained chairman, and creating a situation similar to that existing in the Fraktion.[6] At the same time, two members out of five who had been elected as paid members of the executive were dropped: Fritz Heine, responsible for press work, and Herta Gotthelf, head of the executive's office for political work for women. The new organization statute provided that only the chairman, deputy chairman, and treasurer would be elected as paid officials, although the executive has apparently felt free to pay others as it has seen fit.[7]

---

5. Erler, quoted in *Der Sozialdemokrat* (Frankfurt), December 1957.
6. *Protokoll, 1958.*
7. The 1958 party congress refused to accept a proposal of the executive to elect paid and unpaid members of the executive in separate ballots, for the reason

Respondents to my interviews agreed that these changes in the leadership could be considered as fulfillment of the demand for separation of the Apparat and the political leadership. The Apparat was defeated at least symbolically, and a new and more diverse leadership established. As noted before, this meant less a changed power position for the bureaucracy than a change in leadership qualities.

The Leading Candidates

The most dramatic changes were made in the party's candidates for major political office. It seems to have been understood as early as the 1958 congress at Stuttgart that Ollenhauer would no longer be a chief candidate in coming elections, although this was not officially announced until more than a year later. The delay worked in favor of Willy Brandt who in 1959 did not yet figure prominently in the overt shifts within the party. At this time Carlo Schmid appeared the most likely candidate on the basis of the general respect he had earned as vice-president of the Bundestag. He was in fact nominated in 1959 for president of the Federal Republic when Theodor Heuss, a respected liberal, was obliged to retire after two terms. Popular though he was, Schmid failed to be elected because the election was held in the CDU-controlled electoral assembly which, after much confusion and political muscle-flexing by Adenauer, elected CDU-man Heinrich Lübke.

Schmid's nomination to the politically more important chancellorship would have marked a departure for the party, since Schmid's reputation lay as much outside as within the party. The ultimate choice of Brandt in 1960 was, however, a more spectacular departure because he had emerged into the political limelight so suddenly. Brandt represents a new type of strong personality

---

that such a practice would give the former some kind of special status. Except for the paid members who were dropped from the executive altogether, however, the immediate practical effect was very small. Nau and Eichler continued to be paid members of the *Vorstand,* the first as treasurer and the second as leader of the Cultural Department of the executive.

in the SPD. His style of political action, the manner in which he rose to prominence, and the kind of appeal he strives to make are all sharply different from his two immediate predecessors as chief party candidate, Schumacher and Ollenhauer.

Brandt's early career did not mark him out in any way.[8] He was active in party youth organizations during the Weimar period, and when the SAP, a left-wing splinter party, broke off toward the end, he was among its members. Like Schumacher, who was the editor of a party newspaper in Stuttgart and a member of the Landtag and Reichstag, he could thus be considered a party militant. Like Ollenhauer, who had achieved prominence as the head of the party's youth organization, Brandt had his early political experience with the subsidiary political organizations of the party.

During the war, Schumacher was interned, Ollenhauer rose to a post on the executive and went into exile with that body, and Brandt went into exile in Norway where he became a Norwegian citizen. Unlike the others, Brandt broke his ties with the SPD, although he became active in the Norwegian Socialist Party. He returned to Germany first as a journalist, then as an attaché with the Norwegian Embassy. There he met Ernst Reuter, the popular mayor of Berlin. His first job with the party came "on Schumacher's suggestion" (Brandt's words)[9] as the delegate of the party executive to Berlin in 1948, a post appointed by the party leadership. Here again, his career was not notable in SPD annals since he was rising through the central party institutions.

Brandt's identification with Reuter, whose authority in the party derived from his very prominent position in the municipal–international politics of Berlin, provided a better steppingstone to power than his position in the party bureaucracy. He became embroiled in the factional disputes between Reuter and the head of the party organization in Berlin, Franz Neumann, and became Reuter's protégé. The party recognized Brandt's claim on leadership only after he had become the president of the Berlin Chamber of Deputies and, in 1957 (on the death of Otto Suhr, Reuter's successor), governing mayor of Berlin. The national and inter-

8. See Willy Brandt, *Mein Weg nach Berlin* (Munich, 1960).
9. Ibid.

national prominence which that post gave him during the successive crises involving Berlin attracted public attention and press coverage—familiar enough reasons for promotion in other parties but unusual in the SPD. Even his rise within the party organization—when he defeated Neumann for the chairmanship of the Berlin *Landorganisation*—was based on his identification with Reuter and was successful only after he had become mayor. He was the only one of the postwar SPD *Kanzlerkandidaten* who employed popular success, rather than support within the party organization, to win that post. He had played his cards boldly, appealing to the pro-American sentiments of the German people (which contrasted with sentiments of militant party members) by touring the United States in early 1959 and winning a favorable reception as the mayor of Berlin. Over and over again in public appearances, he has made a point of subtly dissociating himself from the party organization whenever possible.[10] His speech accepting the party's nomination for the chancellorship at the party convention on November 25, 1960, includes, for example, the following passage:

> I am perhaps not making a statement that will win easy popularity when I declare here that I cannot simply be an instrument for expressing the will of the party, but that after earnest thought and on my own responsibility, I shall have (if elected) to make decisions which are vital to the interest of our nation. But I know that the Social Democratic Party, whose confidence I enjoy, will guarantee me that freedom of decision which this office (the chancellorship) requires under the Basic Law.[11]

10. Brandt was even able to maintain his "above-party" status in his occasional speeches to the Bundestag, where he could appear as observer from the Bundesrat. His many statements on foreign policy were made as mayor of Berlin, and his appearances at party congresses—especially after his rise to prominence in 1957–58—were generally brief. He spoke only once at Bad Godesberg, for example, making a relatively mild statement in favor of the acceptance of the new program. *Protokoll, 1959*, p. 74. His prominence was such, however, that he shared the headlines the next day with Ollenhauer.

11. *A Policy for Germany*, Speech to the Hannover party congress on November 25, 1960 (Bonn, 1960).

The contrast between Brandt's style and Schumacher's is thus clearest in their relations with party members and voters. Uniformly, respondents to my interviews discussed Brandt as a instrument for winning votes whether they admired him or not. His ability to challenge Adenauer, the champion vote-getter, was the basis of his selection.[12] Brandt seeks simply voters; they need not be converts. He seeks not to mobilize people for the cause but to win their confidence. He is therefore probably the most dramatic manifestation of the party's new style in leadership.

The choice of Brandt over Schmid indicates the party's willingness to adapt not only to the general system of values but also to the situation of the moment. The party chose the shooting star over the fixed one in order to exploit the existing wave of sympathy with the 44-year-old Berlin mayor, as well as take advantage of whatever doubts there might be about the 85-year-old chancellor.

As I have noted, one of the objectives of the reformers was to put in the most visible positions of party leadership men who would show the diversity of party members. The most literal achievement of this goal was the *Mannschaft* (team) which the party put forward as a device in the 1961 campaign. The team was comparable to the "shadow cabinet" used in Britain. Suggestions were made in public throughout the 1957–59 period for the establishment of a shadow cabinet,[13] but the idea was ultimately rejected and the "team" was presented in its place in September 1960. The precise reasons why the cabinet idea was abandoned are not clear, but it is apparent that the party was able to draw a wider circle of prominent members—some of whom seemed unlikely ever to accept posts in the government—

12. Public reactions have of course not been unanimous, but press opinion has probably been more sympathetic to Brandt than to any other SPD leader in the postwar period. *Die Welt*, June 27, 1960, published an article by its columnist Sebastian Haffner entitled "Ein Kronprinz aus der Opposition?" in which the author suggested that Brandt was the best candidate available to carry out the general line of foreign policy initiated by Adenauer. *Die Welt* is normally pro-CDU.

13. Cf., for example, the article by Hermann Volters, senator from Berlin, in *Vorwärts,* October 1957.

into the team. The team included, for instance, Max Brauer, pre-1933 mayor of Altona, émigré to the United States and from 1945 to 1961, with one four-year interruption, mayor of Hamburg. Brauer had already announced his intention to retire from his post. It was possible that this long-time *Kommunalpolitiker* (municipal politician) might be persuaded to accept a government post, but the reasons for including him on the team unquestionably had more to do with his generally good reputation among the people and among the elites in Germany than with his possible future participation in an SPD government.

The team represented, according to a party publication,[14] a "cross-section of German Social Democracy." The party identified the members of the team in the following way, indicating the kind of diversity it hoped to show:

Willy Brandt . . . heir . . . of Ernst Reuter . . . great political capacity . . . fairness in conflicts with people with different ideas . . . clarity of political ideas . . .

Carlo Schmid . . . recognized that the intellectual should not only talk about democracy, but should also help shape it . . . [he has] undisputed significance for Germany in the postwar period.

[Fritz] Steinhoff [ex-minister president of Nordrhein-Westfalen], [Georg August] Zinn [minister-president of Hesse], and Brauer have stood for decades in leading positions in German Land politics. What they have done . . . contradicts all those lies which say that one only hears a "no" from Social Democrats. Hamburg and Hesse . . . [are] leading examples of progressive social, economic, and cultural policy.

Käte Strobel who, when asked for her occupation, says modestly "housewife," has won a reputation in her political work for her expert knowledge of the economics of food.

14. *eilt*, September 1960.

Fritz Erler, Dr. Heinrich Deist, and Wenzel Jaksch have long been leaders in . . . the Fraktion . . . [and] command great knowledge in special fields, but also general knowledge, which wins the recognition in debates of even their political opponents . . . Jaksch [is] a representative of the refugees . . .

The DGB [German Labor Union Federation] chairman, Willi Richter, is a man of practical social and labor politics. For years he participated in a leading position in the Bundestag in the shaping of the social and labor legislation of the postwar period . . . he unites the knowledge of the worries and hopes of the working men with the strong consciousness of the representative of the freely organized workers.

Alex Möller is a man of business [*ein Mann der Wirtschaft*] . . . general director of a large insurance concern, recognized by the world of specialists [*Fachwelt*] and respected as the leader of the social democratic Landtagfraktion in democratic *Musterländle* [model Land] Wurttemberg-Baden.

The expert, the experienced administrator, the representatives of influential groups appear among the candidates the party put forward. The team was not very representative of the party leadership, however, and included no party secretaries.

Top Organization Leaders

In contrast to Schumacher and Ollenhauer, Brandt did not become simultaneously chief candidate and chairman of the party. The role of the top leadership was somewhat more complex. Ollenhauer remained chairman, with Wehner and Von Knoeringen as his deputies. The first two for different reasons were unacceptable as major candidates for the party—Ollenhauer because he had lost twice and Wehner because of his vulnerability to attack as a former functionary in the Communist Party.

Ollenhauer's position seemed to be that of administrator, and perhaps symbolic concession to the older party faithful, a symbol that all had not been lost to "these young men" (as an older member of the party described the present leadership to me). Except in party affairs, he largely retreated into the background.

During the period of Nazi rule, Wehner spent considerable time in the Soviet Union. While there he became disillusioned with Communism and during the war went to Scandinavia, returning to Germany right after the war. Chiefly on the basis of his role in the Bundestag he has risen through the party rapidly since that time. Adenauer used every opportunity to recall Wehner's Communist past, however, and he has been a focal point for attacks on the SPD.

Although apparently frustrated in his ambition for high government office, Wehner has become clearly the most dynamic and important personality within the party organization. He has become a strong proponent of a more open, expansive party structure.[15] He is also an excellent speaker (although his speeches read terribly, they are delivered with a fine sense of emotional impact), and is the party's chief spokesman for working-class audiences. Although accused of being a dangerous radical by opponents of the SPD, and occasionally falling into a radical form of speech, he is clearly convinced of the need for a new party style. Judging from my interviews and the response to his speeches, he seems to have the confidence of a wide segment of the party, including many who are openly critical of the new course he has done much to further. He has consequently been used— at the Godesberg congress and in the foreign policy debate of the summer of 1960, for example—as the defender of the executive against the complaints of the radicals.

Like the other two members of the party triumvirate, he has

15. Particularly indicative of his position are the speeches before the Arbeitsgemeinschaften selbständige Schaffenden (see note 17, Ch. 4) and a collection of speeches and writings he apparently issued himself at the time of the change of leadership in 1957–58, perhaps as campaign material within the party; it was entitled "The [Party's] Attraction for Other Groups in the Population Depends on the Greatest Possible Unity Among the Working Population."

disavowed any intention of taking political office. As a strong personality in an older style, yet tamed to contemporary circumstances at least for the present, he represents the biggest question mark in the future development of the party. He may, if he stays behind the scenes, become something of a political manager.

Von Knoeringen is a poor third with respect to public reputation. It could be said that he represents the younger generation of party organization leaders, having stepped up not through the Bundestag but through the Bavarian party organization. He has specialized in the fields of education, science, and youth, all of which are chiefly relevant in Land politics. His responsibility within the executive includes coordination with the regional governments.[16] One can speculate on the basis of these facts that his strength lies in his position as coordinator and representative of the newly influential, successful party leaders in the Land governments, and in his appeal to the highly unrevolutionary "radicalism" of contemporary youth, who reject Marxian formulations. Whether youth will long be impressed by the odd "utopia" he describes of a "politically educated" German people—his most consistent theme—remains to be seen.

No clear trend emerges from an analysis of this triumvirate, and the characteristics of future party chairmen remain uncertain. However, some light can be thrown on the criteria used in selecting the elite by turning from the personalities themselves to the attitudes of the members. Their evaluation of the skills to be desired in their leaders can be discerned in the debates over the reform of the party and in the responses to my questions about party leaders. Four leadership types emerge: (a) the intellectual, capable of inspiring followers, (b) the expert, who has mastered a complicated policy field, (c) the administrator and/or compromiser, and (d) the figure popular among nonparty elites and the general public. As might have been expected, these four types reflect the characteristics of past and present leading personalities in the party.

16. As a member of the presidium, he has responsibility for cultural policy, coordination of Länder politics, propaganda and recruitment, Young Socialists, and youth policy.

The first, obviously patterned after Schumacher, was commonly mentioned as most desirable by the minority who opposed the Godesberg Program and look for a rejuvenation of the old party style. One respondent complained in an interview that the present leaders lacked "real authority": they lacked the breadth of perception to comprehend the totality of the historical situation. Beyond this, he asserted, they lacked the intellectual gifts that would enable them to reduce these complex relationships to simple terms that could be communicated to the rank and file. The current leaders, he concluded, "led" simply because they held the appropriate offices.

The second type, the expert, has its obvious prototypes in Erler and Deist. It appealed most to those of my respondents who held responsible posts in parliament or government. Highly impressed with the complexity of legislation and administrative policy, and suspicious of "dogmatic simplifications," these party members considered it absolutely necessary that people highly qualified in specialized areas such as defense, social legislation, and economic affairs be represented in the highest councils of the party. The contrast between these first two types marks again the contrast between the two styles of party. The expert is never considered by the new group to stand alone. He is part of the team, though at the highest level of policy making. For the older members and those younger men who demand a more traditional approach, experts, when they are necessary, should play a role subsidiary to that of the leader.

The third ideal, the administrator and compromiser, clearly has Ollenhauer as its prototype. The administrator as leader is also seen as part of the team, as a sort of linchpin around which various factions can move. This type answers the needs of a broad segment of the party, for the most part those who place a high value on unity and those who are completely involved in parliamentary politics. Some of the latter appear to want the party organization to have as small a role in policy making as possible.

The fourth type, the popular leader, recurred often as an ideal among virtually all but the most intransigent opponents of the present trend. It is surprising, however, in view of the rise of

Willy Brandt, how begrudgingly popularity with the voters at large was conceded to be necessary *except* for the one post of Kanzlerkandidat. Emphasis was placed instead on the quality the Germans call *Umgänglichkeit,* or "sociability"—the ability to get around in society, to establish contacts with the influential, and to win confidence. These characteristics were often mentioned as necessary for the party leader.

Again, not unexpectedly, the emphasis on popularity and Umgänglichkeit came most strongly from party members who held elective office, and, perhaps less obviously, from the party secretaries. Once again, it was the opponents of the new program, the members who appeared most closely identified with work within the party organizations or the unions, who treated both general popularity and Umgänglichkeit with some contempt. Among these, scorn for Willy Brandt as a "pure opportunist" would occasionally break through. In general, even among the most ardent reformers, Brandt has not achieved a very close link with party members. That link is perhaps even less strong than it seemed in my interviews. I suspect that the prospect of criticizing to an outsider the by then (early 1960) leading contender for the candidacy for the chancellorship was felt as a kind of breach of party discipline. Otherwise, I would probably have been exposed to more negative judgments of the young mayor of Berlin. At the same time Brandt's apparent popularity (with women, for example, who have consistently voted more heavily for Adenauer than have men) is generally conceded to be a necessary and desirable electoral attraction.

The Structure of the Party Elite and the Process of Selection

Further understanding of the process of elite recruitment in the SPD can be gained from consideration of the methods by which most leaders reach their positions. For purposes of analysis, we may take as the party elite the holders of major party and parliamentary office, since there is no evidence that any behind-the-scenes group has appreciable influence over the party.

The major offices of the SPD have been described in the previous chapter. At the top is the party executive with its smaller presidium, the executive of the Fraktion, and the party's candidates for leading government offices. The next rank includes the remaining members of the Fraktion and the members of the party council. There are many instances of double office holding, so that, in 1961 for example, the small group at the top numbered only six: Ollenhauer, Brandt, Fritz Erler, Heinrich Deist, Carlo Schmid, and Herbert Wehner. The total number of persons in the Fraktion executive and the party executive was 42, of which 14 were members of both. The total number of members of the Fraktion and the so-called "little party congress," i.e. the executive, the council, and the *Kontrollkommission,* was 255, of which 39 were members of both.[17] These 255 could be considered the party elite at the national level.

The formal methods for election to the elite group are of two kinds: party elections and party nominations to public office followed by a successful election campaign. The formal party elections follow a highly traditional pattern. Leaders are elected by secret ballot at party conventions on the basis of a list submitted by the existing leadership, occasionally augmented by nominations from the floor. Of the 255 mentioned above, the executive (33 members), and at least 20 of the Bezirk representatives to the council (probably all 58 members) were elected in this way. That makes a maximum of 91, or about a third of the total, including all six of the very top leaders. Selection of candidates for the Bundestag and Landtage is accomplished by secret ballot, in either a Bezirk or Land congress. At least 195 and probably closer to 215 of the 255 at some point passed this test. All 255 therefore went through some kind of election by a wide circle of party members.

Actually, of course, the most important factor in rising to membership in the elite is approval from the existing members. In party elections, the executive maintains a strong position in determining its own future composition. In the nomination of

17. As of the end of 1959. Cf. *Jahrbuch der SPD, 1958–59.*

candidates to public office, it is commonly asserted that the influence of the party executive is felt by the Bezirk or Land executive in the selection of approximately 40 per cent of the Bundestag Fraktion.[18] This 40 per cent includes experts, Fraktion leaders, and probably "deserving *Genossen* (comrades, i.e. members)" too. In addition, the Bezirk or Land executive unquestionably plays the major role in determining who shall stand for the party. The presidium and the Fraktion executive are formally elected by the elite from the elite.[19] Only the chairman, the two deputy chairmen, and the treasurer of the party are elected to the presidium, ex officio, by the general party congress; the others are elected by the executive.

These formal and semi-formal procedures have changed little from earlier times. Looking behind the formal requirements which, by party statutes (and by German law with respect to the selection of candidates[20]), provide the general pattern for choosing leaders, there are a few aspects of party practices and performance that throw some additional light on the structure of the party.

Kitzinger, in *German Electoral Politics,* and some scattered references in party yearbooks suggest that in nominations and even elections within the party organization the successful individual campaigner is gaining recognition at the expense of the party functionary. The German electoral law provides for two methods by which a man may enter office—as a constituency candidate or as a list candidate. In the first case, he runs in a particular district and is elected on the basis of a simple majority. In the second situation, he runs as a member of the list which the party prepares on the Land level and is elected by proportional

18. The figures cannot, of course, be exact. Cf. Wildenmann, *Partei und Fraktion,* p. 140, and Kitzinger, *German Electoral Politics,* pp. 66 f.

19. Prior to 1958, the party congresses elected, from lists provided by the executive, a small group of paid party leaders sometimes called the "presidium." The changes of 1958 had the effect of transferring the election of this small group, now officially called the presidium, to the executive.

20. The legal stipulations on nominations do not seriously affect the SPD since they coincide with normal party practices. They call, for instance, for a secret ballot in the appropriate party organizations for constituency and list candidates. Kitzinger, *German Electoral Politics,* Ch. 2.

representation. The voter has two votes, one for a candidate in his local constituency and one for the party of his choice on the Land level.

Kitzinger notes that the SPD, even more than the CDU, has tended to give favored treatment to constituency candidates especially those who have run well. This has been manifested in two ways. First, the party has assured incumbents who have won their seats in the constituencies an almost certain opportunity to run again. Kitzinger notes that only one of 44 incumbent constituency candidates failed to win renomination when he expressed the desire to do so. The second method of favoring this group has been based on the fact that one may be a candidate both in a constituency and on a list. With favorable treatment from the party he can have two chances of election. Kitzinger notes that the SPD, more than the CDU, has generally placed the constituency candidate relatively high on the list.

The value placed on campaigners is given added emphasis and made an organizational objective in the following passage from the opening pages of the report on the organization in a recent party yearbook:

> the policy of the organization is to make effective the principle of helping the right man or woman to the right place for them, that is, to the place where their political strength can develop in the most effective way . . . the efforts . . . must be continued to avoid letting the candidates who were active in communal or Land election campaigns, and who generally contributed a significant amount of personal campaign effort go back, when they are not elected, to their former functions . . . [Rather, we must] help them stay in the foreground and thereby come into increasing contact with wider circles of the population.[21]

This emphasis on campaigners shows that the party is very much concerned to adapt campaigns, and party activity in general, to local relationships. Kitzinger reports that local nominating

21. *Jahrbuch der SPD, 1958–59*, p. 237.

committees maintain considerable autonomy in their selection of local party candidates, within a basic framework of candidates from the executive. The same party yearbook, too, reports somewhat proudly that the help the party was able to give local areas in running campaigns had been accomplished without "schematization," that is, without an inflexible line that would conflict with variations in electoral districts. It reports, too, that the party has started a file on each of the electoral districts that will provide the leadership with detailed knowledge of their structure and will allow, for instance, a more rational distribution of speakers from party headquarters.[22]

Turning to party leadership at the regional level, there is no single pattern describing the special role of party leaders as compared with parliamentary ones, although there is enough evidence for some tentative hypotheses. A few examples will give an idea of the variations.

In the west-central Land of Hesse, there are two Bezirke. Hessen-Süd is the larger of the two. Its center is Frankfurt. Hessen-Nord, with headquarters in Kassel, is smaller and more rural. Georg August Zinn, present member of the party's "team," member of the executive, and minister-president of the Hessian government, has been the Bezirk chairman of Hessen-Nord since 1951. The Hessen-Süd Bezirk has been headed since 1954 by Willy Birkelbach, who until 1958 was a member of the party executive and is now a member of the Bundestag and chairman of the Socialist Fraktion of the European Parliament. He was also for many years the director of the Deutsche Gewerkschaftsbund (German Union Federation) school in Hesse. At the Godesberg congress Birkelbach emerged as one of the chief spokesmen of the critics of the new program. His particular strength lies in his intellectual capabilities.

Max Brauer has long been mayor of Hamburg, but he has not been the chairman of the Hamburg Landesorganisation (Hamburg is technically not a Bezirk, but it has virtually all the attributes of one), a post held by Karl Vittinghoff, who is a more

22. Ibid.

traditional party leader. His background lies in the labor movement; for many years he was a functionary in the unions. Unlike
the chairmanship of the Hessian Bezirk, his post is a paid one.
Vittinghoff appears to be closer to a manager of the organization
than either Zinn in Hessen-Nord or Birkelbach in Hessen-Süd.

In the case of Berlin, which has a large, diverse organization,
the situation appears to have changed with the advent of Brandt.
Reuter, like Brauer, was not chairman of the party organization.
According to Brandt's testimony, he was a popular and effective
mayor but had little talent in the field of party work. Brandt
writes:

> Achievements, even recognized and successful achievements
> [*Leistung*], are not alone sufficient to win influence in a
> large and well-organized party. Ernst Reuter was a clear
> and warning example. He used an excessive part of his
> strength in a small steady war with single members of his
> own party. Reuter's strength did not lie in the sphere of
> purely party work. He had an especially difficult time be-
> cause his contact with Schumacher [thereby] suffered, and
> above all because the then chairman of the Landesorgani-
> sation scarcely helped him, but often met him in crass
> rivalry.[23]

For many years there was not only a division of labor in the
Berlin organization between the head of the party organization,
Franz Neumann, and the Social Democratic government, but
also a split in opinions and a conflict in personalities. Neumann
appears to have been a party organization leader who sought to
maintain considerable influence over the determination of policy.

In the mid-fifties, at first under Reuter's tutelage and then on
his own, Brandt was a candidate for the leadership of the local
party as the head of an anti-Neumann faction. Finally, in 1958,
having moved up the ranks in the parliamentary life of the city
(he became president of the Berlin House of Deputies in 1954 and
mayor in 1957), he became leader of the party. In Berlin, there-

23. *Mein Weg nach Berlin,* p. 278.

fore, the change brought a shift in the party leadership from a man of the organization to the party's highest local elected official.

It is clearly hard to generalize from such diverse patterns, but I will hazard a hypothesis that the pattern of leadership in the SPD in the coming decade will move toward one of two situations, both having similar consequences. Either office holders will become party leaders, or party leaders will become only managers. Both solutions depart from the older style in that the political leadership—the leadership that takes the most active part in the formulation of policy—rests with the party leader most closely associated with the regional governing body or parliament. He may be the nominal head of the party organization as such (Zinn and Brandt, for example) or not (Brauer).

Another role is filled by the party organization leader or his lieutenant, who is in effect a kind of manager. "Secretary" is probably too narrow a word for someone like Vittinghoff, if used in the SPD sense of paid permanent staff. He is the relatively neutral manager of party business with respect to two spheres of party activity. He is the manager of local election campaigns and of the local sector in national campaigns, and he is also the manager of activities of the party organization that deal with national policy.

The older type of organizational scheme still seems to exist in Hessen-Süd and characterized Berlin before 1958. In this form the political and organizational leadership is in the hands of a party leader who seeks to control local elected officials of the party but is essentially interested in national problems and often in ideological concerns. This pattern emphasizes the dividing line between the party and the government. In Hessen-Süd, of course, the situation is special because the Bezirk does not correspond to the Land. The pressure to conform to the newer pattern is therefore not so great.

In general, at virtually all levels, positions of leadership are widely held to require more and more the ability to deal with persons outside the party. One respondent dated this from the time the party began to "assume responsibility," i.e., to win a

160

significant share in government responsibility. In the early days, according to this respondent (a longtime party functionary), it was important to be in touch with organizations that formed the other sections of the labor movement: the unions, the cooperatives, and other workers' organizations. Now a member of the Hamburg *Bürgerschaft* (city parliament), he finds it necessary to make a very wide variety of contacts ranging from local organizations interested in social policy (his field) to the many individuals who look for help from the man who is "in the same party as Brauer" (the mayor). Another respondent declared, somewhat ironically, that a party functionary used to "go everywhere . . . before he would ever be seen speaking in a church—but now they invite him to speak there!"

7. Organization and Membership

A massive organization of rank-and-file members is the distinguishing mark of the mass party, of which the SPD has often served as prototype. From the turn of the century to 1933, as we saw in Chapter 1, the SPD not only built up its own membership but also sponsored affiliated organizations whose functions ranged beyond the realm of politics altogether into such fields as insurance, education, and child care. Many of these organizations either atrophied or became independent after World War II, including the most important of them, the trade unions. However, the party organization itself—the network of local and regional units—has remained and still comprises over 650,000 dues-paying members. The changes the party has undergone in the last decade have, however, raised questions about the organization and its structure and functions.

In the movement type of party, the party membership represents a high level of commitment to the "cause," and the party organization is a means of strengthening the members' solidarity, proselytizing, and providing a way for militant members to guard the purity of the doctrine. The SPD's abandonment of an ideological orientation, its emphasis on winning independent interest groups and general public sympathy, and the increasing prominence of vote-getters among its leadership suggest that this is no longer a suitable function. Three possible alternatives suggest themselves: the party's membership organizations may continue in the old way and in conflict with the new orientation, or may follow the steps of the other groups affiliated with the party and slowly atrophy, or may undergo some kind of transformation that will allow them to play a new role in the activities of the party.

There is almost no evidence that any of the members of the party, reformers or radicals, publicly advocated the apparently natural idea that the organization should dissolve since it has finished the task of integrating and educating the working class. Only once did I see such a suggestion made openly, by a group of lawyers associated with the party in Hamburg who proposed in effect that the party become a series of committees of notables.[1]

The regularity with which party leaders have asserted that the party would not abandon its character as a membership party may indicate that such proposals have been more common than is apparent from accessible materials.[2] The sentimentality of the older members and the vested interests of the party secretaries probably acted as a brake on publicizing such radical suggestions. Essentially, however, there were too many reasons to retain the organization to make this idea acceptable. First, the financial security and independence that membership dues provide could not be lightly thrown away in favor of uncertain contributions from moneyed interests or even more uncertain disbursements that might be forthcoming from the public treasury if some suggestions for party legislation were put into effect.[3] Secondly, *some* form of organization is needed to meet the competition of the highly professional and elaborate apparatus with which the CDU mobilizes voters.

SPD party members often refer to the *Hilfstruppen* (auxiliary troops) of the CDU,[4] including also the churches (especially the Catholic Church) and the wide variety of ad hoc and "educational" organizations founded by people sympathetic to the CDU

1. "Haben die Juristen Recht?" *Der Sozialist* (Hamburg), March 1954.
2. For example, Ollenhauer in *Der Sozialist* (Hamburg), February 1958; Wehner in a radio talk reproduced in *Der Sozialist* (Hamburg), January 1958 (speech of November 11, 1957).
3. For the party's finances, see Appendix.
4. For example, Erler in a speech reported in *Der Sozialist* (Hamburg), November 1958, justifies the suggestion by the SPD Fraktion that party members should make contact with and even join units of the new army in order to prevent it from becoming the "propaganda instrument of one party" through the training agencies set up to prepare the new soldiers "psychologically."

and financed with money from business circles or sometimes even from the government itself.[5] Deputy SPD Chairman Herbert Wehner, now especially concerned with organizational questions, has repeatedly cited this competition to justify not only the retention of the organization but its reinvigoration.[6] In an article written for internal party consumption in January 1958, using characteristically old-fashioned socialist language, he writes:

> There are still today materially privileged upper strata [*Oberschichten*] which are very desirous and very much in a position to limit or influence the democratic order for their own interests and to the detriment of the interests of the broad masses [*breiten Schichten*]. So long as such upper strata exist, a broad membership party is necessary, one which knows how to keep itself financially independent in order to avoid the danger of becoming financially tied [to special interests] and therefore sold out.[7]

Broad agreement on the necessity of an organization has not prevented argument about its form and activity. One of the reform manifestos of 1953 sums up one aspect of the problem (in good Teutonic style) as follows: "The present form of the political community life [*politische Gemeinschaftsleben*] of the SPD can no longer appeal to the young people."[8] Many have condemned (and others defended) party symbolism, such as the familiar form of address, the flag, and the term "comrade" (*Genosse*), as both repellent to outsiders and too easily confused with Communist usage. Another tack was taken in the measured words of the 1956–57 yearbook:

> A stronger and more vigorous life for the *Arbeitsgemein-schaften* [working groups of members with special interests]

5. One of the services of the party magazine *eilt* is to identify "opponents' organizations," of which 60 are listed in the index for 1959.

6. E.g., cf. Wehner, note 2 above.

7. *Der Sozialist*, January 1958.

8. *Beitrag zur Erneurung.* (Note 15, Ch. 3.)

must be achieved in the large cities . . . the organization by areas in which the members live . . . no longer suffices.[9]

It is apparent that these criticisms indicate real problems, and steps have already been taken to solve them.

Organizational Structure on the Regional and Primary Levels[10]

The party organization throughout the country is made up of many kinds of groups which are more or less well integrated in the party organization and include new groups added to old ones associated with the party for many years. According to the statute, the party is "made up of Bezirke [regional organizations] which are composed of local organizations [Ortsvereine]."[11] The latter are the primary groups, but the 20 Bezirke, which cover the entire area of West Germany, can be considered the key organizations, since only at their level does one find represented (and coordinated) all the types of party structures.

Immediately after World War II, the Bezirke had great freedom in determining their own structure, even in such matters as the amount of dues assessed the members.[12] It was not until after the founding of the Federal Republic and the first Bundestag election in 1949 that the party leadership began to centralize and standardize the organization, slowly establishing a uniform pattern throughout the regions.[13] Some differences in the organization of the Bezirke remain, but they are in degree and not in kind and result from the occasional situation in which a Bezirk

9. *Jahrbuch der SPD, 1956–57*, p. 242.

10. The following analysis is based on information gathered in interviews in the South-Hesse and Hamburg party organizations and by examination of the yearbooks available at party headquarters in Bonn, which covered 14 of the 20 party Bezirke.

11. Organization statute, Article 3.

12. See Schütz, in Lange et al., *Parteien in der Bundesrepublik*.

13. The landmark in this process was the declaration of the *Herner Beschlüsse*. Cf. *Jahrbuch der SPD, 1948–49*, p. 141 (decisions of a meeting of the executive and council on November 16 and 17, 1949).

does not correspond to a Land, or from the higher level of specialization that is possible in the larger Bezirke.

The central organs of the national organization—the executive,
the council, and the congress—were described in Chapter 5. The
Bezirk is organized and operates in much the same way. The
subordinate organizations for which these provide the leadership
include four groups roughly distinguishable in functions and
operation. These are the secretariat, the policy advisers, the
groups representing special interests, and the traditional units
organized on the basis of the residence of members.

The Secretariat

Although much is made, even by Social Democrats, of the bureaucracy of the party, the paid staff is small relative to the size of
the membership, or even in comparison with the number of
elected, unpaid functionaries. In the Bezirk of South-Hesse, for
example, all of the party organizations taken together employ
about 50 people, of which only 20 are party secretaries, the rest
being clerical, janitorial, etc. The party as a whole reports that
288 secretaries were employed by the party (below the national
level) in 1959.[14]

In the organizations under the Bezirk level, only the next in
line, the Unterbezirk, normally has a secretary, and he is usually
the only employee at that level. All the party secretaries are
employed by and responsible to the Bezirk executive; in some
cases the Bezirk congress also has to take action to approve the
activities of the secretary.

As is true of party agents in Britain, the SPD party secretary
is a professional who, in the normal course of events, remains a
party secretary throughout his life, although he may be nominated by the party for political office too. It does not seem uncommon for secretaries to hold at least a minor elective post.[15]

14. *Jahrbuch der SPD, 1958–59*, p. 266.
15. Many party secretaries have been party leaders in East Germany, suggesting that such work is sometimes deliberately given to refugees. Party journals
regularly have advertisements for party secretaries. They are by no means drawn
only, or even usually, from the immediate area in which they serve.

The chief officer in the secretariat is the Bezirk secretary. Working with him are others who specialize in particular areas of party work. The number of these and the specializations they represent depend on the financial strength of the party and the size of the Bezirk. The South-Hesse Bezirk, for example, has six secretaries,[16] one assigned to each of the following areas: communal politics, union and factory work, women's organizations, relations with the press, youth groups, and finance. Each secretary provides an office and support for a variety of loosely related fields. The secretary for communal politics in South-Hesse, for example, also serves as the secretary for the agricultural policy committee and for the Arbeitsgemeinschaften for doctors, lawyers, and teachers.

The routine work of the secretary appears to involve subordinate tasks, such as handling the arrangements for meetings, distributing and sometimes writing and publishing internal party publications, and managing equipment used by the party. His role in policy making appears to be slight, except for decisions concerning changes in the organization and management of programs and campaigns.

There is no evidence that the party secretaries represent a traditionalist bloc, wed to their inflexible rules, within the party. If such is the case, their attitudes are completely hidden under their self-assumed role of subordinates to politically responsible, elected superiors. It may be that once the demands to reform the organization (and thus their jobs) had been satisfied without any threat to their status they no longer felt defensive and convinced that only the status quo offered them security. In other words, there may have been a drastic change in the last few years. In any case, the secretaries seem to be interested in the new style of the party organization and in the challenge and potential for building a more open and more effective organizational structure. Their professional interest seems to have overcome any fixed attachment to a particular form of organization.

16. *Jahrbuch der SPD Bezirk Hessen-Süd, 1958,* and ibid., *1959.*

Advisory Groups

The advisory groups to the Bezirk executive include a variety of organizations ranging from committees similar to those attached to the national executive, which bring together leading members of the party particularly interested in specific areas of policy making, to the Arbeitsgemeinschaften, which are made up of both members and nonmembers and have the dual function of rendering advice and recruiting members and voters among the groups they represent.

The committees are generally composed of experts who are coopted[17] by the Bezirk executive and whose functions relate solely to policy making. There is considerable variation among Bezirke in the number and activity of these committees, depending partly on the size of the area involved. Weser-Ems, for example, a small and largely rural Bezirk in the north, reports only one active committee (for communal politics) and even that was organized only recently.[18] The large Berlin party organization, on the other hand, reports fifteen *Fachausschüsse*.[19] The committees vary, too, according to whether they emphasize policy making for a legislature in which the party is participating or whether they concentrate on drafting programs for the party organization itself for use, for example, in election campaigns. Many of the committees in Berlin act somewhat like legislative party caucuses, drafting and reviewing legislation for the party representatives in the assembly and in the city government, which has been dominated by the SPD. In South-Hesse, where the Bezirk does not correspond to a Landtag, the committee's policy concerns are more limited, and its preoccupation with organizational questions is proportionally greater. The contrast can be seen in the following list of committees in the two Bezirke[20]:

17. "Cooption" may mean persuasion rather than selection. Several of the yearbooks report efforts to find suitable men.
18. *Geschäftsbericht, 1956–57,* SPD Bezirk Weser-Ems.
19. *Jahresbericht, 1957–58,* SPD Landesverband Berlin.
20. *Aus der Arbeit eines Jahres, Jahresbericht, 1958,* SPD Bezirk Hessen-Süd.

In Berlin

Communal policy	Cultural policy
Economic policy	Political education
Housing	Legal policy
Traffic	All-Berlin questions
Agriculture and food	Youth
Labor	Sport
Health	Recruitment and propaganda
Social affairs	

In South-Hesse

Communal policy	Women's organizations
Agricultural policy	Youth
Cultural policy	Refugees
Social policy	Press, film, radio, and TV
Party work in the factories	

A variation on the committee system involves groups sometimes called *Arbeitskreise* and sometimes *Arbeitsgemeinschaften* (not to be confused with the units of the same name to be discussed below), which concern themselves not with specific policies but with general topics and broad program declarations. For example, a 50-member *Sozialpolitischer Arbeitskreis* in South-Bavaria (around Munich) is described as a "loosely-knit community of specialists" who contribute to the "overcoming of social contradictions [*Gegensätze*]" through their "fundamental investigations." Their contributions have taken the form of reports and discussions on broad problems of social policy, discussions of federal legislative policies, and the drafting of a proposed social policy section for the party's program in Bavaria.[21] Similar groups can be found in Bielefeld and Berlin.

The Arbeitskreise are a modern, specialized version of the groups of intellectuals who argued party ideology and social theory in the past. Now, however, there is no hard and fast line between these groups and the committees that discuss particular

21. *Geschäftsbericht, 1956–57,* SPD Bezirk Südbayern.

policies. Furthermore, as theoretically oriented (one might almost say academic) groups, they appear to lead a struggling existence, thriving only when particularly interested individuals have been very active.[22]

Even the committees, as a matter of fact, have ups and downs as individuals come and go. In one case, a committee was reported to have ceased operations when its chairman was called away to become an official of a Land ministry.[23] Normally the committees are the more permanent institutions; they meet anywhere from twice a year to once a month, considering legislation or plans for organizational activity, and drafting reports on policy which are often, it appears, simply taken over by the executive.

Special Interest Groups

According to the general guidelines laid down by the national party executive, the Arbeitsgemeinschaften "form advisory bodies for the responsible organs of the party; in addition they give attention to certain tasks of the party in order to exercise a stronger influence within particular social groups."[24] Although the Arbeitsgemeinschaften are not "constituent organs" of the party, i.e., collect no dues and elect no delegates to party congresses, they are membership organizations in the sense that they are open to all who are interested. They form a hierarchy of local, regional, and sometimes national organizations. Many of them accept as members persons who are not members of the party, although their officers must be members and, further, must usually be approved by the corresponding party executive. Their finances are controlled by the Bezirk, and the latter's executive is responsible for their coordination with other party affairs. The activities

22. An interesting group originally formed as a kind of committee and then expanded into a group holding regular meetings open not only to party members but also to the public is the *Arbeitsgemeinschaft sozialdemokratischer Akademiker* founded in Munich by Von Knoeringen. It brings together a wide circle of intellectuals and reports that about 2,000 people regularly attend its meetings. Ibid.

23. *Jahresbericht, 1956–57*, SPD Bezirk Ostwestfalen-Lippe.

24. *Jahrbuch der SPD, 1956–57*, pp. 342–43.

of the different groups in this category are so varied that before any generalizations are offered it will be useful to consider some of them individually.

One type of Arbeitsgemeinschaft brings together refugees from East Germany and/or Eastern Europe. Similarly, another unites Social Democrats who experienced political persecution by the Nazis or the Soviets.[25] These groups are slowly decreasing in importance as the refugees are integrated into the prosperous German society and as the importance of persecution recedes for the individuals involved. At the present time, groups such as these still serve the party in an advisory capacity on questions dealing with restitution, "equalization of burdens," and other complicated legal arrangements made in the aftermath of the war. They also serve as technical advisers on these questions for individual members, since the latter are often faced with a maze of requirements, forms, and special situations. Many Bezirke hold regular office hours for this purpose. Only rarely do these Arbeitsgemeinschaften hold regular meetings of their membership. Berlin, with its very high concentrations of refugees, is an exception. Usually such activity is left to the well-organized nonparty refugee organizations which conduct social, sentimental, and occasionally political meetings.

One of the oldest types of Arbeitsgemeinschaften brings together professional persons sympathetic to the party. In the normal Bezirk pattern, there is usually one group for doctors, one for lawyers, and one for teachers.[26] They have regular meetings, at most about once a month and sometimes only two or three times a year, at which a member or an invited expert addresses the group on some phase of local or national legislation, followed by a general discussion and question period. From time to time, the executive committee of the group will formulate a proposal or statement, which will be discussed and approved by the

25. *Jahresbericht, 1957–58,* SPD Landesverband Berlin. In Berlin this group became most active when the flood of returning prisoners from Soviet concentration camps arrived following Stalin's death. They had been taken to Russia from East Germany in the immediate postwar period.

26. In the 14 Bezirke I studied, the doctors had such organizations in 7, the lawyers in 9, and the teachers in 9. The teachers' group was founded in 1919 and then refounded in 1947. *eilt,* April 1960.

membership and forwarded to the executive of the local party organization or to the appropriate Land or Bundestag delegation. Often, too, the group will receive proposals from the party concerning future policy and will subject it to critical review.

The *Arbeitsgemeinschaft selbständige Schaffenden* ("independent producers" or "independent businessmen") has only recently been activated. Although the party acknowledges the existence of Social Democratic groups for the economically independent before 1933, and of other groups formed spontaneously after World War II, a national organization was not formed until 1953[27]; in the Bezirk yearbooks of the 1955–58 period, there is still little or no activity reported on the part of these groups. Only the organizations in Berlin, Hamburg, and a Land-wide organization in North Rhine-Westphalia appear to have undertaken much. Initiative has recently been coming from the top, however, and there promises to be an increase. Biennial conventions are held, and members are sent a magazine, *Der Selbständig Schaffende,* containing articles written by leading personalities of the party in the fields of economic and social policy and described as "of interest to the *Mittelschichten* [middle classes]." According to the most recent yearbooks, the activity of local organizations is being encouraged.

The guiding principles (*Leitsätze*) for the work of this group, issued by the party executive in 1959, declares that its tasks are:

a. to spread the influence and knowledge of Social Democratic opinions among the members of the middle classes in all spheres, in their professional organizations, etc.,
b. to discuss in their meetings the special economic and social problems that concern members of the middle classes, and
c. to strengthen the understanding of middle-class problems in the party and interest in Social Democratic policy [concerning them].[28]

---

27. *Jahrbuch der SPD, 1952–53*, p. 334.
28. *Jahrbuch der SPD, 1958–59*, p. 457.

The *Jungsozialisten* (Young Socialists) represent another kind of Arbeitsgemeinschaft, one found more generally throughout the party. They have been associated with the party for many years. After the war, the reconstruction of party youth groups was met with some suspicion because of the experience the party had had with their radical politics in 1931, when they were dissolved as having "lost contact with the party."[29] Nevertheless, the Young Socialists were reestablished and sponsored by a central working committee as early as 1946.

The Young Socialists are local groups of interested men and women under 35 years of age. Members do not have to be members of the party, although officers must be. Their activities are varied. What has kept them alive has been the often expressed need for some means by which young people can participate in party work without being overwhelmed by the influence—and style—of the older members. Officially they are described as organizations in which members are trained. The 1959 "Guidelines for the Work and Organization of the Young Socialists" states their goal to be "to provide the young party member with the tools for an active and responsible participation in political life through intensive political schooling."[30] A further function, formulating policy on questions of youth legislation, which was apparently urged by the party executive in 1949,[31] seems recently to have been deemphasized and is not mentioned in the 1959 "Guidelines." Instead, they are to "work among the youth advocating Social Democratic policies," "devote themselves to the special political enlightenment of the young voters," and, finally, establish contacts with other youth groups in Germany and abroad.

Before 1959, the Young Socialists had no elected national organization, but only a secretariat led by an appointee of the party executive. The reason for this was perhaps to avoid pro-

---

29. Schütz, in Lange et al., *Parteien in der Bundesrepublik*, p. 187.

30. *Arbeits- und Organisationsrichtlinien der Jungsozialisten in der SPD*, distributed by the Federal Secretariat of the Young Socialists (pamphlet).

31. Schütz, in Lange et al., p. 188.

viding a national forum for possible radical tendencies. Even now, the leaders of the individual local organizations and the Bezirk chairmen who make up a national committee, although elected, are subject to approval by the corresponding party organizations.

As indicated earlier, the Young Socialists in some areas have shown a tendency toward radicalism. In Frankfurt, for instance, the Young Socialist organization, led by a hard-working young man who calls himself a "neo-Marxist," has adopted a traditionally radical invective and Marxist analysis. In general, however, most of the Young Socialists have been relatively moderate.[32] Some, in fact, have been active in furthering the reforms discussed in this study, and in 1953 and 1957 some of the manifestos advocating reforms came from groups that included Young Socialists.[33]

In many of their organizations, judging from observation in Wiesbaden and Bad Godesberg, the Young Socialists have been content to express their youthful idealism in approved forms of activity. Success for these groups has consisted in winning recognition of their efforts from the party, seeing their representatives chosen as candidates by the party, and, finally, winning members for the party.

Typically, in addition to regular lecture-discussion meetings and social affairs, the Young Socialists emphasize schooling in a variety of subjects, ranging from basic economic and social questions to public speaking. Discussion of the new basic program stimulated considerable interest in these courses, which are usually run on weekends and may take place four or five times a year. In the Bezirk Hessen-Süd, which is probably a bit above average, the local Young Socialist group has a meeting of some kind once every two or three weeks and a public meeting once every two or three months. Increasingly popular for the latter, especially in rural areas, are both political and nonpolitical movies.

Young Socialists also help during election campaigns, usually as active assistants to the regular organization rather than as an

32. Ibid.
33. See above, p. 60.

independent group. The extent to which they provide such assistance depends on their relations with the local party organization. Relations between the two are sometimes so cool, for personal more often than for policy reasons, that the regular organization does not call on them for help. In other cases, however, the willingness of the younger people to carry out the *Kleinarbeit* of putting up posters and handing out leaflets serves to ingratiate them with the regulars.

Student groups are a source of difficulty for the political leadership of many countries. That this possibility exists in Germany is illustrated by the case of the Socialist German Student Federation (SDS). Not formally affiliated with the SPD, it recognized the party as the leader of the socialist movement and the party informally recognized it as its representative among the students. In 1960, after the SDS had succeeded in embarrassing the party on several occasions with statements on foreign policy, advocating, for example, a more flexible and friendly approach to the East German regime, the party formally disavowed it and urged students who sympathized with the SPD to join a new group, called the *Sozialistische Hochschulbund* (SHB). Conflicting reports about the relative success of the two organizations make it difficult to judge how successful the party has been in its stratagem.

The Young Socialists, on the other hand, despite initial hostility, suspicion, or apathy on the part of regular party members,[34] seem to have retained their place in the party and to be developing a style of activity that avoids independent political activity and emphasizes cooperation with the regular party. In explaining their success, note should be taken of two factors that have influenced their growth. First, they have been competing with a very active youth organization connected with the CDU, the *Junge Union,* and secondly, they have also been supported by money disbursed by the government to youth groups in many Länder for "political education."[35]

34. *Rechenschaftsbericht, 1958,* SPD Bezirk Hannover.
35. In Hesse, this money is distributed in one large lump sum, plus an additional amount proportional to the strength of the parties in the Landtag. Nord-

Another type of organization with a long history is the women's group. In 1959, the party reported that 19.2 per cent of its members were women, and that 1,647 *Frauengruppen* had been formed in the approximately 9,100 local party organizations.[36] Both the percentage of women members and the number of groups vary greatly from area to area. The percentage of women members in Berlin, for example, is 30.2, whereas in the Saar it is only 9.6.

It is generally acknowledged that the party has done a poor job of winning the woman's vote, and it would seem natural for the women's organizations to be assigned a large role in reversing the trend. Much criticism is reported of their activities, however. The general tenor of the criticism is that the "Women's Movement" (*Frauenbewegung*) has become ingrown and largely serves the needs of women functionaries who are already fully involved in party work.

As Klaus Schütz points out, citing the organization statute of the Berlin SPD,[37] the aim of the women's organizations was to make themselves unnecessary by achieving equal rights for women. The implication of the criticism is that they, or at least their most active functionaries, have been more concerned with winning equal rights for women within the party than outside and have given least attention to the most pressing task, namely, attracting the female vote. Schütz says, for example, that the meetings of the groups above the lowest level appear to devote more time to planning for party elections than they do to planning activities of and for women in public.[38] The yearbook reports on the Frauenbewegung, as a matter of fact, use the number of women elected to party executives and put up as candidates by the party as indexes of success.

Emphasizing the failure to serve a real function in recruiting

---

rhein-Westfalen, Hamburg, Bremen, and Baden-Wurttemberg have similar arrangements.

36. *Jahrbuch der SPD, 1958–59*, p. 297.

37. Schütz, in Lange et al., p. 184.

38. Ibid., p. 185.

new women members, a Berlin yearbook notes the bad public image the female party functionary has and notes that only women who joined the party before 1933 participate in group activities. Other yearbooks speak in more guarded terms about this traditional element of socialist political action, but again and again criticism is expressed. That this occurs in the stronghold of organizational orthodoxy, the party yearbooks, is probably strong evidence of the extent of the failure of the women's organizations.

Since about 1957–58, when the revolt against the Apparat swept Herta Gotthelf from her position as the chief director of the women's organizations, there has been some change in approach. Attempts have been made to make the meetings and lectures more attractive to the woman voter who is not a party member. In Frankfurt, for example, the local group has sponsored a fashion show. It would appear, then, that the Frauenarbeit is in a state of transition. Still to be resolved are the conflicting demands of the older women functionaries, the party leaders anxious for votes, and women in the party who need special help to feel at home in this "man's party." The basic question of what will appeal to the women has yet to be answered. Meetings tailored to feminine interests are one approach, but perhaps attractive candidates such as Willy Brandt will in the long run prove more effective.

Another type of group found in party organizations throughout the country is the *Betriebsgruppe* (factory group). It may seem strange that the SPD, long closely connected with the workers, should in the 1960s be undertaking to expand its influence among the workers by building up party organizations within factories. But this is in fact what is happening. The reason is simple: the election results of 1957 showed that a great many German industrial workers voted for the CDU. Political work in the factories after the war has been conditioned by several factors. One is that the unions have become above party in their new united federation, the *Deutsche Gewerkschaftbund* (DGB). Another is that the last important efforts of the Communists to retain influence in West Germany have taken place in the factories.

The SPD has had a peculiar relationship with the unions—a relationship determined by its desire both to support the non-party union idea,[39] and to maintain the party's predominant influence therein. The party has consistently underplayed its political role in the factories in order to avoid creating disunity or encouraging counterorganizations of the CDU and the KPD. At first, winning votes among the workers did not seem to be a very important problem since most were already SPD voters, and those who had voted for the KPD had either shifted after the war or were deprived of that possibility when the Communist Party was made illegal. The main problem was seen to be not that of getting votes in general elections but of getting control of the workers' representatives on the factory councils set up under the codetermination laws to provide for a measure of self-government in the factories. The chief aim of the party in this connection was not so much to put SPD supporters on the councils as to prevent Communist domination.[40]

The organizational forms used were the *Soziale Arbeitsgemeinschaften* (SAG) and the Betriebsgruppen. The first was simply a group of Social Democratic functionaries in the labor unions, while the Betriebsgruppen were (and are) composed of all the Social Democrats in a particular factory or office. Judging from the testimony of my respondents, as well as from the party yearbooks, both of these organizations, by and large, became active only during the elections to the factory councils.[41]

By the early 1950s, according to the SPD's own report, the threat from Communist infiltration, while still a problem, was reduced to the level where it was merely a nuisance.[42] During the last decade, threats to the party have taken a different shape and have come from a different source—the CDU-sympathizing group which has sought to form a rival Christian union. Although

39. Wilhelm Mellies is reported to have told a meeting of the SAG (SPD union men in the DGB) that their first task was "the preservation and promotion of the united labor unions (*Einheitsgewerkschaft*)." *Jahrbuch der SPD, 1958–59*, p. 478. Cf. also a series of articles on workers' council elections in *Der Sozialist* (Hamburg), January and February 1959, and February and April 1958.

40. *Jahrbuch der SPD, 1958–59*, p. 479.

41. Ibid., p. 478.

42. *Jahrbuch der SPD, 1952–53*, p. 355.

the attempt to split the DGB had largely failed by 1960, the CDU had managed to form its own factory groups, especially at the time of the 1957 election, and for this and other reasons had won many working-class votes. The orientation of the SPD's efforts in the factories has therefore been shifting.

Herbert Wehner, speaking over the radio in 1957, noted that while the CDU had had some considerable success in organizing groups in the factories,

> the SPD scarcely dared to develop its *Sozialen Arbeitsgemeinschaften,* often out of consideration for what is called the political neutrality of the unions . . . [but the party must] develop the effectiveness of its recruitment for its ideas.[43]

The 1958 party congress reemphasized the need for active political work in the unions.[44] With regard to organization, the party executive issued in April 1959 a document drafted by its Committee for Factory and Union Questions and entitled, "Guidelines for Factory Group Work."[45] It recommended the creation of conferences of functionaries which would bring the following together within any particular area:

a. representatives of the party from small factories where no regularly established factory group can be formed,
b. the membership of the leading elements of the factory groups of the party,
c. the members of the factory councils and personnel councils [the counterpart of the factory councils in large administrative offices] who are members of the party,
d. the leading members of the union organization of the factory who are also party members,
e. the members of the administration of the local union and the local office of the union federation, including the paid secretaries of both, and
f. . . . representatives of the executive of the local party organization.

43. In his collection of speeches and writings; see Ch. 6, note 15.
44. *Protokoll, 1958,* p. 505.
45. *Jahrbuch der SPD, 1958–59,* pp. 402 and 481.

The expectation was that an organization bringing together the party's representatives in both the factories and the unions would reinvigorate the effort to make a political appeal to the workers.

The party has also stepped up its distribution of materials printed specifically for workers and has even established special newspapers for several large firms.[46] The fragmentation of the party's appeal probably has no clearer example than this. It could count at one time on its local organizations and its ties with the unions to provide a direct and comprehensive channel through which appeals could be made to the workers. Now the party must develop special techniques to reach them.

The last party activity involving special interest groups to be discussed here involves the making of policy for, and the coordination of, *Kommunalpolitik,* i.e., the political activity of the party's representatives in city, town, and rural governments. The existence of a communal policy committee at the national level of the party has already been noted, but naturally it is in the regional organizations of the party that the problems assume greatest importance. In contrast to some of the other organizations, which have developed as a result of the initiative of the national party organization, the groups involved with communal policy appear to have arisen spontaneously as a result of the demands on the vast number of party members who hold office on the local government level. This number is so large and so close to the total number of party members who can be considered as continuously active that there is good reason to believe that, on the local level at least, the SPD has become the party of *Kommunalpolitiker.*[47]

The importance of the local politician in the party does not indicate, however, as it might in the United States, that the party

46. The party publishes a monthly pamphlet entitled *Arbeit und Freiheit,* which consists principally of reprinted speeches and articles by SPD leaders. About 800,000 copies are distributed annually, though there is reason to doubt that it is carefully read. Hessen-Süd reported a distribution of 139,500 copies of 7 different factory papers in 1959. See *Sozialdemokratische Politik in Hessen-Süd, Jahresbericht, 1959,* SPD Bezirk Hessen-Süd.

47. The party yearbook lists 42,366 local politicians active in the party and notes that the list is not complete. *Jahrbuch der SPD, 1958–59,* p. 489.

has become simply a loosely connected holding body for independently powerful local bosses. Paradoxically, the centralization of the SPD is shown most clearly with respect to local politics. In the American party system, the national or regional party organization plays little or no role in determining local policy. In the SPD, however, local policies adopted by local politicians have usually been worked out at the Bezirk level or higher.[48] Issues dealt with by local officials in Germany concern housing (very important in the period of reconstruction after the war), schools, local finances (a source of perennial problems, since the local communities have little taxing power of their own), health, welfare, and traffic. In order to equip local party representatives to handle the technical and legal questions arising in connection with these issues, the national party publishes a bulky monthly magazine, *Die Demokratische Gemeinde,* and the Bezirk arranges weekend and week-long schools. The Bezirk Hannover, for example, reports that it conducted 397 sessions over a two-year period, with an average attendance of 30.6 persons.[49] Berlin reported one set of courses involving 120 participants and another series of five courses with 83 participants, and it looked forward to the establishment of a relatively permanent seminar.[50] For the year 1958, the Bezirk Hessen-Süd organization reported that some 1,410 mayors, council members, and others had completed week-long courses at the Bezirk's Academy for Communal Policy.[51] The Academy reported that over its 15-year history some 20,000 persons had attended its courses.[52] A sampling of the courses given in 1959 included:

Furthering Youth Development
Procurement of Building Land

48. Cf. Schütz, in Lange et al., *Parteien in der Bundesrepublik,* p. 214. He notes that policies are formulated at a higher level and then passed down, although he asserts that functionaries at the higher level take into account the known wishes of local politicians.

49. *Rechenschaftsbericht, 1958,* SPD Bezirk Hannover.

50. *Jahresbericht, 1957–58,* SPD Landesverband Berlin.

51. *Aus der Arbeit eines Jahres, Jahresbericht, 1958,* SPD Bezirk Hessen-Süd.

52. *Sozialdemokratische Politik in Hessen-Süd, Jahresbericht, 1959,* SPD Bezirk Hessen-Süd.

Legislation Relating to Developments
Financing Problems for Town Purposes
Measures for a Concrete Agricultural Policy in Hesse
Responsibilities and Tasks of the Towns in Road Traffic

There have been some attempts to create an Arbeitsgemein-schaft for communal politicians, but these seem not to have taken hold in the two Bezirke that reported them. Apparently local officials are motivated more by the need for technical assistance and policy guidance than by the feeling of solidarity and common interest that would provide the basis for such an organization.

The communal policy committees of the Bezirk executives play an active role in the evolution of general lines of policy for small communities. In addition, they serve to help coordinate the demands of local officials who want to influence actions taken by the national government. In the committee reports, there is often mention of contacts with the "peak organizations" (*Spitzenverbände*), especially the Congress of German Cities (*Deutsche Städtetag*) and the Congress of German Towns (*Deutsche Gemeindetag*), which constitute nonpartisan pressure groups. The chief paid official of the latter is, in fact, the chairman of the Communal Policy Committee of the Bezirk Hessen-Süd and a member of the Bezirk executive.

By means of these committees and schools, the party organization provides a training ground for local politicians and administrators, an agency for intertown and intercity cooperation, and a means through which policy can be coordinated. The traditional German attitude toward city government has not normally given the parties a very large role in decision making and has favored instead a neutral, technical administration.[53] According to one reliable source within the party, the role of parties on the local level has in fact been hampered by this attitude not only among voters but among city officials as well.[54] At the same time, how-

53. To a greater extent than citizens of other countries, Germans seem to appeal not to local party authorities when they want something done but rather to the bureaucracy.

54. Hans Muntzke, "Die politischen Parteien in den kommunalen Parlementen," *Die Demokratische Gemeinde, 11,* No. 10 (1960), p. 870. Muntzke

ever, he notes an increasing acceptance of the role of parties, based on an appreciation of practical and technically sophisticated party policies adapted to the local situation in contrast to the ideological concerns of the past. This suggests that the party's role in policy making on the local level, through the agencies which have been discussed here, has assumed more important proportions.

Local Party Organizations

The organizations discussed so far have been built around special interests. The basic local unit of the party, usually called the *Ortsverein,* is made up of members who live in a particular area. It is basic in the sense that it is the smallest unit to participate directly in the formal electoral processes within the party and have the right to submit proposed resolutions to the party congresses, privileges not enjoyed by the organizations discussed in the preceding pages.

The local organizations elect their own officers, which normally include a chairman, his deputy, a treasurer, and an executive. There is frequently an officer in charge of propaganda. The Ortsverein also has a system of *Hauskassierer* (literally, "house treasurers," although perhaps better translated "house-to-house treasurers"), who collect dues from (and distribute materials to) the members in assigned areas. Traditionally this position, which provides a key contact between the organization and its members, is the first rung on the ladder for aspiring party officials.

In 1959, the 9,100 local organizations averaged 69 members apiece.[55] This means, of course, that by far the largest number of organizations associated with the party, and therefore the greatest number of meetings, public and private, carried out under party auspices, are conducted by these groups. Schütz calls the Ortsverein the locus of the "real political life" of the party,

---

is the member of the South-Hesse Bezirk executive and managing director of the nonpartisan group mentioned above.

55. *Jahrbuch der SPD, 1958–59,* p. 269.

where the money is taken in and the political line explained and discussed.[56]

The following figures for the Bezirk West-Westphalia, which includes the heavily industrialized Ruhr region and is the largest SPD Bezirk with about 85,000 members, give some idea of the number of meetings held by the Ortsvereine as compared to the special interest groups in the same area.[57]

Bezirk West-Westphalia
NUMBER OF MEETINGS REPORTED IN YEARBOOKS

Type of Meeting	1955	1956	1957	1958
Members (Ortsvereine)	4789	5157	4707	4424
Public "	272	721	835	646
Women's groups	2370	2634	1955	1911
Young Socialists	774	703	984	1037
Factory groups	629	501	425	515
Arbeitsgemeinschaft—Teachers	9	16	19	15
" —Lawyers	11	6	11	13
" —Doctors	8	5	0	8
Other meetings	775	702	954	902
Committee meetings	173	554	388	359
Party School Sessions				
Women	54	48	68	97
Functionary schooling	110	121	155	88
Young Socialists	ND	ND	97	102
Communal policy	ND	ND	20	23
Public speaking	ND	ND	3	2

Note: 1955—no election   ND=No data given
1956—local elections
1957—national elections
1958—Land elections

56. Schütz, in Lange et al., p. 177.
57. Report to SPD Bezirksparteitag, Bezirk Westl. Westfalen, April 27, 1957 (mimeo.) and *Jahrbuch, 1959*, SPD Bezirk Westl. Westfalen.

Since there were 643 Ortsvereine in this Bezirk, the figures show that they met on the average between 6 and 8 times per year, with the more frequent figure marking the year in which local elections were held. In spite of this apparently high rate of activity among the local organizations, many party members expressed doubts about their usefulness or significance.

In analyzing the reasons for this pessimism, we may begin by noting that in general there are three functions performed by the local organizations, one of which usually dominates. First, they can serve simply as the means through which members maintain contact with each other. Secondly, they can serve as agencies for recruiting the public through propaganda and public meetings. Thirdly, they can be committees of locally important party leaders charged with the conduct of local elections and filling the posts won by the party in local government.

In the conduct of elections, the local organizations are important only in those areas where they correspond to the local administrative and electoral divisions. In the cities, elections are carried out on a citywide basis, and nominations and the campaign are organized at a level one or two steps removed from the local party organization, so they play a small role both in planning and in patronage. In the small towns and rural areas, however, the local organization is at its strongest. Perhaps more accurately, the local executive is at its strongest, for the role of the membership at large in these cases seems to be very limited; in fact, several of my respondents characterized the party's units in the rural areas as organizations comprised almost solely of actual and potential office holders. One member even charged that deliberate restrictions were placed on membership to maintain the monopoly and maximize the patronage available to the few. Others, however, explained the generally small membership on the basis simply of lack of interest. Whatever the reason, local organizations in the rural areas generally seem to take on a special character, not unimportant but considerably different from the ideal function of "spreading the socialist message."

Even where the role of local notables is not so pronounced, local organizations show a very uneven pattern as institutions

185

through which members can meet and discuss policy and undertake programs to win new adherents. Scattered figures on attendance at membership meetings show that only between 10 per cent and 25 per cent of the members are usually present. An interesting set of figures was produced by the Schleswig-Holstein Bezirk in 1956, based on a questionnaire sent to local organizations.[58] The figures may be somewhat inflated due to the methods used to obtain them, and the categories are not precise, but they can serve to indicate broad variations in the activity of members as measured by attendance.

Schleswig-Holstein Bezirk
ACTIVITY OF MEMBERS IN DIFFERENT TYPES OF LOCAL ORGANIZATIONS

Percentage of members who are:	*Cities* Large	Small	*Housing Developments*	*Rural Areas*	*All*
Fully active	4.8	8.5	16.5	15.4	8.8
Partly active	8.0	6.9	25.6	16.5	10.0
Occasionally active	10.1	4.8	4.3	17.2	9.9
Seldom or never active	77.1	79.8	53.6	50.9	71.3

The low rates of participation in the cities are probably explained in part by the fact that the party clearly has a much larger number of members there, though the common assumption has always been that they are more militant. Ease of communication in the housing developments probably explains the relatively high rate of participation there. Unfortunately the figures are not broken down far enough, nor are enough facts available, to arrive at firm conclusions, but one fact does stand out, namely, that one-half to three-quarters of the membership never turns out for party meetings or other party activities. Other evidence bears out this general conclusion.

The most common pattern for a meeting is to build it around a talk on an important topic in current affairs, usually national rather than local in scope, given by a member of the local group

58. *Jahresbericht, 1955–56,* SPD Bezirk Schleswig-Holstein.

or an invited party member with special qualifications. The speech is followed by questions from the floor.[59] The essential purpose seems to be informative—to acquaint members with the policies of the party and events in national politics.

A variation on this pattern occurred in the period prior to the adoption of the new fundamental program at Bad Godesberg. The importance of this event created an unusual amount of excitement, and often dissent, with the result that a large proportion of the amendments sent in to the Godesberg congress were formulated in the Ortsvereine. Many were originally formulated in special committees of interested persons within the local organizations, but they were at least voted on, if not necessarily discussed in detail, by the whole group.

The other major type of meeting is one in which members nominate candidates, elect officers, and select delegates to the party congresses. Indications are that these are more likely to call forth a high level of attendance and produce controversy than meetings involving policy discussions.

The record therefore seems to show a fairly respectable pattern of activity in the membership meetings of local organizations. Why then are they criticized? The problem is that many of the meetings have degenerated into social affairs for the older members of the party. They have become occasions for conversing with old comrades, recalling old exploits, and falling into easy communication with the Genossen in a friendly environment.

---

59. One meeting I attended in Frankfurt—which was represented to me as typical, although it was probably a relatively active group—had the following pattern:

It was a Distrikt meeting. Of the 400 members, 50, mostly in the 50- to 60-year-old age bracket, were in attendance. The chairman, a longtime socialist who had gone into exile to escape persecution for his underground activities, introduced a discussion on the new laws the Adenauer government had introduced on health insurance. A very competent union expert on the subject lectured for over an hour. Another short speech was given by a member of a union delegation which had gone to see members of the Bundestag on the issue of insurance laws. The subject was one on which the assembled party members could all agree (i.e., in their hostility to the government proposals) and there was no conflict, but about 20 per cent of those present asked questions, chiefly of an informational nature. The meeting closed with remarks of the chairman concerning future meetings, including the announcement of an excursion that was being planned.

Even the earnestness of speakers discussing the crises of contemporary Germany fits into the familiar pattern. The meetings are often dominated by older members with, and for the sake of, old emotional ties.

Because of this, both reformers and radicals can and do criticize the meetings. The reformers complain that, because of the predominance of old members, the meetings do not attract new members, especially individuals able to go out and explain the policies of the party convincingly and attractively to a wider audience. (Most of the new recruits for the party are, in fact, not won through the Ortsvereine but through the factory groups.[60]) For radicals who seek within the party a place for effective political discussion, the overwhelming weight of tradition and the stereotyped terminology, symbols, and ideals make the meetings impossibly bland. Little real discussion occurs because the agreement of the members on the old slogans is complete. Apparently the diversity of members within a geographic area has been submerged under the party's efforts to promote unity. As a result, both left and right wings within the party look to the specialized organizations as a better channel for political action.

The decline in the importance of the local organization seems to be particularly noticeable with respect to its function as a party agency for influencing the public. In addition to failing to attract new members, the Ortsverein is being progressively outmoded as a propaganda agency by developments in technology. The growth of independent mass media, and even more the prevalence of mass entertainment, has provided such competition for the party's local organizations and public meetings that virtually every party report and critic calls attention to this. The public is either distracted by television or other forms of entertainment or so accustomed to close-up views of nationally prominent leaders that people turn out in force for local meetings only when one of the major party leaders is speaking.

60. Almost every yearbook that mentions the organizations making the first contact with new members cites the factory groups as the most active. A speech at the 1960 Bezirk party convention in Hamburg, however, suggested that this source of new members was becoming less and less important in that city.

Nevertheless, it would be a mistake to jump to the conclusion that local party organizations are simply victims of the general trend toward a mass society in which isolated individuals can relate to their environment only through impersonal means of communication. This is not the view of the party, if one is to judge from its attempts to find remedies for the situation by making the public meetings of local groups more attractive. The party apparently believes that it is not the mass media alone that render local meetings unattractive but the poor showing the meetings make in comparison. The party has sought to play down the image of a closed party by arranging meetings that present different and contrasting points of view. In other cases, the use of films and various kinds of entertainment are being employed.[61] Finally, mention should be made of the institution of the *Werbehilfer* (recruitment and propaganda helpers),[62] specially trained and supplied with material, who try to establish the kind of person-to-person contact which members of the local organizations were originally supposed to handle.[63]

These efforts certainly do not indicate that the party believes it is dealing with a mass society, but rather that it finds the particular form of the local organization, especially the traditional *Versammlung* (meeting), inadequate in appealing to the public. There is no sign that the party is about to abandon the local organizations. They still provide the dues on which the party lives, in many but not all cases conduct local elections and support local politicians, and occasionally realize their potential as a training ground for rising members of the party. Though deemphasizing them by relying heavily on specialized organizations, the party is seeking to reform them but has no thought of abolishing them.

---

61. Both the South-Hesse and the Hamburg party organization yearbooks mention film services. The Hamburg organization even runs a regular course for projector operators. Some of the films are very good—for instance, "Hiroshima, Mon Amour" was shown, perhaps for obvious reasons.

62. Cf. *eilt*, 1959 and 1960, in which the recruiting of volunteers is continually urged.

63. Person-to-person contact is generally considered to be the major justification—after dues—for retaining the membership character of the SPD.

The Changing Meanings of "Education"

The SPD has been said to have a "pedagogical mission."[64] In the early days, education at the lower levels in the party was an essential part of its activity.[65] Many times in the course of my research, I was reminded by members of the party that it had originally been based largely on the "educational societies" established for the workers. Courses were offered at night to give the ambitious worker the education he had been unable to take advantage of in the state or other schools because he had to begin working at an early age. In contemporary Germany, however, workers are generally able to take advantage of the public school system, and when additional schooling is needed, changes can usually be brought about through legislation (for example, lengthening the time spent in school) rather than supplementary effort by the party. Basic education has therefore largely passed out of the hands of the party.

Another form of education important in the early days of the party was the provision of the basic skills necessary for aspiring party functionaries. This educational effort of the party still continues, but to a diminished degree. The party's new style is reflected, however, in the relatively greater emphasis given to the skills needed in dealing with the media and, in general, in influencing mass public opinion.

The kind of education traditionally associated with Socialist parties has always had a more ambitious goal, namely, developing or changing the perception of society among a large segment of the population in such a way that political decisions will be made more "rationally." In the past, this objective has been connected with the effort to increase class consciousness among the workers and to teach them to think along socialist lines. This approach appears occasionally now in modern dress in party

64. Cf. Leiserson, *Parties and Politics,* in which Socialist parties are considered distinctive because of this "pedagogical mission." Such comments are very common in statements of party leaders.
65. Cf. Johannes Schult, *Die Hamburger Arbeiterbewegung als Kulturfaktor* (Hamburg, n.d., probably 1954).

190

writings which assert that a massive educational program is necessary to counteract the "ideology of the classless society" propagated by the "ruling classes" for their own ends.[66]

More often, however, the rationale for political education, as it is expressed today, rests fundamentally on liberal grounds, that is, the need to keep the voter well informed and, especially in this modern age, to counteract the effects of scientific techniques of mass persuasion made possible by "mass and depth psychology." The "hidden persuaders" are as well known in Germany as in the United States.[67]

Part of the educational program of the party is directed toward providing general knowledge that will presumably make the voter and party member more "rational." Courses in German history of the last century, relating especially to the Nazi period and the development of the SPD, instruction in basic economics and sociology, and courses on developments within the Communist bloc are provided by the party in many areas. In some Bezirke there are secretaries charged with political education along these lines, and in lower organizations there are sometimes functionaries specifically assigned to carry out such programs. There are also two schools rather closely connected with the party which draw students from all over Germany. The Georg Vollmar School in Bavaria and the Bergneustadt School in northern Germany offer a wide variety of courses as well as provide facilities for conferences and meetings.[68]

The party's major effort at general education is carried out by the specialized groups—the factory groups, Young Socialists, and, to a lesser extent, the women's organizations. Even these, however, are not very ambitious programs, judging by any standard of pedagogy. They consist for the most part of weekend sessions in which a series of two or three related lectures are followed by discussion. The course subjects vary somewhat from area to

66. Cf., e.g., Abendroth, "Warum Parteiprogramm?" *Neue Gesellschaft*, 3, 1956.

67. Vance Packard's book (*The Hidden Persuaders* [New York, 1957]) is in Young Socialist libraries.

68. *eilt* regularly reproduces lists of the courses, which range from the history of Nazism to practical education for party functionaries.

area and group to group, as the following two examples show. The first agenda has a bias toward history, the second toward current events:

The Concentration of Economic Power
The Opportunities for Socialism in the Age of
  the Second Industrial Revolution
Socialization in Germany after 1918 and 1945
The Economic System of the Soviet Union and the
  People's Democracies
History of the Labor Movement
> (From a list of courses run by the
> Young Socialists of South-Hesse)

Theory and Practice in the DDR (East Germany)
The Situation in the West and the Developing Countries
The Working Man in the DDR
Human Relations in the DDR
The Fundamental Program of the SPD
> (From a list of courses run by the fac-
> tory group secretariat in Hamburg)

Compared with American parties, the SPD carries on political education at a very high level. Nevertheless, these courses represent a very small step toward achieving the political education goals announced by the party. To begin with, about half the Bezirke appear from their own reports to have conducted very few or no courses of this kind despite their traditional appeal. Furthermore, the programs that do exist reach a very small proportion of the party membership, much less the general public. In fact, the main function of the kinds of courses listed above appears to be to "train functionaries," that is, give the active and potentially active members of the party training in political argumentation. With respect to this kind of education too, then, the party has in fact, if not in rhetoric and ideals, given over responsibility to the public and nonpartisan private organizations.

Despite the many general statements in the yearbooks and at party congresses concerning the necessity of political education, about one-fourth of my respondents denied that the party had any special message, responsibility, or resources to carry on this task. In contrast, however, the minority opposed to the Godesberg Program were much more likely to emphasize the need for an extensive educational program in order to rebuild a real political movement. Others were content to repeat the slogans without much conviction either way.

The Membership

According to the organization statute, a person joins the party when he "accepts [*bekennt sich*] the basic principles of the party and has earned membership [*die Mitgliedschaft erworben hat*]. The local organization's executive decides on questions of accepting members."[69] A member can be expelled for "persistent action contrary to a resolution of a party congress or party organization . . . dishonorable activity or gross offense against the principles of the party."[70] He can be stricken from the rolls for nonpayment of dues over a period of three months.

In practice, with respect to expulsions, the party is very lenient. Almost without exception, it has expelled only members who have openly abetted Communist propaganda. In 1958–59, 62 persons were expelled.[71] Death, nonpayment of dues, and "disappearance" (moving without reporting to the party) actually account for virtually all losses of membership.[72]

The gross figures for party membership are shown in Table A. The general trend—a high point in 1948, a slow decline after the currency reform until 1955, and then a slow rise which is still continuing, although it has not reached the 1950 level—quite

69. Articles 1 and 2.
70. Article 27.
71. *Jahrbuch der SPD, 1958–59*, p. 268.
72. Taking a Bezirk at random, out of 47,298 members in Franken Bezirk at the beginning of 1959, 803 died, 1,249 left the party, 429 were dropped for nonpayment of dues, and 742 moved out of the area of the Bezirk, while 5,062 new members entered the party and 372 moved in from other Bezirke. Only in the last half dozen years, of course, have the figures generally worked out to a net gain. The general turnover seems very large.

literally traces the lifeline of the party. In its long period of decline, the party was dying out. The recent rise has been due to one membership campaign after another, and presumably also to the party's new style, which has made it more attractive to younger members.

Table A. OVERALL MEMBERSHIP

Year	Total Membership
1946	701,448
1947	875,497
1948 (June)	896,275
1948 (December)	846,518
1949	736,218
1950	683,896
1951	649,529
1952	627,817
1953	607,456
1954	585,479
1955	589,051
1956	612,219
1957	626,189
1958	623,816
1959	634,254
1961 (February)	664,551

Note: All figures for December 31, unless otherwise noted.
Sources: Yearbooks of the party, except 1961, which is from *eilt,* April 1961.

The party no longer publishes analyses of its total membership —since 1955, it has kept detailed records only on new members —indicating the emphasis placed on the present rather than the past appeal of the party. Its concern in the early 1950s over the advancing age of party members is still echoed by speakers who make a special point of calling attention to increased membership among young people and to any accomplishment by them.[73] The figures in Table B indicate some improvement in the age levels attracted, while Table C shows that new members are still drawn most heavily from the working class.

Table B. AGE DISTRIBUTION OF
NEW MEMBERS—PERCENTAGE UNDER 40

October, November, and December 1955	52.1%
Total, 1956–1957	52.9%
Total, 1958–1959	55.7%
February 1961	60.0%

Sources: Yearbooks, except 1961, which is from *eilt,* April 1961.

It is apparent from what has been said so far in this study that the character of membership is many-sided and takes many forms in this complex organization. Participation in party activity can follow many different patterns, and in many cases the participant need not even carry a membership book, e.g., in many of the

Table C. SOCIAL BACKGROUND OF NEW MEMBERS

	Oct.–Dec.					Feb.
	1955	*1956*	*1957*	*1958*	*1959*	*1961*
Workers	53.7%	54.4%	53.5%	55.0%	54.9%	57.4%
Employees	13.8	15.9	13.8	13.2	11.7	11.7
Officials	3.4	3.8	7.8	7.8	8.2	8.4
Pensioned	7.3	6.6	6.2	5.4	6.4	5.8
Independent businessmen	4.9	5.3	4.6	4.1	4.7	4.9
Professionals	2.8	3.3	3.8	3.3	2.9	2.5
Housewives	14.3	10.7	10.3	11.2	11.2	9.0

Sources: As above.

73. The election of Dr. Hans Jochen Vogel, 34 years old, as the mayor of Munich in 1960 let loose a veritable flood of optimistic, enthusiastic claims that the party was becoming the party of young people.

Arbeitsgemeinschaften and in the newly emphasized public meetings. There is clearly no one type of member. The original Marxian conception of a party member was that he was among the most politically conscious representatives of the working class, but this seems always to have been simply an ideal and to have applied to very few. Michels, writing in 1905, refers to the difficulty of finding members with a good knowledge of socialism, and Gay refers with some scorn to the theoretical capacities of the leaders themselves at the turn of the century.[74] In any case, even as an ideal, agreement on socialist theory or on a world-view is no longer relevant and cannot serve as a defining characteristic of the membership.

The emotional solidarity of party members, however, has and does play an important role. It was loyalty and obedience to the party in a hostile environment that enabled the SPD to survive (if not overcome) government suppression under the Empire and the Nazis and made possible the incredibly fast reconstruction of the party after the war. There is no question but that this kind of solidarity still exists, especially among older members. Schütz, writing in 1954, says:

> The majority of the party members live still with the idea of the necessity of forming and maintaining a closed organization against a hostile environment. "Solidarity," however fragile it may have become in practice, is the tie which should hold the members together, and even where the concept has become a fiction, it still fulfills its emotional function.[75]

About three-quarters of my respondents differentiated between the SPD and the CDU on the basis of the "closer relationship" and the collective commitment of the members of the SPD. Significantly, most of them said there are still such ties.

An index to this feeling is the party's symbolic usages and customs—the familiar form of address among members, the songs

74. Michels, *Political Parties,* and Gay, *The Dilemma of Democratic Socialism.*
75. Schütz, in Lange et al., *Parteien in der Bundesrepublik,* p. 206.

still sung at the end of party congresses, the red flag, and the use of the term *Genosse* (comrade) for party members. Among the various proposals for reform have been suggestions that these symbols be dropped because, while they might represent significant emotional ties for older members, they are repellent to outsiders. A long-drawn-out debate—inconclusive and emotional on both sides—was carried on in 1960 in the pages of the party's weekly newspaper, *Vorwärts*. Protests against the suggestions for reform poured in. In one of his infrequent contributions to open discussion, Erich Ollenhauer wrote, "The party without the red flag would be a party without a heart . . . behind all of our activity and work in public must stand always the man completely committed to the movement."[76] He added, however, "it is not necessary . . . to go out into the open market with our symbols and beliefs (*Bekenntnissen*)." He admitted that the party's symbols were misused by the Communists, and continued:

> The party stands on three pillars, on the great traditions of the labor movement, on the unchanged historical necessity for the creation of a social order that will enable the workingman and the socially weak to live a life free from need or fear, as well as our readiness to put into action our whole idealism, in order to accomplish the great tasks of the reconstruction, with all our mental and political capacity.

The question of party symbols has not been raised publicly by the leadership since 1956–57, apparently to avoid arousing emotional opposition to the party's new style, but in practice they have been increasingly underplayed. It is no longer considered necessary to drape congress halls entirely in red—one small flag will suffice.

In general, the bond of emotional solidarity seems to be declining among the members. For the older ones, especially those who grew up in the party organizations of the Weimar period, it is no doubt still an important factor. The younger members,

76. Ollenhauer, writing in *Neue Rhein Zeitung,* quoted in *Der Sozialist* (Hamburg), December 1953.

however, are drawn to the party and remain with it for other reasons—because there are opportunities to discuss the important political issues of the day, because there is still an element of excitement in the party, still a small amount of daring in becoming a socialist in a mildly hostile environment, and because the party retains a kind of idealism, unlike the "pure opportunism and *Personalpolitik* (job-seeking)" of the CDU and most of its members.

These sentiments nevertheless indicate a different degree of attachment from the full-scale commitment to which Ollenhauer referred, and the basis for them is more often the successful or potentially successful party in which "something is going on."

There is probably still another reason for looser ties among members: many party members hold political office of one kind or another and are forced to work in the party as a means to an end. The party yearbook lists 42,366 members who hold local office in the cities, towns, or rural areas, and this figure does not include two special categories of officials found in some Länder.[77] Added to the number of members who are in the Bundestag and the Landtage, these form almost 7 per cent of the total party membership. An even higher percentage is common in predominantly rural areas.[78] Measured against the figures for membership activity, we are led to the conclusion that one out of every two or three active Social Democrats is a parliamentarian or an administrator. Not all, of course, are without emotional ties to the party, but if my sampling of communal politicians is representative they tend to be pragmatically motivated.

The party's overwhelming emphasis on winning wider influence among potential voters has therefore led to tolerance and acceptance of a looser form of membership. There has been increasing agreement on the need to whittle down the boundary line between members and nonmembers, so that outsiders whose sympathy the party wishes to win will not feel threatened. The following quotation from the beginning of the education section of

77. *Jahrbuch der SPD, 1958–59*, p. 488.

78. Often 10 per cent or more of the members in these areas are officials. Cf., e.g., *Jahresbericht, 1955–56*, SPD Bezirk Schleswig-Holstein.

the yearbook issued by the Berlin party organization in 1957 clearly expresses this point of view:

> Our future cultural–political activity will remain without response if we are not ready to engage in thoroughgoing and planned efforts to build up sympathy and trust in the social life which we have as our goal . . . Most important, we must enrich our organization with real life, by organizing those who sympathize with us without necessarily bringing about their enlistment in the party. That means that at first our recruitment of members for the party must be undertaken without using the application for membership, and [it means] engaging in discussion with those who stand outside the party without organizational purposes.

Although no absolutely certain prediction can be made, it seems likely that as the new style of the party evolves and the older members pass out of the picture the looser conception of membership will gain ground, and members of the SPD will no longer be expected to give themselves up to the movement, but will have a more instrumental relationship, from which both members and the party will benefit.

199

8. The Party and the Public

A large part of any major party's time and effort is spent seeking public support and, ultimately, votes. In Chapter 4, an indication was given of the general character of the SPD's public relations. We noted that the party had abandoned in large part the older objective of integrating an ever-increasing proportion of the population into the party, and instead seeks the potentially much larger group which might vote for the party if convinced that it provides a reasonable and useful alternative to the present government. In this effort, party leaders have sought to change the party's image among the electorate.

The Party and the Electorate

The election figures for the postwar period reveal the SPD's problem. In the four general elections between 1949 and 1961, the party's share of the popular vote rose slowly from 29 per cent to 36 per cent. At the same time, the CDU's share climbed at a much faster rate from 31 per cent to a high point of slightly over 50 per cent in 1957, and then back down to 45 per cent in 1961, still considerably ahead of the SPD. The number of parties represented in the Bundestag dropped sharply, from 11 in 1949 to 6 in 1953, 4 in 1957, and 3 in 1961. Thus, in the national elections (although not so much in the Land elections), the smaller parties, with the exception of the Free Democrats (FDP), have seen their votes wasted or absorbed by the CDU. In absolute numbers, the turnout of voters has steadily increased. While holding its own and even increasing its strength, the SPD has failed to keep pace with the CDU, and a governing mandate has seemed further and further away.

Information provided by voting records and polling agencies indicates the more subtle dimensions of the situation facing the SPD.[1] Workers, both urban and agricultural, are more likely to vote for the SPD than for any other party, although only around half of those officially so classified do so. Every other category— employees, public officials (*Beamte*), self-employed (*selbständige*), farmers, and pensioners (*Rentner*)—is more likely to vote for the CDU.[2] The SPD has done as well as it has only because the workers constitute about 40 per cent of all voters. They provide the SPD with about two-thirds of its voting strength.[3] The pre- dominantly working-class character of SPD voters no doubt ac- counts in large part for some of the other characteristics of the SPD electorate. For example, the party's strength declines as the level of education among the electorate increases.[4]

Religious affiliation, especially when coupled with regular church attendance, also works against the SPD. This is true not only of Catholics, but also of Protestants, though to a lesser de- gree. The two wings of the Christian church claim almost equal proportions of the population as members, although, as one might expect, the rate of churchgoing is much higher among Catholics.[5] Overall, it is affiliation with the Catholic Church that provides the greatest obstacle to the SPD, even in working-class districts.

---

1. Aside from the official statistical publications of the German Statistical Office, the following sources have proved useful: DIVO, *Untersuchung der Wählerschaft und Wahlentscheidung 1957* (Frankfurt, 1958) (mimeo.); DIVO, *Basic Orientation and Political Thinking of West German Youth and Their Leaders: Report on a Survey* (Frankfurt, 1956) (mimeo.); DIVO, *Fragen und Antworten: Ergebnis einer Meinungsbefragung* (Frankfurt, 1957) (mimeo.); DIVO, *SPD, Eine Politische Studie* (Frankfurt, 1956) (mimeo.); Wolfgang Hirsch-Weber et al., *Wähler und Gewählte* (Berlin, 1957) (A study of the 1953 election); and Kitzinger, *German Electoral Politics.*

2. The figures are shown in several places. See, for instance, Hirsch-Weber, Part III, Ch. 7, citing results of a 1953 EMNID poll.

3. Hirsch-Weber.

4. Ibid., p. 255.

5. Cf. Kitzinger, pp. 222 ff.

There is also a difference in the age groups that support the various parties. Older voters are more likely to vote for the CDU, while younger voters, especially from 30 to 45, are more likely to vote SPD. Sex also appears to be a determinant in the pattern of party voting, with women, especially older women, more likely to vote CDU than SPD. Finally, a person is more likely to be an SPD voter the larger the town he lives in, although there is a slight reverse trend in the very largest cities.[6]

The party's electorate therefore continues to show the characteristics of most Socialist parties, distinguished mainly by a working-class identity and traces of socialism's long-standing hostility to the churches.

In an analysis of the 1953 election, a German political scientist suggested that the German electorate could be divided into two blocs, not the "ins" and the "outs" but a very stable bloc of socialist voters and a *bürgerlich* bloc which included almost everyone else. Within either bloc, voting shifts appeared to occur easily, but they were very unlikely between them.[7] The gradual absorption of minor parties by the CDU while the SPD vote remained relatively constant seems to bear this out.

According to this thesis, there are two characteristics of the socialist bloc. First, although it is fairly large, there are rather definite limits to its potential for expansion. In the Weimar Republic the socialist bloc included the Communist Party (KPD) and the leftist splinter parties. In the first years after World War II, there was some transfer of allegiance from the declining KPD to the SPD, but the hard core of Communists are not now in the socialist bloc,[8] and after the outlawing of the KPD in the early '50s its supporters apparently scattered their votes among many parties. In any case, the number involved is small and does not offer the SPD any hope for growth. At present the socialist bloc is made up almost exclusively of persons already voting for the SPD; there are virtually no new groups to tap.

6. Hirsch-Weber, p. 216.
7. Ibid., pp. 155 ff.
8. Ibid., pp. 177–79.

Secondly, the socialist bloc is more homogeneous and has a higher degree of solidarity than the bourgeois bloc. One indication of this is that SPD voters have a more homogeneous environment than other voters in terms of party affiliation in their families and, especially, in their places of work.[9] Another indication, according to a 1957 survey by the polling organization DIVO, is that the SPD has a much higher proportion of constant voters, who do not shift their allegiance between elections or during campaigns.[10] The solidarity of these faithful voters appears to rest on the ideological character of the party and its identification with the working class.[11] According to DIVO's researchers, constant voters (compared with shifters) are more likely to judge parties (both negatively and positively) on the basis of their ideology and their social class identification than their policies or the personalities of their leaders. All voters tend to view the SPD in terms of ideological and sociological criteria, whereas the CDU is more likely to be judged by more flexible criteria. This is no doubt a result in part of Adenauer's leadership and the fact that the CDU has held office, but the consequence for the SPD is perpetuation of its image as a movement.

This situation has two aspects. The party may be said to generate stronger loyalties among its followers than other parties or it may be said to have failed to attract a significant portion of the large bloc of voters who shift parties or vote for the first time. There is an embarrassing rule of thumb (rarely admitted publicly by the SPD) that the lower the turnout the higher the SPD share of the vote. When the Berlin Land elections combined a high turnout with a high proportion of SPD votes in 1958, this was proudly cited as evidence of the effectiveness of the new style of party activity, of which the Berlin leaders were among the most active proponents.[12]

9. DIVO, *Untersuchung*, p. 152.
10. Ibid. The constant voter is also more important in the cities than in the countryside.
11. Hirsch-Weber, pp. 166 ff. Interestingly, in those areas where the proportion of Catholics is especially high, the CDU voter also tends to be constant. See DIVO, *Untersuchung*.
12. *Jahresbericht, 1957–58,* SPD Landesverband Berlin.

To break out of the minority position in which the party has found itself, it has had to find some way to appeal to voters having no predisposition toward loyalty to the socialist bloc and no reason to vote SPD because of class or group affiliation, as well as those who are in the working class but fail to vote for the party.

To take an example, the refugees, who by the 1950s included every fifth West German, were an important group. They seemed to be ripe for some kind of radical doctrine, and at least one observer suggested that they might provide a new "crisis strata" in postwar Germany.[13] In fact this did not happen, most likely because the high level of prosperity in Germany provided a basis for their rapid integration into the economy. In the competition for their votes, the Social Democrats did not do well, except possibly with those who had a strong traditional affiliation with the SPD in East Germany or a socialist affiliation elsewhere. In 1953 and 1957 the League of Expellees (BHE), a party especially oriented toward this group, won a good portion of the refugee votes, but by 1957 its strength was declining and there appeared to be no market for such a specialized party. The DIVO analysis of the 1957 election shows that refugee support went heavily to the CDU.[14]

More disturbing to the SPD was the DIVO finding that among unskilled workers (in contrast to skilled ones) the SPD did poorly in 1953 and even trailed behind the CDU in 1957. This suggests that only those workers whose allegiance to the party was reinforced by their commitment as skilled workers to their trade, and even more by trade union affiliation, could be counted on to vote SPD.

Other groups having no special commitment to the party or its program were more often than not lost to the CDU—older people, including those on pensions, white collar employees, public officials, and women.

The evidence therefore suggests that when the voter is not

13. Sigmund Neumann, "The New Crisis Strata in German Society," in Hans Morgenthau, ed., *Germany and the Future of Europe* (Chicago, 1951).
14. DIVO, *Untersuchung*.

firmly in the SPD column, and when he is subject to even relatively slight cross-pressures from other quarters, he tends to give his support to the SPD's competitors. The solidarity of the SPD is a fact, but it has been achieved at the cost of turning away the uncommitted.

To avoid becoming a permanent minority party, the party leaders must discover a method of reversing the trend which is consistent with their conception of the party, or find a conception of the party which is consistent with a method of reversing the trend. As has been indicated earlier, the latter course has been chosen.

Three Approaches to Increasing Support

There is no disagreement within the party on the need to break the "30 per cent barrier" (roughly the high-water mark of the party's electoral strength since 1920) nor on the basic reasons why the party has so far been unsuccessful in doing this. The same reasons have been given over and over again, falling roughly into three categories:

1. The satisfaction of the German electorate with economic prosperity and the identification (most party members would say incorrect identification) of that prosperity with Adenauer and the *Sozialmarktwirtschaft* (social market economy) of his economics minister, Ludwig Erhard.

2. The refusal of many to vote for a party that might follow policies threatening their security both in foreign affairs (e.g. negotiations with the Soviets for reunification, abandonment of the NATO alliance) and in domestic economic affairs (e.g. reorganization of the economy). These fears have been heightened by the inaccurate image of the SPD as a radical party bent on such drastic measures as the nationalization of all private property.

3. The CDU's well-run election campaigns, buttressed by its ability to draw on the financial and organizational resources of industry and the Catholic Church as well as the state apparatus itself, and assisted by shrewd psychological moves such as the 1957 slogan, *Keine Experimente!* (No experiments!)

There is less unanimity on the conclusions to be drawn from this situation and the assignment of blame for the party's inability to respond effectively. Three sets of ideas can be discerned. The first two can be called the "left" and the "right" approaches, both still based on a more or less Marxian analysis of society. The third lies behind the new style and might be called the "merchandising" or "pluralist-plus-public-relations" approach. It should be emphasized that the distinction is not between revolutionary or radical methods of winning power and democratic ones, but rather between methods of securing the support of a larger number of people *within* a democratic framework.

The common element between the first two ways of defining the problem is that both conceive of society as essentially stratified, that is, divided into social classes determined by economic situations and associated in turn with differences in prestige, rewards, opportunities, and so forth. Both also conceive of the party's role as representing one or a combination of these classes and articulating its interests.

What distinguishes them is that the left believes in increasing the party's basis of support by enlarging the working-class representation, while the right seeks the same end through the formation of a coalition of classes (or subclasses).

The left approach is most often found among a minority of younger socialists, a group of those connected with the party's traditionally affiliated organizations, and, in a less active sense, older members of the party with a sentimental attachment to the organization and its ideas. There is a good deal of idealism in this approach, and it demands a concentration of effort on one single conception of man's modern "alienation," which should dictate the party's policies, propaganda, strategy, and its choice of the group in the population it should work to win. Its proponents have been articulate in demanding a coherent party theory, but in the absence of a new definition of socialist goals they have tended to call for a renewed concentration on the working class. It is not always easy, of course, to know just what group in society is meant by the designation "working class," and use is often made of such vague terms as *Arbeitnehmer* (employee) or *Schaf-*

206

fender (producer), which can cover extremely wide ranges of people.

Concrete demands for action to improve the party's base of support include closer identification and cooperation with the trade unions[15] and mobilization of the workers by means of popular movements, for example protests against atomic armaments or government proposals hostile to the welfare state. The party has engaged in both kinds of activities to a limited extent. They are considered valuable not only in themselves but even more because they bring into the open the sharp division assumed always to exist between the masses and finance capital, or the ruling classes.

Shortly after several thousand workers had met in a noisy meeting organized by (but outrunning the expectations of) a local union federation to protest against health insurance reform,[16] one articulate staff member of a large industrial union complained that the party (and the unions as well) had failed to exploit mass discontent with the policies of the Adenauer government. The chairman of a local party organization subsequently exhorted party members to exploit the popular discontent revealed in the demonstration by showing other people how the whole chain of foreign policies, welfare policies, and economic policies of the Adenauer government was essentially hostile to the workers and favorable to *Grossindustrie*.

An advocate of the left approach is Wolfgang Abendroth of the University of Marburg, one of the most articulate proponents of a return to a Marxist program, who wrote in 1957 that the

15. Here again we see the reversal of positions from earlier periods in the history of the SPD. The unions constitute now a focal point of "radical" or "left" resistance to the changes in the party, in contrast to the conservative, gradualist position for which they were noted earlier. The reasons for this are clear—the unions form the last major social force in which purely working-class interests find institutional expression. This is not to say that the DGB is a radical organization by any means, but simply that one must look within the large industrial unions to find the remnants of radicalism in Germany. Although it is due for change in the near future, the DGB program still retains demands for nationalization of basic industries.

16. Cf. *Frankfurter Allgemeine Zeitung*, February 19, 1960.

SPD and the DGB had failed to use the "only spontaneous mass movement of a political-opposition character since the war—against remilitarization"—in order to organize and build the "consciousness of the workers." A generally left-wing member of the Bundestag told me in answer to a question concerning the functions of the party organization that the essential task was to support every opposition movement against the government.

For this group, the key element in the postwar failure of the party and in future strategy is the socialist concept of class-consciousness, that is, the consciousness of the members of the working class of their common interests and their willingness to join in political activity to promote them collectively. As the workers in the early stages of industrialization were drugged by the opium of liberal ideology, conservative religion, and even social reform movements, the present working classes are being doped by the opium of the absolute (but not relative) increases in their standard of living and by the ideology of the classless society. To win wider support the party must increase, by a special kind of political education, the number of those who are subjectively "working class." Abendroth, while admitting that a great part of the technical means for carrying out an extensive educational program, i.e., the older organizations of the movement and the party press, were much diminished in their potential, nevertheless insists that "the SPD must be the political opinion-forming center and leadership of the workers in their politico-social conflict with finance capital." It must make itself, he asserts, into a "crystallization point" for the consciousness of the worker.[17]

Many who share this general attitude, however, are pessimistic or fatalistic. One older member said, "we are right in our ideas, but we have come very much too early for the voter . . . we must wait until the voter understands by himself."[18] Or another said, when asked how best to influence voters (and clearly thinking of

17. Wolfgang Abendroth, "Das soziale Selbstbewusstsein wieder wecken," *Der Sozialdemokrat* (Frankfurt), December 1957.

18. Joachim Kleist (member of the Hamburg *Bürgerschaft*) in *Der Sozialist* (Hamburg), February 1958.

1933), "We shouldn't influence them, simply tell them the truth so that they can't say they didn't know when things go wrong."[19] Others feel that the temptations of prosperity are too great and that *Wohlfahrt macht faul* (Well-being makes one lazy).

In addition, in recent years, the pessimism of this element of the party has extended beyond the voter to the party itself and its new style. Most of the advocates of a left point of view are not prepared to abandon the party yet, or, as they say, "put the party in question,"[20] but one member predicted that as the parties move more and more closely together (as he interpreted the present trend) in ten years, or sooner in the case of an economic collapse, this left would break away and would be able to take with it 10 per cent of the SPD's representation in the Bundestag. Others have discounted this possibility and have predicted that a break-away movement would fail to win any seats at all.

What I have called the right-wing approach is more diffuse and less articulated within the party today, except insofar as it harmonizes with the present dominant style. It represents the kind of approach characteristic of the party leadership at the time of Schumacher's chairmanship, 1945–52. It begins with substantially the same basic conception of the class society, but differs from the left-wing approach in that it goes further in accepting existing subjective class identifications and concludes that the party must find new groups to win, particularly in the middle classes.

After the war, such an effort was felt by many leaders to be

19. This opinion, conveyed in an interview, was accompanied by a self-righteous attitude toward the party's behavior in the early '30s, when the slogan, "Who votes for Hitler votes for war," was considered prophetic and, for this respondent at least, justification for the party's action or inaction.

20. In one of the few dramatic moments at the Godesberg congress, Dr. Peter von Oertzen, one of several spokesmen for the opposition to the new program, stated: "a part of the delegates here, and a part of the comrades in the party, have had their task of representing this program with their whole heart and with full conviction made very difficult . . . [however] the unbreakable bonds of those who cannot in the end give their approval to this program is not put into question. Our faithfulness and our ties to the party will not be influenced in a negative sense through this debate." *Protokoll, 1959,* p. 308.

not only expedient but morally imperative. Schumacher wrote in 1945:

> Socialism is no longer the affair of the working class in the old narrow sense of the term. It is the program for workers, farmers, craftsmen, tradesmen, and the intellectual occupations. They all stand in unbridgeable opposition to the real exploiting groups. That the groups in the so-called middle classes (*Mittelstand*) were taken in by the propaganda of the reactionaries, the militarists, and the Nazis, and thereby let themselves be used as political cannon fodder against democracy and socialism, led to national and economic catastrophe . . . The German future depends on what kind of position the middle classes take with respect to Social Democracy.[21]

Ernst Reuter, mayor of Berlin during the early postwar period, outlined the same general strategy, emphasizing that the reason for the success of Nazism in 1933 was in large part the "great isolation of the Social Democrats from the middle classes, which, since Bismarck's fateful efforts [were successful] had lost their own political will."[22]

After the postwar wave of socialist sympathies failed to materialize, however, the party directed its appeal to small businessmen, shopkeepers, artisans, farmers, and so on by means of a series of largely unrelated demands. In the minds of party members these demands, especially in the early period, *were* related by the fact that they all represented claims against the ruling classes. Although Schumacher rejected anything resembling a "dictatorship of the proletariat," or, in other words, the repression of any class,[23] he still represented the idea that there was a kind

---

21. *Turmwächter der Demokratie*, 2, 39 ff. The quotation is from the 1945 *Aufruf*.

22. Ernst Reuter, "Aufgabe und Funktionen der SPD," in *Das sozialistische Jahrhundert*, April 1947.

23. Cf., for instance, Schumacher, p. 297: "Die Wandlungen um den Klassenkampf" (1946).

of class conflict that demanded a party appealing to groups whose prime concern was that conflict.

As the party has undergone changes in leadership and organization in the last decade, these tactics have given way to the new style. The present active leaders of the party refuse to accept the pessimism of the left or its faith that economic collapse will bring voters to the party. It has been pointed out, for instance, that if the experience of the 1930s was a guide hopes for a sudden growth in socialist sympathies in a depression are clearly unrealistic. On the other hand, the new leaders find the tactic of an "opening to the right" to be an insufficient, if not completely useless, device.

The major innovation of the new style is to focus on the general reputation of the party rather than on its group structure. The new leaders are particularly concerned at the negative image of the SPD which German voters apparently have. The following passage from a Berlin party yearbook reflects the new approach:

> We know that socialism exists in the public consciousness as a regulator of society, but not as a manifestation (*Repräsentanz*) of it. It appears as the doctor at the sick bed of society, whom one doesn't ask for advice in periods of health. As disturbing "world-betterers" it appears to be developing easily misunderstood decisions in an isolated organizational life which seems provincial to the intellectual and destructive to the ego of the small citizen (*Kleinbürger*). The image of the Social Democrat is therefore negatively determined in the minds of the people. We can see waves of antipathy produced by decades of propaganda against us.[24]

Concern for the party image reflects a rather different picture of the political universe from that indicated by the left-wing and right-wing approaches. Judging from some of the comments of party members, the chief teacher of this new view may have been Konrad Adenauer.

24. *Jahresbericht, 1957–58,* SPD Landesverband Berlin.

The reasoning seems to run as follows: The party's success at the polls depends only slightly on the planks in the party platform. For the present, and most likely for a good while to come, the party must first take into account the voters' general conceptions and prejudices concerning the kind of society they live in and the kind of leadership they want, regardless of their special interests, beyond the general health of society. In particular, the party must concern itself with the views people have of the SPD in the light of these conceptions and prejudices. At election time the party must reckon not with group demands, whether objective or subjective, but with a mixture of emotional and rational attitudes and beliefs arising from cultural traditions created by the "completely accidental boundaries drawn by the Westphalian peace of 1648,"[25] from the general identification of prosperity with Erhard's social market economy, from the desire to secure personal economic success, and from the determination to avoid war and the Bolshevization of Germany. These considerations are especially important to the occasional voter, now particularly important to the SPD, who generally shows little interest in the details of political bargaining.[26]

In order to win this voter, the party must create general sympathy for itself, disarming prejudices that stamp it as "dangerous" or "unacceptable." Once this is done, the party will be in a position to capitalize on the shifting trends of opposition to the government that develop with fast-moving international and domestic political events. Opposition is sometimes based on group interests and sometimes on the ineffectiveness of the government; it is rarely based on just those issues a movement has made its particular concern.

25. The quotation is from an analysis of the party's need to obtain a better understanding of the ideas held by the population and to employ modern techniques of influencing ideas. It is one of the few such party documents completely in touch with modern social science. Heinrich Braune, *Mittel und Methoden der Meinungsbildung* (mimeo.), reprint of a speech given at the Hessen-Süd Bezirk party congress, April 1960.

26. Braune cites figures from a survey of Hamburg which show that 74 per cent of the people never attended meetings at which political or economic questions were discussed, and 66 per cent were neither officers nor members of an association, a union, or a party.

212

This line of reasoning does not necessarily imply the abandonment of the "opening to the right." It does suggest that this tactic will remain fruitless until the prejudices against the party are destroyed and that, in any case, the "opening to the right" constitutes only one step forward.

The "new style" approach is therefore based on three assumptions quite different from those held by proponents of the other two tactics. First, it includes general values and attitudes as well as group interests among the factors conditioning voting behavior. Secondly, because of this it rejects the effort to build a bloc of one or more classes or groups because no such bloc exists or could exist without a drastic realignment of public attitudes. Thirdly, it rejects any narrowly representational view of the party's role. The new party program proclaims that the party has become the party of the people (*Volkspartei*). What this really means is that the party has moved toward becoming the party of no one in particular, and in the process of bidding for votes seeks to become the embodiment of shared values, the vehicle of diverse interests, and the advocate of respected policies.

Earlier I called this the "pluralist-plus-public-relations" approach—"pluralist" because of the attempt to win over shifting groups and "public relations" because of the effort to maintain an open channel to the people by creating an acceptable image. To create this image—the most pressing task facing the party—it has had to neutralize hostility from the churches and the "bourgeoisie," calm the fears of prospective voters that the party has hidden motives or a reckless, irresponsible nature, and, finally, accentuate the positive qualities the party has—its sober, constructive, progressive thinking, tested by experience.

Neutralizing Hostilities—
The SPD and the Churches

One of the drawbacks of a century-long tradition of opposition is that the party must reckon with the hostility of the groups it has fought. The SPD's enemies of the past are many, but perhaps none has such immediate importance as the churches. The party's recent efforts to make peace with religious institutions can serve as an example of its more general efforts to neutralize hostility.

Before the election of John F. Kennedy, it would have been difficult for an American to understand the antagonisms aroused in Europe by the relationship between church and state. The hostility of Socialists to the church goes back to the time when the Protestant church in Prussian Germany was the pillar of a stratified society and so closely identified with the state as to be part of it. Party hostility to the church was therefore a byproduct of Socialist conflict with society and state authority, though it was also reinforced by an anti-religious ideology. Ludwig Metzger, member of the SPD executive and at the same time a member of the Synod of the Evangelical Church in Germany, summed up this historical background in the following passage defending the formulations of the Godesberg Program:

> in the preceding century, there was a gulf between the social-ist workers and the churches. At that time, since the churches were largely still bourgeois churches, the socialist workers had to feel outside them, just as they felt outside bourgeois society.[27]

The Catholic Church, then (and still) a minority church in Germany, was not part of the Establishment but found itself in conflict with the Socialists over ideological questions (because of the latter's materialist and egalitarian ideas) and in competition with them as the sponsor of a rival political organization (the Center Party) and rival trade union organizations. For a time under Bismarck, during the *Kulturkampf,* the Catholics shared the honor of persecution at the hands of the state, but this failed to produce any long-lasting bond.

In the Weimar period, despite the frequent association of the Center Party and the SPD in the Weimar Coalition, the emergence of a fringe of religious socialist groups, and increasing church

27. Ludwig Metzger, in *Protokoll, 1959,* p. 272.

interest in social doctrine, the Socialists and the churches were never reconciled.

The situation has been changing in the Bonn Republic. The CDU was built on the foundations of the old Catholic Center Party, but it has tried to form a union of both Catholics and Protestants. Thus the churches and the Socialists, as the two political forces least compromised in the Nazi period, provided the bases for the two major parties after the war. This would seem to have set the stage for a resumption of hostilities between them, but in fact the kind of conflict typical of the nineteenth century has not ensued. The basis of their hostility—their respective positions with regard to the state and society—has altered fundamentally. Reduced by the division of Germany to a bare majority of the religiously affiliated people of West Germany, and commanding a great deal less loyalty from their communicants,[28] the Protestants have been a junior partner of the Catholics in the CDU. Many Protestants have been outspoken critics of the Adenauer government. As a result, Protestant relations with the Socialists have been relatively cordial. Metzger notes that "open discussion between them as equal partners [has been] carried on intensively . . . from the time of the collapse of National Socialism."[29]

Catholic hostility to the SPD has however increased, and communications between them have been correspondingly less successful. Although competitive organizing has declined since the formation of the DGB, the CDU has from time to time sought to recreate the Christian trade union movement, thus keeping the issue alive. Disagreements over policy questions, such as the nature of a united Europe, and ideological differences have also kept feeling high. Christian social doctrines had a new popularity in one wing of the CDU,[30] but in the main this created not a bridge to the Socialists but a bulwark against them. Catholics have

28. Kitzinger, *German Electoral Politics,* cites figures showing 51 per cent of the population as registered Protestants, 45 per cent as Catholics. From 50 to 60 per cent of the Catholics attend church regularly, however, as compared to 10 to 20 per cent of the Protestants.

29. *Protokoll, 1959,* p. 273.

30. Cf. Heidenheimer, *Adenauer and the CDU.*

cited the 1931 Papal Encyclical "Quadrigesimo Anno," in which the following passage appears, to justify their hostility:

> Socialism, whether as a teaching, as a historical event, or as a movement, even when it gives room for the truth and for justice in . . . parts, remains forever irreconcilable with the teaching of the Catholic Church . . . It is impossible to be at the same time a good Catholic and a genuine Socialist.[31]

Although the party can prove that many Catholics have voted for the SPD,[32] Catholic votes have gone much more heavily to the CDU, and the problem of changing this situation has been made more difficult by Catholic priests speaking from the pulpit in favor of the CDU during election campaigns.[33] The party attempted for a time to counteract this by attacking the hierarchy and trying to persuade individual Catholics to disobey their priests. Kurt Schumacher, in his vituperative style, seems to have led the way in this strategy.[34] In the 1950s, however, the tone and objectives of party activity with respect to the Church changed. The party is now concentrating on disengaging the Church from politics, especially of course from the CDU, one technique being to ridicule the CDU's identification of itself as the only Christian party. SPD leaders often speak ironically of the CDU as the party with the "big C."

31. Quoted in "Der Katholik und der SPD," pamphlet published by the SPD executive (Bonn, December 1959), p. 19.

32. "In recent elections, the SPD has succeeded in making a not inconsiderable dent into the strata of Catholic voters. For example, in the communal elections of 1956 in North-Rhine Westphalia, the SPD could win the absolute majority in many city and rural districts which had an overwhelming majority of Catholics in the population, and in the total result won 44.2% of the . . . votes." Ibid., p. 6.

33. A pastoral letter in 1959 from the bishops of Speyer, Mainz, and Trier read: "in the fulfillment of their electoral obligations [Catholics] should support those believing men and women who have ordered and built the Land according to Christian standards . . . There are enemies of the church from whom one can hear again and again now the call for the so-called 'deconfessionalization' of public life." *eilt*, May 1959, p. 28.

34. Schumacher's occasional outbursts against the Catholics were criticized in Klaus-Peter Schulz, *Sorge um die deutschen Linke.*

On a more fundamental level, the party has sought to convince Catholics that they may work politically through any party and that there is no basis for opposition to the SPD on grounds of principle. One step in this process has been to assert and emphasize the compatibility of socialism and Christianity and the consequent possibility that Christians may become socialists without violating their faith.

As mentioned above, there were groups of religious socialists even before the Nazi period. After the war, an effort to reduce the "cross-pressures," from socialism and Christianity, on the voter and member was undertaken. In a speech in 1946, which was often quoted in the debates over the Godesberg Program, Kurt Schumacher maintained that:

> It is all the same whether one becomes a Social Democrat through Marxist methods of economic analysis, or through philosophical or ethical grounds, or in the spirit of the Sermon on the Mount. Everyone has the same right in the party to the preservation of his intellectual personality and to his own motives.[35]

In the Godesberg Program itself (slightly varying from the language of the Aktionsprogramm of 1952), the party went further, declaring:

> Democratic Socialism, which in Europe is rooted in Christian ethics, humanism, and classical philosophy, declares no last truths—not from lack of understanding or indifference to world-views or religious truths, but from consideration for the differences in men's beliefs, the contents of which neither a political party nor the state determines.

> Socialism is no substitute religion . . .

> The party is always ready for cooperation with churches and religious societies on the basis of a free partnership.[36]

35. Quoted by Ollenhauer, *Protokoll, 1959*, p. 59.
36. Ibid., pp. 13 and 25.

Defending this language at the convention, Metzger explains:

> It is important to indicate now that the situation has changed, that the workers and the socialists no longer feel that the socialist movement is a substitute for everything that the church could mean. Above all, this formula [that socialism is not a substitute religion] will also make clear that the political party and the churches operate on two different levels, even if cooperation is desired and necessary.[37]

The party subsequently sought to make these declarations more explicit for Catholics in a pamphlet, *The Catholic and the SPD,* in which, among other things, the authors (Waldemar von Knoeringen and Willy Eichler) dissociated the party's brand of socialism from the socialism condemned by the "Quadrigesimo Anno."

These varied attempts to allay the hostility of the Church have been accompanied by a number of meetings, conversations, and debates which have brought Socialists and Catholics together for discussion and exchange of views.[38] The questions raised at such meetings are profound—although the answers sometimes fail to reach that level. At one meeting, for example, the term "partnership" was disputed by Catholics on the ground that the Church was on the same level as the state and could not therefore enter into a partnership with a political party. Clearly, much time will elapse before the SPD receives the blessing of the Catholic hierarchy. The party has, however, been able to call on a few Catholic social theorists, such as Professor Oswald v. Nell-Breuning, S.J., to point up the similarities in the political outlook of the Church and the party.[39]

37. Ibid., p. 272.

38. Two such conferences were (1) a meeting of representatives of the Social Democratic parties of Germany, Switzerland, and Austria with representatives of the Catholic Church in 1959 at Langenargen am Bodensee, and (2) a meeting of the German counterparts only at Königstein im Taunus, March 5, 1960.

39. Professor Nell-Breuning is so often quoted in party discussions of this subject that he has become something of a focal point of party theorizing. *Vorwärts* paraphrases an article by Nell-Breuning to the effect that "it is impos-

The delicate nature of the task of seeking a rapprochement with the Church led the party in December 1959 to issue "guidelines" for contacts with the churches. Members are encouraged to participate in discussions with Catholics but are warned that only persons authorized to do so can speak for the party. Others must clearly state that they are speaking as individuals.

The effort to change Catholic attitudes toward the party has not, of course, prevented the party from opposing the Church on particular issues; there is a continuing battle over secular versus religious education. The Basic Law left education to the Länder, and in practice the regional branches of the party have often gone a considerable distance toward meeting Church views. For example, in Bavaria, a particularly strong Catholic area, the SPD has accepted the idea of government support of parochial schools. In general, the party has tried to remove the traditional ideological overtones from this issue and to substitute pragmatic judgment, although this has been difficult for Catholics and Socialists alike.[40]

The party's new style vis-à-vis the Church is to find a *modus vivendi* involving mutual recognition of separate fields of interest. It has sought to confine clashes to relatively low-intensity questions of practical policy.

Calming Fears—Socialism, Communism, and Foreign Policy

The most common explanation for the party's poor showing in the 1957 elections was summed up in the CDU slogan for that

---

sible to deny that free democratic socialism, especially of the German variety, has come very much closer to Catholic social teaching than that which Pius XI in 1931 recognized in revisionist socialism." *Vorwärts,* February 2, 1960.

40. The all-West-German meeting of representatives of the Church and the party mentioned in note 38 was characterized by rather sober and intellectual discussion until the question of Church schools arose, at which point the theologians and ideologists were displaced by the politicians among the participants, with a considerable increase in heat. The *Frankfurter Allgemeine Zeitung* (March 9, 1960), reporting on the meeting, headlined its article, "Obstacles Between Catholics and Social Democrats: The School Question in the Middle."

campaign, *Keine Experimente!* It was a slogan with a variety of meanings—don't change horses in midstream, don't allow the SPD to embark on dangerous innovations in foreign and domestic policy.

Citing the results of a survey undertaken for the party in 1956, Heinrich Braune, an editor of a newspaper close to the SPD, noted that:

> the winning party would be the one that was ready to secure the well-being which had been achieved, with the least risk for the individual and for the economy. Adenauer's slogan for 1957, "No experiments," was the slogan that suited [these demands]. . . . The party's own slogan, "security for all," was, on the basis of the image millions of voters had of it, not sufficiently legitimized, because the party often gave too varied and uncertain answers to particular questions.[41]

One of the greatest ironies was the notion, furthered by the CDU, that a vote for the SPD would help the Communists. It was ironic because the party has been engaged in a long-drawn-out battle with the Communists ever since the two parties split apart after the First World War. As recently as the immediate post-World War II period, the SPD fought to keep Berlin from falling to the Communists, first by preventing the formation in Berlin of a united Socialist-Communist party, the Socialist Unity Party (SED), and later by providing the leadership that held out, with Allied help, against the blockade.

The damaging effect of the innuendos spread by the party's opponents can easily be comprehended in the light of the over-whelmingly negative attitudes of the great majority of German voters toward Communism. The fact that millions of West German citizens are refugees from Soviet regimes in East Germany and elsewhere, added to the long-standing hostility of the German middle classes to Marxism (a theme exploited by the Nazis) is

41. Braune, *Mittel und Methoden der Meinungsbildung.*

explanation enough, without a recital of the long train of hostile Soviet acts.

These attacks on the SPD take two general forms (sometimes implicitly combined in the same statements): first that there is a wing in the SPD favorable to Communism and to the East German regime which would gain in influence if the party won, and second, that the policies of the SPD, especially with regard to negotiations with the U.S.S.R. and the creation of some kind of neutralized, reunited Germany, would lead inevitably to a Soviet take-over in West Germany.[42] The party has undertaken to meet both of these criticisms. To avoid being compromised by left-wing members, it has cracked down on those within its ranks who have shown themselves sympathetic to the East German regime. Expulsion from the party is a seldom-used sanction and is now undertaken almost exclusively against members who have openly shown such sympathy. Almost all of the 62 expulsions in 1958–59 were for this reason.[43] The disavowal of the socialist student federation (SDS) in 1960 was also clearly intended to avoid having the party compromised by the leftist statements of that group's leadership. To guide members who fail to comprehend the importance of the party's image or might unintentionally compromise the party by lending their names to the seemingly harmless cause of "East-West contacts," the party has laid down explicit regulations concerning relations with representatives from the Communist East, in effect prohibiting them unless they take place under official party auspices.[44]

The party has also sought to allay public suspicion that Socialists are really Communists by constant and repeated declarations of the party's hostility to Communism. A pamphlet was published recounting the history of the party's conflict with Communists.[45]

42. Cf. Kitzinger, *German Electoral Politics*.

43. *Jahrbuch der SPD, 1958–59*, p. 268.

44. Ibid., p. 407, which reprints a decision of the executive of January 30, 1960, which in turn substantially repeats the points made in an article by Herbert Wehner in 1959 entitled, "Keine Aktionseinheit: Gegen den Missbrauch der Arbeitersolidarität durch die SED," published (among other places in party publications) in *Der Sozialist* (Hamburg), March 1959.

45. *Die Alternative unserer Zeit, Auseinandersetzung der Sozialdemokratie mit dem Kommunismus*, published by the SPD executive (February 1960).

The most dramatic attempts to change the party's image have been the shifts in party policy, especially those associated with Willy Brandt (who is, incidentally, unceremoniously lumped together with "Western militarists and revisionists" by Communist propaganda). The new foreign policy of the party has sought to assure the German people that the SPD, too, would fight Communism with military means and would rely, as Adenauer has done, on the U.S.–NATO deterrent to preserve German security. The party has therefore accepted the currently popular definition of the requirements for peace. This change has involved a repudiation of pacifism which, although never directly embraced by the party, was tolerated by and found considerable support among party members in the Weimar period and during the initial stages of German rearmament in the early 1950s. This repudiation, cryptically embodied in the following formula from the Godesberg Program, "The party approves the defense of the country,"[46] touched off one of the few controversies during the Godesberg convention.

These changes in policy have taken place in a very short time. As recently as early 1959, the party issued the *Deutschlandplan,* commonly ascribed to Herbert Wehner, which attempted to answer the criticism that the SPD did not state its policies clearly enough by specifying the particular steps by which negotiations could be carried on with the East German regime in order to achieve the reunification of a Germany unaligned with either East or West.[47] It would require extensive analysis to assess the realities of the situation and the practical value of the plan, but in any case the reaction in Germany was clear. The plan met with considerable hostility, especially of course from CDU sources, which condemned it as a *lebensgefährlich* (life-endangering) plan. Only one year later, in a statement issued by Wehner,[48]

---

46. *Protokoll, 1959,* p. 16, and *New York Times,* November 25, 1960.
47. *Deutschlandplan der SPD,* published by the SPD executive (April 1959).
48. In *Vorwärts,* March 18, 1960. Wehner's role in this shift was especially useful to the party. He was naturally responsible for both promulgating and retracting the Deutschlandplan since his field of special interest in the Bundestag has been policy toward East Germany. Identified with the left wing of the SPD, he was able, as spokesman for the shift to the right on this issue, to pacify dis-

the party reversed itself, dropping the plan and adopting a common stand with the Adenauer government on most points of Cold War strategy. At the Hannover congress in 1960, for instance, Brandt insisted on "the absolutely binding . . . declaration that we will be faithful to the alliance [NATO] and will do nothing to jeopardize it."[49] To explain its earlier position, the party maintains that negotiations with the Soviets would still have been possible in the early 1950s. By 1960–61, in any case, the party had abandoned that view and was vainly seeking a joint review of foreign policies with the CDU.

Accentuating the Positive—
Making the Party *Glaubwürdig*

Complementing the party's efforts to erase its image as risky in the eyes of the German voter has been the attempt to create an impression of responsibility and close identification with the nation. Willy Brandt's statement in 1960 emphasizing his responsibility to the entire nation rather than to party directives should he win the chancellorship is one example of this. Another is the use of the team (discussed in Chapter 6), which emphasizes the extensive experience of leading party members in the Land governments and in the Bundestag.

To counteract the impression of disunity, fuzziness, and monotonous opposition to government policies which the SPD feels it has given the German public, the party has undertaken to formulate detailed and positive programs. The series of plans noted in Chapter 3 constituted one of the first steps in this effort.

Giving the party a "profile," i.e., drawing up and publicizing coherent party policies, has been one of the continuing demands of party reformers, both on the left and on the right. The left sought to do this by means of a new program. The right, on the

---

satisfied party members on the left and at the same time to counteract the CDU's attempts to picture him as a radical. He played the same role in the foreign policy debate in the Bundestag in July 1960.

49. *New York Times,* November 25, 1960.

other hand, thought the solution lay in eliminating the traditional language of Marxism from the generally moderate proposals actually put forward by the party.

The Godesberg Program was important in creating a common frame of reference for all the important areas of policy making, especially the most sensitive and sensational ones. The plans demonstrated the party's ability to go beyond negative criticism and to present workable proposals.

But the Godesberg Program was still not enough to prove the party's *Glaubwürdigkeit,* or "trustworthiness," as it is referred to in party discussions. This refers to the voter's perception of the party as competent to carry out popular demands in a responsible way. The requisites for achieving this reputation appear to be connected in the minds of reforming party members with a kind of dramatic unity of the party. That the party has failed to give the impression of such unity is substantiated by Kitzinger, who states in his study of the 1957 elections that the CDU, although a much more loosely constructed party, was able to convey a unified impression while the SPD gave the impression of diffusion.[50] One of the reform documents from the 1953 period indicates that the problem was even then on the minds of some party members:

> The SPD must . . . break into wide strata of the population . . . this cannot be achieved, however, by dividing the ideas of the party into isolated sections and within these sections . . . speaking to each separate group. This attempt, which is often evident today, is condemned from the start to *Unglaubwürdigkeit.*[51]

The unity demanded involves more than logically coherent party policies; it requires a few clear, simply stated themes that can be understood by the public and will distinguish the SPD from the CDU. Many, including Fritz Erler, consider this to be one of the major needs of the party.

50. Kitzinger, *German Electoral Politics,* p. 104.
51. *Beitrag zur Erneurung.* (Cf. note 15, Ch. 3.)

The efforts to improve the party's image have of course benefited from many of the changes in party structure mentioned in previous chapters—the new emphasis on personalities, the increasing use of the independent mass media, the reformed style of meetings, and the employment of public relations experts.[52]

Many of these techniques could, of course, be construed simply as opportunism, and there are members of the party who are quick to use that term. Protests have been made against the use of the tools of mass manipulation, and members have argued that the party's task is to educate, not manipulate.[53] However, insofar as the new approach enables the party to mobilize the shifting currents of discontent with the party in power—discontent not always or even usually arising from traditional socialist grievances —the party may be developing a channel through which special interests within the broad arena of public opinion but not the concern of a professionalized interest group may be articulated and made effective.

52. Professionals are engaged not only at the national level but also at the regional level. Cf., e.g., *Aus der Arbeit eines Jahres, Jahresbericht, 1958,* SPD Bezirk Hessen-Süd. It is proudly noted there, however, that the party's apparently successful slogan for the Landtag elections, "Ich bin für Zinn" (G. A. Zinn, minister-president of Hesse), was the creation of a party secretary.

53. Cf. the discussion at the Bezirk congress of Hessen-Süd, April 1960, in Braune, *Mittel und Methoden der Meinungsbildung.*

9. Conclusion

The Social Democratic Party of Germany was one of the first political parties in the world to develop on the basis of a systematically organized mass membership. As the new industrial working class emerged in the nineteenth century, it sought to win a decent standard of living, a respected place in society, and the right to participate equally in the political process. When these efforts were frustrated, the workers' political representative, the SPD, tightened its discipline, adopted an ideological position to rationalize the workers' demands, and slowly built a network of organizations to provide independently for their needs.

The ideology and the massive organization commanded the loyalty of the membership and held the party together through the upheavals of the First World War and the Revolution of 1918–19. In the Weimar period, Germany's first experiment with a formal democratic parliamentary regime gave the SPD its first chance to govern, but the emergence of strong radical opposition both on the right and the left, and the fragmentation of the political society in general, made the successful operation of the government impossible. In the process the pressures toward solidarity within the party were reinforced.

It was only after the establishment of a relatively stable and prosperous Germany in the post-World War II period that the fundamental conflict of German society abated, and defense of the movement ceased to be the SPD's overriding motive. The bases for solidarity within the party were greatly weakened: the working classes began to enjoy relative prosperity, many of the party's affiliated organizations dissolved or became independent, and, in the political atmosphere following the excesses of Nazism, the appeal of ideologically based invective diminished. At the same time, the problem of winning power (something which had always been confidently expected as the result of historical processes) also became more difficult. The strengthening of the chancellorship and the fabulous success of the CDU at the polls (in contrast to the SPD's performance) meant that the party had to increase its popular support drastically in order to win power. To do this—to appeal to Catholics, the middle classes, and refugees and pensioners—the party has had to separate itself from those very features that once made it distinctive and gave it its character as a movement. The party's ideology and its exclusively working-class orientation—the factors that had maintained the solidarity of its traditional supporters—produced only hostility among the new groups it courted.

Supported by a majority of the politically active members of the party, reformers have undertaken changes which have done more than simply modify the party line on particular policies or even create a coalition of groups forming a somewhat larger proportion of the electorate. They have changed the character of the party altogether. They have begun to replace outmoded ideology with a flexible policy-making process capable of exploiting the demands of many groups and capitalizing on shifting trends of public opinion. They have changed the pattern of leadership recruitment to produce men who will win popular support and respect among German elites rather than simply the devotion of party militants. They have begun to transform the membership organization from an ideologically motivated "in-group" to a flexible tool able to maintain contact between the leaders and the public and train political "technicians."

The SPD is therefore undergoing a quiet revolution. It is not the revolution in German society planned by the founders of the party, but a revolution that the changing society itself has forced upon the party. To those whose emotional and intellectual loyalties remain with the labor movement and a socialist view of society, this revolution naturally seems to be either a betrayal or a blatant exhibit of opportunism, for the changes now in process can no longer be explained away as simply bringing the movement up to date. As an idea, a philosophy, and a social movement, socialism in Germany is no longer represented by a political party. If it is to exist as an active political force, it will have to find a new relationship to politics, a new organ through which to act and be heard.

Although the SPD now has a reputation for "reformism" among Socialist parties, the kind of reformation it has undertaken has actually been in process in almost every Socialist party in Europe. In Scandinavia and elsewhere, the transformation has been set in motion less dramatically through more or less extended periods of government responsibility. The continued, though deemphasized, use of traditional symbols and programs by northern European Socialist parties is a luxury the SPD cannot afford, nor has the SPD been able, as they have, to shunt radical militants into government jobs, for the SPD has always been outside the government. The SPD's leaders have had to make their departures from tradition more public and more dramatic to keep in the public eye and establish the party's new image. The Socialist parties of France and Italy, on the other hand, although they have also been out of power, have not been able to adopt the overt tactics of the SPD, for well-organized and powerful Communist parties could exploit any failure to perform the rituals of working-class politics.

Perhaps the most interesting contrast is with the Labor Party in Britain. Once considered on the right of European socialism for its "revisionist" tendencies, it now seems more militant than the SPD because of the strength of its left wing. Hugh Gaitskill, in fact, endeavored to change the British Labor Party in much the same way as the SPD, although the impact and the success of his maneuvers have been impeded by the tactics of the militant left, supported by a few influential leaders like Frank Cousins in the trade union movement. Among the explanations for the apparent reversal of positions of the British and the German Socialist parties along the "left–right" scale are the following: The division of Germany has made West Germans more hostile than the British to any form of Communism, and the similarity in language used by Communists and Socialists often works to the latter's disadvantage. The separation of the SPD from the trade unions, in contrast to the continued close organizational ties between the British unions and the Labor Party, has weakened the leftists' organizational base in the German party. Further, the larger gap in voting strength between the major parties in Germany has necessitated more drastic disciplining of the SPD's left wing. Any complete explanation would also have to account for the rather surprising lack of significant intellectual activity in Germany among leftist thinkers, but an analysis of this situation would take us beyond the bounds of our inquiry here.

The changes in the SPD are not, of course, complete or irreversible. An evenly matched intraparty struggle, like the one that seems to have paralyzed the party in Britain, or a reassertion of traditional radical feelings in the SPD, might undo what has been done so far. If, for example, a major economic crisis were to occur, repolarizing German society along class lines, the rationale for a new radical socialist doctrine would be reestablished. Or if the present leadership fails to produce results at the polls (the 6 per cent increase in the popular vote in 1961 was impressive, but still leaves the party almost 10 per cent behind the CDU), the conservatives (leftists and traditional socialists) might reassert themselves, recreating the old pattern for its own sake or in hopes of future vindication. Thus a failure at the polls— whether caused by the public's unwillingness to accept the party in spite of change, by the party leaders' ineptness in handling their machine, or simply by the continual success of the CDU in satisfying basic popular desires—might well prove to be the undoing of the party's new style.

A reversal that frustrated the party's effort to establish a more open and flexible relationship with other political groups would be unfortunate for the development of a stable and democratic German political system. The relative absence of basic conflict within the society means that the political parties must adopt a new role in the political system in order to avoid creating friction where none need exist. The CDU led the way, moving far away

229

from its early ideological inclinations, becoming an organization that brought together a variety of interests, provided a professional and effective political machine, and mobilized wide support behind the generally acceptable foreign and economic policies of the chancellor and his economics minister. But the SPD still commands the loyalty of a very large segment of the German population and is equipped to act as spokesman for a set of interests often ignored by the governing party. The autocratic tendencies of Konrad Adenauer, too, pointed up the danger of single party monopoly, no matter how loosely constructed, over effective power. Not only is the transformation of the SPD necessary to avoid the possibility of perpetuating the debilitating conflict of major social groups which has so marked German political history in the twentieth century, but it is also necessary to provide the competition the CDU needs in a democracy. To offer this competition, the SPD must accept the pluralistic character of German society and challenge the CDU where the latter has been most successful—in the competition for political support from the uncommitted and the effective elite. It is in this direction that the party has been moving.

From a long-range point of view, the success of the party in making the transition from an ideological, class-based party to one capable of operating flexibly in a two-party system would mark the closing phase of one of the most serious problems facing Western societies in the last century. Ever since the creation of nation-states, the political systems of Europe have suffered periodic shocks as various segments of their populations have sought entry into the governing process. As industrialized and interdependent societies have developed, and, more recently, as the functions of the central government have expanded, larger and larger elements of the population have become vitally interested in, and capable of, taking an active part in the making of decisions. The integration of the working class has been one of the most difficult steps in this process, resulting in some of the most serious cleavages in European society. The changes in the SPD constitute an attempt to transform a party that represents a class seeking entry into the political system to a party that performs within a broadly based system in which no major group remains outside society or outside politics. The party's pragmatic approach, its effort to appeal to widely shared values of large groups, and its desire to be accepted as a legitimate leader of society are measures of the integration which has already been achieved.

The development of the party is relevant to yet another aspect of European political history. The abandonment of a clear, single, class identification in favor of greater flexibility, and the abandonment of an ideological point of view for a more pragmatic one, provide only the minimum conditions necessary for an effective and democratic political system. More is required than a stable executive, a working parliament, and a two-party system. The evils of the fragmented political system, characterized by multiple, intransigent political parties, should not lead us to think that watering down party policies and eliminating all but two parties are sufficient to secure a legitimate and effective political system. Also required are methods of taking account of all significant political demands within the society, arriving at policies that will achieve national objectives, and ensuring the most effective employment of the resources of the governmental apparatus in carrying out policies.

The stage in the development of Western societies when parliamentary institutions and elections were sufficient to carry out these functions has long passed, however indispensable they remain. Political parties—those agents of the decline of parliaments—have also proved inadequate insofar as they limit themselves to their traditional roles as either representatives of class or status groups (as in Europe) or as the organizers of elections (as in the United States). Politically relevant society has become too complex for these traditional (although in some cases only recently accepted) political institutions. On the one hand, the increasing number of interest groups and the diversification of their channels of access and, on the other hand, the tremendous increase in the size of the central bureaucracy have increased the problems of successfully linking government and society far beyond the capacity of these relatively rudimentary organizations.

231

With differing degrees of success, modern governments have adopted many devices, some old and some new, for regulating this relationship. The Soviet Union, rapidly modernizing under a revolutionary regime, has built the Communist Party into a mammoth organization which controls the government, but this has been accomplished at the expense of free expression of the varied interests that must exist despite the unanimity stressed by party leaders. In the West, political systems are increasingly marked by direct, informal contacts and consultations between the administrative apparatus of government and the multiplying, organized interest groups within the community, and by the increasing importance of even those very tenuous contacts which individual leaders such as DeGaulle, Macmillan, Adenauer, and even Kennedy established with the public.

The developments in the Social Democratic Party of Germany suggest that political parties constructed on a new pattern may have a significant role to play in providing an adequate institutional basis for democratically linking the people of a country with their government. To appreciate this potential, it is necessary to avoid using an almost implicit typology to analyze political parties. The "electoral" party, loosely organized and impermanent, constitutes one type, and the "mass" party, organized around a particular ideology or class interest, forms another. What Duverger calls the "cell or militia party," typified by the Communist and Fascist parties, may constitute a third. This rough categorization of parties has encouraged the assumption that mass parties must offer their active members an ideology, a cause, and, in fact, a way of life. Otherwise, it is implied, only the small group of individuals who actually have a chance at high political office can be induced to take a permanent interest in the party and its activities.

The indications are, however, that the SPD may not fit into any of these categories. It has retained its mass organization, and, in fact, is actively seeking to extend it, while at the same time it is striving for the flexibility of the "electoral" party in terms of policy. In striving to employ its organization to mobilize a wide basis of support, the SPD has in fact created an institution that,

232

potentially at least, serves to bring together numerous groups within the society—including many who have no other representation on a national scale—for training and promoting individuals skilled in dealing with complex legislative issues and for tapping diverse trends of public opinion and group interests in a relatively systematic way. It is too early to estimate, of course, the impact such a "cadre" (as I have called this type of party to distinguish it from the other structural types) will have on the three requirements for a legitimate and effective political system: representativeness, effective policy, and political control of the administration. The SPD may be too hindered by its traditions to make its quiet revolution successful, but the kind of party organization it is trying to develop may in the end prove to be the best method yet devised for maintaining a strong and democratic government in a modern society, while providing a method of mobilizing the intellectual and technical skills of the country to meet the crucial problems of today.

The German Social Democratic Party is thus undergoing a transformation that is not simply helping to complete the development of a stable political system in Germany but is also demonstrating one way in which a stable political system can remain democratic and effective in a complex world.

Appendix: Party Finances

Unlike most political parties, the SPD publishes each year a fairly extensive accounting of its finances, showing in broad categories the money taken in and spent. The finances of the national party and the Bezirke are kept separately, so the figures for the national organization do not include the total amount taken in by the party; the proportions appear to be roughly similar, however, so the figures for the national organization can serve as an illustration.

The income of the national party has risen from about 1.9 million Deutschmark in the first full year after the currency reform (1949) to a high point in 1957 (an election year), when it reached 6.65 million Deutschmark (about $1.66 million at present exchange rates). The sources of this income are shown in Table 1.

The main source of income is the regular dues paid monthly to the *Hauskassierer* in exchange for stamps which are placed in the member's *Mitgliedsbuch* (membership book). This money is sent to the Bezirke where about 15 per cent is forwarded to the national organization. Table 2 shows the scale of dues paid by members, as determined by their monthly incomes. The amounts assessed from the different categories have changed very little since the currency reform, but the party's total income has increased as a result of the general rise in members' incomes (party treasurers have had to engage in continuing campaigns to overcome the tendency not to report higher income), and the additional categories which have been inserted raising the assessment on the upper half of a category.[1]

Table 1. INCOME OF NATIONAL PARTY EXECUTIVE
(in percentages)

Year	Dues[a]	Special Assessments	Fraktion	Contributions	Payments[b]	Other
1946	91.3	5.4		2.0		1.3
1947	64.6	30.0		3.8		1.6
1948 (first half)	69.6	23.6		5.0		1.8
1948 (second half)	22.0	51.2		23.3		3.5
1949	42.2	45.6	1.3	7.3		3.6
1950	49.5	30.0	9.1	7.6		3.8
1951	45.8	33.7	8.7	8.7		3.1
1952	56.9	24.7	7.5	7.9		3.0
1953	65.7[c]	16.7[c]	6.5	9.5		1.6
1954	57.2[c]	24.5[c]	10.7	6.5		1.1
1955	55.9[c]	19.1[c]	10.5	3.1	9.0	2.3
1956	69.9[c]	17.2[c]	7.2	4.1		1.6
1957	84.2[c]	7.9[c]	5.1	1.1		1.7
1958	68.4[c]	16.2[c]	12.2	2.0		1.2
1959	66.5[c]	16.9[c]	14.1	1.7		0.8

a. Transferred through the Bezirke.
b. Payments for property taken from the party during the period of Nazi rule.
c. From 1953 on a special assessment for the election was included in the figures for dues.

Sources: Klaus Schütz, in Lange et al., *Parteien in der Bundesrepublik,* and SPD Yearbooks.

1. For a recent table showing dues assessed according to income levels, see *Jahrbuch der SPD, 1958–59,* p. 257. Unless otherwise noted, other figures in this appendix are from this source.

As of 1959, 80.5 per cent of all dues payments came from members in the lowest income brackets.

Table 2

30 Pfennigs (about 7.5¢) per month—for people in especially straitened circumstances (abolished in 1958) —0.1% of dues payments

60 Pfennigs (15¢) per month—for invalids, unemployed, and pensioners with very small incomes—41.1% of dues payments

1.20 Marks (30¢) per month—for persons with up to 300 DM ($75) monthly income—39.3% of dues payments

Above 1.20 Marks—19.5% of dues payments

Whether or not members always pay the full amount called for, the average rate of collection is high—about 94 per cent. The average member pays his dues 11.3 out of 12 times a year. He would lose his membership if he missed payments three months in a row.[2]

In addition to this regular source of income, the party collects from its members for many special purposes. On these occasions also, collections are made by selling stamps which are affixed in the membership book. The largest of these are the special collections for election campaigns. For the 1961 election campaign, for example, stamps were sold in denominations of 1, 2, 5, and 10 DM.[3] Other special stamps are sold in the Bezirke, for general purposes such as propaganda and political education and for special campaigns such as the "Anti-Atom Action" in 1958. These extra payments are reputed to be "semi-mandatory." At times, especially in election years, they may constitute a much higher proportion of total income than regular dues payments.

2. Organization statute, Article 8.
3. *eilt,* May 1961.

In 1957, for example, the executive received about 1.2 million DM from dues and about 4.7 million DM from special levies. Therefore, although the party still lives primarily on income from its members, their payments are made not only in the form of dues but also in extra contributions that usually provide over half, and sometimes much more than half, of the party's income.

The next source of income listed in Table 1 is the levy paid by the party members of the various parliaments out of their salaries. Dating from a period that called for a material symbol of the subordination of parliamentary delegates to party discipline, as well as their solidarity with the movement as a whole, this practice, as the table shows, has over the last ten years provided from 5 to 14 per cent of the total income of the party executive.

The figures for "Contributions" in Table 1 stand for contributions from individuals and groups, a system that is similar to the one in the United States. The percentage of total income represented by this category rose to a maximum of 9.5 per cent in 1953 and then fell back to around 2 per cent in later years. It is almost impossible to find out just how much these contributions amount to in all, since many of them are given not to the executive but to party organizations in the Länder[4] (many of the SPD leaders in Land governments have probably been more successful than the national executive in winning friends among people who have money to contribute) and, too, because money may be given to individuals rather than to the party organization and therefore not appear in the published tallies. Another source of income not mentioned is the money paid by the Land governments to the party for education and youth activities. Most observers agree, however, that hidden sources of income constitute a small portion of the total.

Looking at the manner in which the party money is spent, a rough generalization would be that for both the Bezirke and the national organizations expenses are divided almost evenly into two categories—first, propaganda and campaign costs, and

4. On contributions in general, see Klaus Schütz, in Lange et al., *Parteien in der Bundesrepublik*, p. 193.

secondly, administrative costs, including both salaries and equipment. About 20 per cent of the latter covers travel and convention expenses, loudspeaker systems, and the like.

Recently there has been a trend to devote a higher percentage (almost 65 per cent) of the budget to elections and propaganda. This was the case in 1959, which was not even an election year. It can be attributed to the increasing use of the mass media and the greater and greater importance being given in national elections to the general "image" managed from the center. This trend is not evident in the Bezirk organizations where in some cases the administrative costs outweigh the propaganda costs.[5]

In summary, one can still describe the SPD as financially dependent on its membership. The rising cost of publicity and the increasing use of centrally managed propaganda are beginning to shift the balance in the outlays of the party, with the bureaucracy taking proportionally (although not absolutely) less of the budget.

The party remains financially independent and can remain so as long as prosperity and recruitment of new members keeps pace. The mounting demands of competition with the far richer CDU campaign machine, however, may ultimately force the party to search for other sources of income.

5. See Bezirk yearbooks listed in the bibliography; also Schütz, in Lange et al., p. 195.

Bibliography

Yearbooks of the Social Democratic Party

National

Jahrbuch der Sozialdemokratischen Partei Deutschlands, for the
years 1946, 1947, 1948–49, 1950–51, 1952–53, 1954–55,
1956–57, and 1958–59 (Hannover until 1950, then Bonn,
various dates).

Bezirke

SPD Bezirk Braunschweig, *Rechenschaftsbericht*
SPD Bezirk Franken, *Jahresbericht, 1958*
SPD Bezirk Franken, *Jahresbericht, 1959*
SPD Bezirk Hamburg-Nordwest, *Jahresbericht, 1958–59*
SPD Bezirk Hannover, *Rechenschaftsbericht Bezirksparteitag, 1958*
SPD Bezirk Hessen-Süd, *Aus der Arbeit eines Jahres: Jahresbericht, 1958*
SPD Bezirk Hessen-Süd, *Sozialdemokratische Politik in Hessen-Süd: Jahresbericht, 1959*
SPD Bezirk Mittel-Rhein, *Bezirksparteitag, 1958*
SPD Bezirk Nord-Hessen, *Bezirksparteitag Bad Hersfeld, 1958*
SPD Bezirk Östwestfalen-Lippe, *Jahresbericht, 1956–57*
SPD Bezirk Rheinhessen, 9. *Bezirksparteitag, 22–23 März 1958*
SPD Bezirk Schleswig-Holstein, *Jahresbericht, 1955–56*
SPD Bezirk Südbayern, *Geschäftsbericht, 1956–57*

BIBLIOGRAPHY

SPD Bezirk Südwest, *Arbeitsbericht, 1956–57*
SPD Bezirk Weser-Ems, *Geschäftsbericht, 1956–57*
SPD Bezirk Westliches-Westfalen, *Bezirksparteitag, 1957*
SPD Bezirk Westliches-Westfalen, *Jahrbuch, 1959*

Other

SPD Landesverband Berlin, *Jahresbericht, 1957–58*
SPD Landesverband Berlin, *Jahresbericht, 1959* (*Zwischenbericht*)
SPD Unterbezirk Frankfurt/Main, *Jahresbericht, 1959*
SPD Landesorganisation Hamburg, *Jahresbericht, 1956–57*
SPD Landesorganisation Hamburg, *Jahresbericht, 1958–59*
SPD Unterbezirk München, *Jahresbericht, 1958*
SPD Unterbezirk Stade (Bezirk Hamburg-Nordwest), *Jahresbericht, 1958–59*

Protocols of Party Congresses

Protokoll der Verhandlungen des Parteitages der Sozialdemokratischen Partei Deutschlands for congresses held on the following dates: 1946, 1947, 1948, 1950, 1952, 1954, 1956, 1958, 1959 (Extraordinary Congress) (title varies slightly)

Pamphlets Issued by the SPD Executive

Programs

Aktionsprogramm der Sozialdemokratischen Partei Deutschlands: Beschlossen auf dem Dortmunder Parteitag am 28. September 1952, Erweitert auf dem Berliner Parteitag am 24. Juli 1954, Mit einem Vorwort von Dr. Kurt Schumacher, Bonn, 1954
Basic Programme of the Social Democratic Party of Germany (Bonn, 1959) (also, in German, in *Protokoll, 1959*)
Handbuch Sozialdemokratischer Politik, Bonn, 1953
Programme der deutschen Sozialdemokratie (Schriftenreihe der Jungsozialisten, March 1959) Bonn, 1959
A Programme for Government, presented by Willy Brandt, gov-

erning mayor of Berlin and chancellor-candidate, on April 28, 1961, at Bonn, Bonn 1961

Other

Agrarpolitische Richtlinien der SPD, Bonn, 1960
Die Alternative unserer Zeit: Auseinandersetzung der Sozial-demokratie mit dem Kommunismus, Bonn, 1960
Deutschlandplan der SPD: Kommentare, Argumente, Begrun-dung, Bonn, 1959
Das IXI der Politischen Werbung, Berlin, 1954
Empfehlung des Parteivorstandes und des Parteiausschüsses zur Parteidiskussion, Bonn, n.d., probably 1954
Gesundheitssicherung in unserer Zeit, Bonn, 1959
Handbuch für Frauengruppen-Leiterinnen, n.p., n.d.
Handbuch für die Ortsvereine, Berlin, 1924, 1930
Herner Beschlüsse: Arbeitsaufgaben für die SPD, Bonn, 1952
Informationsmaterial zur Kommunalpolitik, Bonn, n.d.
Das Junge Mädchen und die Junge Frau in unserer Zeit, SPD Schriftenreihe für Frauenfragen Nr. 5, Bonn, 1959
Jungsozialisten in der SPD, Arbeits- und Organisationsrichtlinien, Bonn, 1959
Der Katholik und die SPD, Bonn, 1959
Der Kleine Wahlhelfer, n.p., n.d.
Kleines Versammlungs ABC, n.p., n.d.
Kleines Wahlkampf ABC, n.p., n.d.
Mitglieder werben—leichter gemacht, Bonn, 1957
Organisationsstatut der Sozialdemokratischen Partei Deutsch-lands, Bonn, 1955
Das Plakat, n.p., n.d.
A Policy for Germany, Speech by Willy Brandt to the Hannover Party Congress, November 25, 1960, Bonn, 1960
Propagandakatalog, n.p., n.d.
Richtlinien für Betriebsgruppenarbeit, Bonn, 1959
Die Selbständigen—Heute und Morgen, Die Schriftenreihe des selbständig Schaffenden Nr. 2, Bonn, 1959
Sozialplan für Deutschland, Berlin and Hannover, 1957

Die technischen Hilfsmittel—unser Helfer, n.p., n.d.
Unser Wahlhelfer, Bonn, 1953
Wir Wollen Was Werden, Bonn, 1959
Die Zukunft Meistern, Arbeitsmaterial zum Thema: Wissenschaft
   und Forschung, Erziehung und Bildung in unserer Zeit, Berlin
   and Hannover, 1959

Periodicals and Newspapers from, or close to, the SPD

Arbeit und Freiheit (monthly)
Die Debatte (irregular)
Die Demokratische Gemeinde (monthly)
eilt: Sozialdemokratischer Brief (monthly)
Geist und Tat (monthly)
Gewerkschaftliche Monatshefte (monthly)
Klarer Kurs: Monatsschrift für die Junge Generation (monthly)
Die Kochel Briefe (from the Georg Vollmar School)
Kommunalpolitische Rundschau für das Land Hessen (monthly)
Mitteilungsblatt, SPD Bezirk Hessen-Süd Jungsozialisten
   (monthly)
Neue Gesellschaft (monthly)
News from Germany (monthly)
Rundbrief: Information über sozialdemokratische Betriebsarbeit
   (Bezirk Hessen-Süd)
Schleswig-Holstein Post–Der Weckruf (monthly)
Der Sozialdemokrat (Bezirk Hessen-Süd) (monthly)
Sozialdemokratischer Betriebsräte-Brief (monthly)
Sozialdemokratischer Personalräte-Brief (monthly)
*Der Sozialist: Monatliches Mitteilungsblatt Landesorganisation
   Hamburg* (monthly)
Das Sozialistische Jahrhundert (biweekly, Berlin, in 1940s)
Sozialistische Politik (bimonthly)—An opposition newsletter
Sozialistische Tribune (monthly, in 1940s, from Frankfurt)
Das Sprachrohr der Automobilarbeiter (monthly)—Special news-
   paper for Social Democratic workers at the Opel automobile
   factory

BIBLIOGRAPHY

Volksstimme, Mitteilungsblatt der Sozialdemokratischen Partei
Gross-Hessen (1946)
Vorwärts, Sozialdemokratische Wochenzeitung für Politik Wirt-
schaft und Kultur (weekly)—Before 1955 known as *Neue
Vorwärts*

Newspapers, Non-SPD

Frankfurter Allgemeine Zeitung
Frankfurter Rundschau
Hamburger Echo
Das Parlament (weekly)
Der Spiegel (weekly)
Die Welt (Hamburg)
Die Zeit (Hamburg, weekly)

General, from SPD Sources

"Arbeitsgemeinschaft sozialdemokratische Akademiker," *Das
Weltbild unserer Zeit,* Nürnberg, SPD, 1954
*Beitrag zur Erneurung der Sozialdemokratischen Partei Deutsch-
lands,* Vorgelegt von jungen Sozialdemokraten des SPD Unter-
bezirk Hamm, Hamm, SPD, n.d., probably 1953
Bieligk, Fritz, et al., *Die Organisation im Klassenkampf,* Berlin,
n.d., probably 1931
Birkelbach, Willi, *Die Grosse Chance:* Diskussionsbeitrage zum
Thema "Demokratischer Sozialismus," Frankfurt, SPD, 1956
Brandt, Leo, *Die Zweite Industrielle Revolution,* Munich, SPD,
1957
Brandt, Willy, *Programmatische Grundlagen des demokratischen
Sozialismus,* Berlin, SPD, 1949
———, *Mein Weg nach Berlin* (aufgezeichnet von Leo Lania),
Munich, Kindler, 1960
Brauer, Max, *Grundsatzliches zur sozialdemokratischen Gemein-
depolitik,* Bonn, SPD, 1956
David, Eduard, *Referenten Führer,* Berlin, SPD, 1907, 1908,
1911, 1919, and 1930

Eichler, Willi, *Lebendige Demokratie: Vom Wesen und Wirken der SPD,* Bonn, SPD, 1957
———, *Der Weg in die Freiheit,* Bonn, SPD, 1955
Erler, Fritz, *Sozialismus als Gegenwartsaufgabe,* Schwenningen, Neckar Verlag, 1947
Ernst Reuter Briefe (Berlin, SPD, 1954)—7 of these appeared irregularly
Franck, Sebastian, *Zur Kritik der politischen Moral,* Schriftenreihe: Wege zum Sozialismus, Heft 3, Offenbach a. Main, Bollwerk, 1947
Jaksch, Wenzel, *Sozialistische Möglichkeiten unserer Zeit,* Offenbach a. Main, Bollwerk, 1947
Kraft, Emil, *80 Jahre Arbeiterbewegung zwischen Meer und Moor,* Oldenburg, 1952
Landesorganisation Hamburg, *Vorstoss zum Volkstaat in Hamburg 1927–1931,* Hamburg, SPD, 1931
Laufenberg, Heinrich, *Geschichte der Arbeiterbewegung in Hamburg, Altona und Umgegend,* 2 vols. Hamburg, Auer, 1911
Die Linke: Sozialistische Informationen zur Ausprache und Kritik (Munich, 1954)—Journal, appeared twice, February and July
19 Thesen für die parteiinterne Diskussion (mimeo.)—Pamphlet issued in 1953 by the executive of the SPD Bezirk Süd-West
Ortlieb, Heinz-Dietrich, *Die Aufgabe der SPD in unserer Zeit,* specially printed by the DGB from the *Gewerkschaftliche Monatshefte,* October 1953
Oschilewski, Walther G., Ernst Paul, and Peter Raunau, *Erich Ollenhauer, der Führer der Opposition,* Berlin, Arani, 1953
Osterroth, Franz, *Chronik der Sozialistischen Bewegung Deutschlands,* Bonn, SPD, n.d., probably 1957
Reuter, Ernst, *Grundsätze und Ziele der Sozialdemokratie,* Berlin, SPD, 1947
Scholz, Arno, and Walther Oschilewski, *Aufgabe und Leistung der Sozialdemokratie,* Berlin, Arani, 1957
Schult, Johannes, *Die Hamburger Arbeiterbewegung als Kulturfaktor,* Hamburg, Hamburger Druckereigesellschaft, n.d., probably 1954

Schulz, Klaus-Peter, *Opposition als Politisches Schicksal?* Cologne, Verlag für Politik und Wirtschaft, 1958
————, *Sorge um die deutschen Linke*, Cologne, Verlag für Politik und Wirtschaft, 1954
Schumacher, Kurt, *Turmwächter der Demokratie: Ein Lebensbild von Kurt Schumacher, 2, Reden und Schriften*, Berlin, Arani, 1953
Specht, Minna, *Sozialismus als Lebenshaltung und Erziehungsaufgabe*, Fulda, SPD, 1951
Stammer, Otto, *Die Freiheit des Menschen in der industriellen Gesellschaft*, Munich, SPD, n.d., probably 1958
Thiemer, Walter, *Von Bebel zu Ollenhauer: Der Weg der deutschen Sozialdemokratie*, Munich, SPD, 1957
Wehner, Herbert, *Die Arbeiterfrage im Grundsatzprogramm der SPD*, Bonn, SPD, n.d., probably 1960
————, *Das Gemeinsame und das Trennende*, Bonn, SPD, 1960
————, and Heinrich Deist, *Selbständig Schaffende und Sozialdemokratische Politik*, Bonn, SPD, 1959
Weisser, Gerhard, *Der Europäische Mensch unter dem Einfluss der Industrialisierung*, Cologne, Land Nordrhein-Westfalen, 1959
Wesemann, Fried, *Kurt Schumacher, Ein Leben für Deutschland*, Frankfurt, Herkul, 1952
Winkler, Erich, *Die Politik und ihre Gesetze*, Jena, K. Zwing, 1930

General, Non-SPD

Alleman, Fritz Rene, *Bonn ist nicht Weimar*, Cologne, Krepenheuer und Witsch, 1956
Almond, Gabriel A., ed., *The Struggle for Democracy in Germany*, Chapel Hill, University of North Carolina Press, 1949
————, and James A. Coleman, *Politics of the Developing Areas*, Princeton, Princeton University Press, 1960
Bergstraesser, Ludwig, *Geschichte der politischen Parteien in Deutschland*, Munich, G. Olzog, 1960

Berlau, A. J., *The German Social Democratic Party, 1914–1921,* New York, Columbia University Press, 1949

Breitling, Rupert, *Die Verbände in der Bundesrepublik,* Meisenheim, A. Hain, 1955

Dahrendorf, Ralf, *Soziale Klassen und Klassenkonflikt,* Stuttgart, Ferdinand Eiche Verlag, 1957

Deutsch, Karl W., and Lewis J. Edinger, *Germany Rejoins the Powers,* Stanford, Stanford University Press, 1959

DIVO, *Basic Orientation and Political Thinking of West German Youth and Their Leaders: Report on a Survey* (Frankfurt, 1956) (mimeo.)

——, *Fragen und Antworten: Ergebnis einer Meinungsbefragung* (Frankfurt, 1957) (mimeo.)

——, *SPD, Eine Politische Studie* (Frankfurt, 1956) (mimeo.)

——, *Untersuchung der Wählerschaft und Wahlentscheidung 1957* (Frankfurt, 1958) (mimeo.)

Duverger, Maurice, *Political Parties,* London, Methuen, 1954

Edinger, Lewis J., *German Exile Politics,* Berkeley, University of California Press, 1956

Eschenburg, Theodor, *Herrschaft der Verbände?* Stuttgart, 1955

——, *Statt und Gesellschaft in Deutschland,* Stuttgart, C. E. Schwab, 1956

Flechtheim, Ossip K., *Die Deutschen Parteien seit 1945,* Berlin, C. Heymann, 1955

Gay, Peter, *The Dilemma of Democratic Socialism,* New York, Columbia University Press, 1952

Golay, John F., *The Founding of the Federal Republic of Germany,* Chicago, University of Chicago Press, 1958

Grosser, Alfred, *La demokratie de Bonn,* Paris, A. Colin, 1958

Heidenheimer, Arnold J., *Adenauer and the CDU,* The Hague, M. Nijhoff, 1961

Heydte, F. A., and K. Sacherl, *Soziologie der deutschen Parteien,* Munich, Isar, 1955

Hirsch-Weber, Wolfgang, *Gewerkschaften in der Politik,* Cologne, Westdeutscher, 1959

——, et al., *Wähler und Gewählte,* Berlin, F. Vahlen, 1957

Hiscocks, Richard, *Democracy in Western Germany,* London, Oxford University Press, 1957

Kaiser, J. H., *Die Repräsentation organisierter Interessen,* Berlin, Duncker and Humboldt, 1956

Kirchheimer, Otto, "The Political Scene in West Germany," *World Politics, 9,* April 1957

————, "The Waning of the Opposition in Parliamentary Regimes," *Social Research,* Summer 1957

Kitzinger, Uwe, *German Electoral Politics,* Oxford, Oxford University Press, 1960

Kosyk, Kurt, *Zwischen Kaiserreich und Diktatur: Die Sozialdemokratische Presse von 1914 bis 1933,* Heidelberg, Quelle and Meyer, 1958

Kuby, Erich, *Das ist des deutschen Vaterland,* Stuttgart, Scherz and Goverts, 1957

Lange, Max Gustav, et al., *Parteien in der Bundesrepublik,* Schriften des Instituts für Politisches Wissenschaft, Stuttgart, Ring Verlag, 1955

Lipset, Seymour Martin, *Political Man,* New York, Doubleday, 1960

Litchfield, Edward, et al., *Governing Post-War Germany,* Ithaca, Cornell University Press, 1953

Matthias, Erich, *Sozialdemokratie und Nation,* Stuttgart, Deutsche Verlags-Anstalt, 1952

Meyer, Heinz, "Zur Struktur der deutschen Sozialdemokratie," *Zeitschrift für Politik,* No. 12 (1955)

Morgenthau, Hans, ed., *Germany and the Future of Europe,* Chicago, University of Chicago Press, 1951

Münke, Stephanie, *Wahlkampf und Machtverschiebung,* Berlin, Duncker and Humboldt, 1952

Neumann, Sigmund, *Die deutschen Parteien,* Berlin, Junker and Dünnhaupt, 1932

————, ed., *Modern Political Parties,* Chicago, University of Chicago Press, 1956

Pinson, Koppel S., *Modern Germany,* New York, Macmillan, 1954

Ritter, Gerhard A., *Die Arbeiterbewegung im Wilhelminischer Reich,* Berlin, Coloquium Verlag, 1959

Rosenberg, Arthur, *A History of the German Republic,* London, Methuen, 1936

Roth, Götz, *Fraktion und Regierungsbildung,* Meisenheim, A. Hain, 1954

Schorske, Carl, *German Social Democracy, 1905–1917,* Cambridge, Harvard University Press, 1955

Speier, Hans, and W. P. Davison, eds., *West German Leadership and Foreign Policy,* Evanston, Northwestern University Press, 1957

Treue, Wolfgang, *Deutsche Parteiprogramme, 1861–1956,* Göttingen, Musterschmidt, 1956

Uhlig, A. W., *Hat die SPD noch eine Chance?* Munich, Isar Verlag, 1956

Wallich, Henry C., *Mainsprings of the German Revival,* New Haven, Yale University Press, 1955

Wildenmann, Rudolf, *Partei und Fraktion,* Meisenheim, A. Hain, 1954

Zimdahl, Hans Heinrich, *Wirtschaftssysteme und Parteiprogramme,* Baden-Baden, Lutzeyer, 1955

Index

Abendroth, Wolfgang, 75 n., 112, 126 n., 207–08

Adenauer, Konrad, 18, 110, 145, 203, 205; on the SPD, 7; and *1957* election, 63–64; influence on chancellorship, 100; Brandt as challenge to, 148; effect on SPD, 211–12; autocratic tendencies, 230

Advisory groups, 168–70

Agartz, Victor, 66

Age, and voting preferences, 202

"Agenda" of politics, 23–27

Aktionsprogramm (1952), 57–60, 61–62, 92

Albertz, Luis, 117 n.

Allgemeiner Deutscher Arbeiterverein, 4

Almond, Gabriel, cited, 40

American political parties, 43, 45, 51

Anticommunism, SPD, 91, 220. *See also* Communism

Apparat: influence protested, 113–14; and changes in party leadership, 144–45

Arbeit und Freiheit, 180 n.

Arbeiterbildungsvereine, 4

Arbeitsgemeinschaft selbständig Schaffender, 106, 111, 172

Arbeitsgemeinschaft sozialdemokratischer Akademiker, 170 n.

Arbeitsgemeinschaften, 124–25, 138, 164–65, 167, 168, 184; role of in party organization, 170–80

Arbeitskreise, 116, 169–70; listed, 122

Arenas of politics, 38–40

Arp, Erich, 78

Aufruf, Schumacher's *(1945)*, 16

Bad Godesberg. *See* Congresses, *1959* (Godesberg); Godesberg Program

Basic Law (Bonn Republic), 100, 219

Bebel, August, 4, 10, 140

Bergneustadt School, 191

Berlin, 11; blockade, 15, 220; postwar party struggle in, 15, 159–60; party organization, 124 n., 168, 169, 171; and rise of Willy Brandt, 146–47; SPD anticommunist action in, 220

Bernstein, Eduard, 5, 8, 98

Betriebsgruppe. See Factory groups

Bevan, Aneurin, 137

Bezirke: organizational structure, 118–19, 165–89; listed, 119; in party policy making, 120; representation in party council, 131, in party congress, 133; executives, 132; educational activities, 192; finances, 235–39. *See also* Regional organization, SPD

Birkelbach, Willy, 67, 75, 92 n., 117 n., 126 n., 158, 159

Bismarck, 4, 6, 7, 11, 103, 214

Bogler, Franz, 117 n.

Brandt, Willy, 132, 139, 142, 155; on foreign policy, 94; attitude toward other elites, 104; rise in SPD, 145–50; compared to Schumacher, 148; on Reuter, 159; and woman's vote, 177; effect on party image, 222, 223

Brauer, Max, 59, 60, 149, 158–59, 160
Braune, Heinrich, 107 n., 212 n., 220
Brenner, Otto, 137
British Labor Party, 19, 136, 138 n., 228–29
Bundestag, 33, 116, 117, 143. See also *Fraktion*
Bureaucracy. See *Apparat*
Bürgermeister-faktion, 59–60
Burgfrieden, 103
"Buro Schumacher," 15, 16
Businessmen, SPD and, 32, 150, 172

CDU. *See* Christian Democratic Union
"Cadre" party, 52
Campaigns, 28 n.; SPD attitude toward, 157–58; financing, 237
Candidates: SPD, 145–50; list, 156–57; constituency, 156–57
Catholic Church, and SPD, 213–19
Catholics, voting preferences, 201
Center Party, 214
"Central Committee" (Berlin), 15
Chancellorship, 100–01. *See also* Adenauer
"Child Protective Commissions," 12
Christian Democratic Union (CDU), 110, 145, 198; *Wirtschaftswunder,* 18; seen as threat to Germany, 89; on SPD power aspirations, 102; effect on political elites, 103; *Hilfstruppen,* 163; youth group, 175; and workers' vote, 177–79; voters compared with SPD, 200–05; as SPD opponent, 205; and the churches, 215–16
Churches: SPD attitude toward, 65, 213–19; use of by CDU, 163
Class movement party, SPD as, 21–34, 39, 112, 162–63
Coalitions: SPD attitude toward, 101, 104 n., 108
Cold War: effect on SPD, 27, 91; SPD policy regarding, 223. *See also* Foreign policy
Committee for the Reorganization of the Top of the Party, 117 n.
Committees, SPD, 120–24, 168–69

Communications: effect of changes on politics, 27–31, on SPD, 113. *See also* Mass media
Communism: SPD accused of being soft on, 94; and SPD image, 110. *See also* Anticommunism
Communist Party (KPD), 10, 15, 202; split off from SPD, 11; postwar party struggle in Berlin, 15; effect on SPD, 89–90, 220–21; activity in factories, 177–78; misuse of SPD symbols, 197
Congress of German Cities, 182
Congress of German Towns, 182
Congress, party, 9; role in policy making, 133–37
Congresses: *1890* (Halle), 7, 9; *1891* (Erfurt), 7, 8, 11; *1946* (Hannover), 16, 17; *1948* (Düsseldorf), 56 n.; *1950* (Hamburg), 64 n.; *1952* (Dortmund), 141; *1954* (Berlin), 61–62; *1956* (Munich), 64, 111; *1958* (Stuttgart), 64–65, 66 n., 81, 115 n., 144, 145, 179–80; *1959* (Godesberg), 66–67, 147 n., 209 n. (*see also* Godesberg Program); *1960* (Hannover), 147, 223
"Constructive vote of confidence," 100
"Corporate" party, 51
Council, party: membership, 131–32; role in policy making, 131–33
Cousins, Frank, 137, 228
Cultural Policy Committee (of SPD executive), 57

DGB. *See* German Labor Union Federation
Defense, SPD and, 65, 91, 222
Deist, Heinrich, 65, 116, 117, 150, 153, 155
Democracy: as SPD goal, 89; within SPD, 113, 128–29
Demokratische Gemeinde, Die, 181
Deutsche Gewerkschaftbund, 177
Deutschlandplan, 93–95, 222–23
Discipline, SPD, 129–30
Distrikten, 131 n.
Dues, 163, 165, 183, 235–38
Duverger, Maurice, 43, 232

INDEX

East Germany, SPD policy toward, 221. See also *Deutschlandplan;* Reunification
Eastern Zone, 15
Ebert, Frederick, 140
Economic inequality, as SPD interest, 89
Economic policy, SPD, 87
Economic prosperity: effect on SPD, 26, 60; effect on politics, 205
Education: SPD interest in, 92, 93; by the party, 184, 190–93
Eichler, Willy, 145 n., 217; on need for new SPD program, 55; on party ideology, 75, 76
eilt, 118
Eisenachers, 4, 6
Elections: *1949,* 19; *1953,* 57, 60, 142, 202; *1957,* 63, 64, 111, 117, 143, 177, 179, 219–20; *1961,* 94; as means to power, 96–97; SPD, 155; work of Young Socialists, 174–75; role of local party organizations, 185; postwar figures, 200–01; financing for, 237
Electoral law, 156
Electorate: analyzed, 200–05; SPD's alternatives for influencing, 205–12. *See also* Voters
Elite, party: recruitment of, 154–61; identified, 155. *See also* Leaders
Elites, SPD relations with, 103–04
Employees, voting preferences, 201
Erfurterprogramm, 7–8, 11
Erhard, Ludwig, 18, 55, 205, 212
Erler, Fritz, 65, 116, 117, 135 n., 143, 144, 150, 153, 155, 163 n., 224; on ideology, 72, 74, 76; interest in defense, 64, 91; on SPD power aspirations, 101–02; on Adenauer, 103; slander against SPD, 111
Executive, party, 9, 133; and new program, 57, 62, 66; as policy-making organ, 115–21; committees of, 120–21; election of, 134; and leadership changes, 143; issue of paid members, 144; composition, 155; influence in party elections, 155–56; income, 236
Executive Committee (exiled), 15

Executives: *Fraktion,* 116, 155, 156; local, 119, 185
Experts, in SPD, 77, 153
Expulsion, from SPD, 193, 221

Factory groups, 177–80, 184; recruiting of new members, 188 n.; educational activity, 191
Farmers, voting preferences, 201
Federal government, in postwar Germany, 100–01
Finance policy, SPD interest in, 93
Finances, SPD, 235–39. *See also* Dues; Income
Foreign policy: SPD interest, 91, 92, 93, 94–95, 142; SPD positions on, 110 n., 205, 222; at local party level, 120
Fraktion, 9, 133; interest in defense and foreign policy, 91; as policy-making organ, 114–17, 120–24; executive, 116, 155, 156; committees, 121–23; leadership changes, 143–44
France, Socialist party, 228
Franke, Egon, 117 n.
Frankfurt, 107, 131 n., 158; Young Socialists, 174
Free Democrats, 200

Gaitskill, Hugh, 228
Georg Vollmar School, 191
German Labor Union Federation (DGB), 137, 150, 207 n., 208, 215
Germany: changes affecting SPD, 24–27, 37–38, 54; possible types of parties, 50–52
Gesellschaft, 127
Goals. *See* Objectives
Godesberg Program, 57, 61, 62, 64–88; defended by Wehner, 90–91; significance, 91–92; opposition to, 112; executive's responsibility for, 118; local party discussions, 187; on cooperation with churches, 217–18; on defense, 222; and the party image, 224
Gotha *(1875),* 4
Gotha Program, 5, 6
Gotthelf, Herta, 144, 177

Hamburg, 11, 107, 131 n., 158, 165 n., 212 n.
Hauskassierer, 183, 235
Heck, Bruno, 102
Heine, Fritz, 117 n., 144
Hessen-Süd, 158, 160; Young Socialists, 174; Academy for Communal Policy, 181
Heuss, Theodor, 145

Ideology, of political parties, 44–45
Ideology, SPD, 6; Revisionist vs. Radical debates, 8, 10; outdated in 1950s, 19; absence of in Godesberg Program, 67–72; in policy making, 72–77; and party unity, 77–80; and the public, 80–83; role of party congress in determining, 135; influence on party policy, 137. See also Program
Image, SPD, 138, 140, 205; attempts to improve, 93, 109–12, 211–13, 219–25
Income, SPD, 1914, 11. See also Dues; Finances
Information, SPD organization for, 120–28
Intellectuals: in SPD, 59, 127, 152–53, 169–70; in SPD and British Labor Party compared, 137
"Intelligence" process, in politics, 40–41, 48
Interest groups: in German political system, 31–34; SPD relations with, 105–08, 138, 182; SPD meetings of, 184. See also Arbeitsgemeinschaften
"Iron law of oligarchy," 50, 70–72
Italy, Socialist party, 228

Jaksch, Wenzel, 150
Journals, SPD, 127. See also eilt; Gesellschaft; Neue Gesellschaft; Neue Zeit
Junge Union, 175
Jungsozialisten. See Young Socialists

KPD. See Communist Party
Kaisen, Wilhelm, 59

Kautsky, Karl, 10
Khrushchev, Nikita, SPD attitude toward, 94
Kitzinger, Uwe, cited, 156–57, 224
Kommunalpolitiker, 87, 104–05, 180–83
Kommunistische Partei Deutschlands. See Communist Party
Kontaktgespräche, 124, 138
Kontrollkommission, 133
Kukil, Max, 117 n.

Labor movement, 3 ff., 89–90. See also Working class
Labor unions. See Trade unions
Länder: politics, 17; and SPD organization, 118–19. See also Regional organization
Länderausschusse, 118
Länderkonferenzen, 118
Landtage, 116
Lassalle, Ferdinand, 4, 5, 6, 21, 103, 140
Lassalleaners, 4, 97
Lasswell, Harold, cited, 40
Leaders: effect on of communications revolution, 29; SPD, 15–16, 31, 64, 135, 139–61; recruitment of, 36–38, 48–49. See also Elite; Elites
League of Expellees, 204
Left, 15, 79, 83; in SPD and British Labor Party compared, 136–37; resistance to changes, 206–09. See also Militants; Radicals
Legien, Carl, 9
Legislation, as solution to problems, 89
Lenin, 21 n., 98 n.
Liebknecht, Wilhelm, 4, 140
Linke, Die, 80 n.
Lobbying, 33
Local interests, in SPD organization, 180–83
Local party organizations, 157–58, 183–89. See also Regional organization
Lohmar, Ulrich, 77
Lübke, Heinrich, 145

Mannschaft. See Team
Marxian theory: in SPD ideology, 6, 7–8, 23, 27, 57, 59, 61, 62 n., 65, 68, 73, 76, 89; among workers, 26–27; on power, 97; on elites, 103; in Young Socialists, 174; on party members, 196; return to advocated, 207–08
Mass media, effect on local party organizations, 188–89. *See also* Communications
Mellies, Wilhelm, 117 n., 143, 144
Membership, SPD, 193–99; figures, 9, 11, 13, 18–19, 194; after World War II, 14–15; activity in local organizations, 186; age distribution, 195; social background, 195
Membership book, 235, 237
Membership patterns in political parties, 49
Metzger, Ludwig, 214, 217
Michels, Robert, 78 n., 128, 130, 135, 196. *See also* "Iron law of oligarchy"
Middle classes, and SPD, 107, 111, 172, 209–10
Militants, 49–50; SPD, 78, 79, 114, 142, 146, 147
Mitgliedsbuch, 235, 237
Möller, Alex, 150
Movement party. *See* Class movement party
Müller, Hermann, 140

NATO, SPD policy on, 205, 222, 223
Nationalization: SPD attitude toward, 65, 76, 87, 92, 99, 205; advocated by DGB, 207 n.
Nau, Alfred, 117, 143, 145 n.
Nazis, and SPD, 14, 74, 90, 210
Nazism, socialist interpretation of, 92 n.
Nell-Bruening, Oswald, 55 n., 218
Neue Gesellschaft, 127
Neue Zeit, 10, 127
Neumann, Franz, 146, 147, 159
Newspapers, SPD, 11. *See also* Journals; Press
"Notables, party of," 48, 51

Objectives, SPD, 83–95. *See also* Ideology; Power; Program
Occupation authorities, 18; and political activity, 14–15, 17; policies on media, 28, 54
Ohlig, Fritz, 117 n.
Ollenhauer, Erich, 63, 64, 116, 117, 133, 155; as speaker, 109; object of reformers, 114; as party leader, 142–51 passim; on party symbols, 197
Opposition parties, 34, 48
Organization of SPD, 5, 9, 11–13, 113–38, 162–93. *See also* Structure
Organization statute, SPD, 17, 115 n., 131, 132 n., 133, 144, 165, 193
Organs, SPD, 115–38
Ortsvereine, 131, 165, 183–89

Pacifism, and SPD, 18, 222
Papal Encyclical "Quadrigesimo Anno," 216, 218
Parliamentary delegation. See *Fraktion*
Parteiausschuss, 132
Parteirat. See Council
Parteitag. See Congress
Parteivorstand. See Executive
Partido Revolucionario Institutional (PRI, Mexico), 51 n.
Parties, political: and the political system, 36–42; structure, 42–50; types, 50–52
Party bureaucracy. See *Apparat*
Party leaders. *See* Leaders
Pensioners, voting preferences, 201
"Plan Z," 93
Planning, as SPD goal, 99
Pluralist approach of SPD, 213
Policy, SPD. *See* Ideology; Objectives; Program
Policy making: in a political system, 36–38; in political parties, 46–48; in SPD, 72–77, 113–38 passim
Political elite, as a political arena, 38
Politics, functions of, 40–42
Popularity, and SPD leaders, 153–54
Power: as SPD goal, 22, 96–112; as goal of political parties, 45–46
Pragmatism, in SPD, 88

INDEX

Presidium, SPD, 124, 125; functions, 117; election to, 156
Press, SPD, 17, 19
Pressure group, SPD as before World War I, 98, 99
Pressure groups. *See* Interest groups
Problem areas of interest to SPD, 88–95
Professional groups, and SPD, 107, 171–72
Program, SPD: before *1953,* 10–11, 16–17, 18, 53–60; *1953–57,* 60–64; after *1957,* 64–67; *1958* draft, on ideology, 77; at local party level, 120. *See also* Ideology; Objectives
Propaganda, SPD, 81–82, 108–09
Property, private, SPD attitude toward, 65, 70, 76
Protestant church, and SPD, 213–15
Protestants, voting preferences, 201
Public, the: SPD ideology and, 80–83, attitude toward, 108–12, relations with, 200–25
Public opinion: as political force, 28–29; as political arena, 38. *See also* Image
Public relations approach of SPD, 213

Radical socialism, 11
Radical Socialist Party (France), 39
Radicalism, disclaimed by SPD, 102. *See also* Radicals
Radicals, SPD: in interwar period, 13–14; and Godesberg Program, 79; resistance to changes, 207 n. *See also* Left; Militants; Young Socialists
Rationalism, in socialist movement, 72–73
Rearmament, 27; SPD policy toward, 64
Recruitment, in political parties, 48–49
Recruitment, SPD: of party elite, 154–61; of women, 176–77; role of local party organizations, 185, 188–89; by factory groups, 188 n.
Reformers: and party program, 61, 63, 64–67; policy toward party militants, 79; tactics in party congress, 135–

36; Ollenhauer and, 142; members of executive, 143; and party leadership, 144, 148; and local party organization, 188
Refugees: SPD and, 107; *Arbeitsgemeinschaft* for, 171; political preferences, 204
Regional interests, role in German politics, 134
Regional organization, SPD, 118–19, 131, 165–89; leadership patterns in, 158–59. *See also* Local party organization
Reichsbannar, 12
Reichstag, as SPD goal, 6–7, 8, 98
Religious affiliation, and voting preferences, 201. *See also* Catholic Church; Catholics; Protestant church; Protestants
Remilitarization, 208
Research organization, demands for in SPD, 127–28
Reunification: SPD policy on, 110, 205; *Deutschlandplan,* 93–95, 222–23
Reuter, Ernst, 59, 146, 149, 159, 210
Revisionist vs. Radical debates, 8, 10, 21 n.
Revolution, not advocated by SPD, 102
Revolutionary movement, SPD as, 21, 22, 82–83
Richter, Willi, 150
Right wing, SPD, 209

Scandinavia, Socialist parties in, 228
Schanzenbach, Marta, 117, 122
Schleswig-Holstein, 186
Schmid, Carlo, 64 n., 116, 117, 143, 144, 145, 148, 149, 155
Schmidt, Helmut, 91
Schoettle, Erwin, 117, 143
Schulz, Klaus-Peter, on reformers, 63
Schumacher, Kurt, 15–18, 63, 90, 104, 133, 139, 209; *Aufruf (1945),* 16; negative toward new program, 56; preface to *Aktionsprogramm (1952),* 57–58; attitude of *Bürgermeisterfaktion* toward, 59–60; on ideology,

73, 75; on foreign policy, 95, 142; as speaker, 109; supported by party militants, 114; characteristics as party leader, 141–51 passim; compared to Brandt, 148; on attracting middle-class vote, 210; and Catholic voters, 216, 217
Schütz, Klaus, 78, 82, 176
Secretariat, in party organizations, 166–67. See also *Apparat*
Secretaries, party, 166–67
Selbständig Schaffende, Die, 172
Self-employed, voting preferences, 201
Sex, and voting preferences, 202
Social Democratic Party (SPD): history, 3–20, 53–54, 96–99, 103, 140, 226–27; possible roles, 34–36, 50–52
Social inequality, as SPD interest, 89
Social market economy, 205, 212
Social policy: at local party level, 120; SPD organization for, 122–23
Social theory. *See* Ideology
Socialism: SPD goal, 89; in Germany, 228
Socialist German Student Federation, 175
"Socialist laws," 4–5, 6, 7
Socialist theory, and SPD, 55 ff., 56, 59, 60, 61, 92, 99
Socialist Unity Party (SED), 15, 220
Solidarity, SPD, 129–30, 196–99, 203, 226
South-Hesse. *See* Hessen-Süd
Soviet Union, 232; postwar pressure in Berlin, 15
Sozialdemokrat, Der, 5
Sozialdemokratische Arbeiterpartei (SAP), 4
Soziale Arbeitsgemeinschaften, 178–79
Sozialistengesetze, 4–5
Sozialistische Arbeiterpartei Deutschlands, 4
Sozialistische Hochschulbund, 175
Sozialplan für Deutschland, 93
Specialists, in SPD policy making, 137–38
Specialization, in SPD, 125–26
Spiegel, Der, 30 n.
Stadtteilorganisationen, 131 n.

Stammer, Otto, on ideology, 73
Steinhoff, Fritz, 149
Strobel, Käte, 149
Structure: of SPD, 6, 17, 130–38; of political parties, 42–50. *See also* Congress; Council; Executive; Organization
Student Federation (SDS), 221
Student groups, 175
Suhr, Otto, 146
Symbolism, SPD, 164, 196–97
Szczerny, Gerhard, 80 n.

Tax policy, SPD interest in, 93
Team, in *1961* campaign, 148–50
Trade unions, 6, 9; now dissociated from political parties, 19; early role in party, 97–98; in Weimar Republic, 99; present SPD relations with, 105–06, 177–80, 207 n.; influence in SPD and British Labor Party compared, 136–37; Catholic, 214; Christian, 215; British, 228

Unions. *See* Trade unions
Unity, party, 77–80, 128–30, 224
Unterbezirke, 120, 131, 166

Veranstaltungen, 4
Violence, not advocated by SPD, 102
Vittinghoff, Karl, 117 n., 158–59, 160
Vogel, Hans Jochen, 195 n.
Volksfürsorge, 12
Volters, Hermann, 148 n.
Von Knoeringen, Waldemar, 117, 143, 144, 150, 152, 170 n., 218
Von Oertzen, Peter, 209 n.
Vorwärts, 197
Vote: figures, 5, 9, 17–18; woman's, 176. *See also* Voters
Voters: analyzed, 200–05; *1957* survey, 203–04; SPD's alternatives for influencing, 205–12. *See also* Electorate

Weber, Max, cited, 48
Wehner, Herbert, 108, 117, 143, 144, 150, 155; on action programs, 90, 93; *Deutschlandplan*, 94–95, 222–23; on

SPD relations with interest groups, 106; on SPD's image, 109, 110, 111; on objectives of *Arbeitsgemeinschaften*, 125; on political activity, 127 n.; as party leader, 151–52; on SPD as membership party, 164; on factory groups, 179
Weimar Republic, 109, 140, 142, 202; SPD in, 12–13, 14, 74, 98–99; socialist interpretation of collapse, 92 n.; socialist-church relations, 214–15
Welfare policy, SPD interest, 92
Welfare state, as SPD goal, 89
Welt, Die, on Willy Brandt, 148 n.
Werbehilfer, 189
West-Westphalia, 184–85
Wilhelm II, 7
Wirtschaftswunder, 18
Women: recruitment of by SPD, 176–77; voting preferences, 154, 202
Women's groups, 12, 17, 176–77, 184, 191

Workers: SPD education of, 190–91; voting preferences, 177, 201
Working class: concern of SPD, 6, 8, 13, 21, 54 ff., 105, 109, 127, 206–09, 226; in German society and politics, 25–27. *See also* Ideology; Labor movement; Trade unions
Working Group of Independent Producers, 106, 111, 172

Young Socialists, 173–75, 184; demand for new program, 60; Marxist ideas, 89; educational activities, 191
Youth groups, 12, 17; CDU, 175. *See also* Young Socialists

Ziegenhain Conference (*1947*), 57
Zinn, Georg August, 149, 158, 159, 160, 225 n.
Zukunft Meistern, Die, 93

Yale Studies in Political Science

1. Robert E. Lane, *The Regulation of Businessmen*. Out of print

2. Charles Blitzer, *An Immortal Commonwealth: The Political Thought of James Harrington*

3. Aaron Wildavsky, *Dixon-Yates: A Study in Power Politics*

4. Robert A. Dahl, *Who Governs? Democracy and Power in an American City*

5. Herbert Jacob, *German Administration Since Bismarck: Central Authority Versus Local Autonomy*

6. Robert C. Fried, *The Italian Prefects: A Study in Administrative Politics*

7. Nelson W. Polsby, *Community Power and Political Theory*

8. Joseph Hamburger, *James Mill and the Art of Revolution*

9. Takehiko Yoshihashi, *Conspiracy at Mukden: The Rise of the Japanese Military*

10. Douglas A. Chalmers, *The Social Democratic Party of Germany: From Working-Class Movement to Modern Political Party*

1-18-67
12-6-69
4-22-73
5-18-73
DEC 3 - 1980